# PEP GUARDIOLA
# THE EVOLUTION

## MARTÍ PERARNAU

First published in Great Britain in 2016 by
ARENA SPORT
An imprint of Birlinn Limited
West Newington House
10 Newington Road
Edinburgh
EH9 1QS

www.arenasportbooks.co.uk

ISBN: 9781909715493
eBook ISBN: 9780857909220

First published in Spain in 2016 by
Roca Editorial as *Pep Guardiola: La Metamorfosis*

*British Library Cataloguing-in-Publication Data*
A catalogue record for this book is available on request from the
British Library.

Designed and typeset by Polaris Publishing, Edinburgh

Printed and bound by Clays St Ives

## ACKNOWLEDGEMENTS

To FC Bayern München; to Markus Hörwick, Petra Trott, Cristina Neumann, Nina Aigner and Holger Quest; to Heinz Jünger and the guards at Säbener Strasse; to Lufthansa and U-Bahn München; to OPTA for their statistical information and to the Wetterstein Hotel, Munich.

Thanks also to Louise Hunter for all her wonderful work translating the original manuscript from Spanish to English and to everyone at Arena Sport for their work on this edition, particular the sports editor, Peter Burns.

# BIBLIOGRAPHY

## BOOKS

Berger, John (2013). *Fama y soledad de Picasso*. Madrid: Alfaguara.

Bin, Sun (1996). *El arte de la guerra II*. Madrid: Edaf.

Brady, Frank (2015). *Endgame. Bobby Fischer's Remarkable Rise and Fall*. Madrid: Teel Editorial.

Castellano, Julen; Casamichana, David (2016). *El arte de planificar el fútbol*. Barcelona: Fútbol de Libro.

Clay, Catrine (2010). *Trautmann's Journey: From Hitler Youth to FA Cup Legend*. Yellow Jersey Press.

Clayton, David (2012). *Manchester City. A Nostalgic Look at a Century of the Club*. Haynes Publishing.

Couto Lago, Álex (2014). *Las grandes escuelas del fútbol moderno*. Barcelona: Fútbol de Libro.

Csanádi, Árpád (1984). *El fútbol: técnica, táctica y sistemas de juego, preparación física, entrenamiento*. Barcelona: Planeta.

Escher, Tobias (2016). *Vom Libero zur Doppelsechs: Eine Taktikgeschichte des deutschen Fußballs*. Rowohlt Verlag GmbH.

Fox, Norman (2003). *Prophet Or Traitor? The Jimmy Hogan Story*. Parrs Wood.

Green, Geoffrey (1974). *Soccer in the Fifties*. Ian Allan.

Hawking Stephen, W. (1989). *A Brief History of Time*. Barcelona: Editorial Crítica.

Herrera, Helenio (1962). *Yo, memorias de Helenio Herrera*. Barcelona: Editorial Planeta.

Honigstein, Raphael (2015). *Das Reboot. How German football reinvented itself and conquered the world*. Yellow Jersey Presse.

Ibarrondo, Imanol (2015). *La primera vez que la pegué con la izquierda*. Madrid: Editorial Kolima Books.

Jackson, Phil (2014). *Eleven Rings*. Barcelona: Roca Editorial.

Joy, Bernard (1956). *Soccer Tactics*. Phoenix House.

Kaspárov, Garry; Greengard, Mig (2008). *How Life Imitates Chess: Making the Right Moves, from the Board to the Boardroom*. Arrow Books.

Kerr, James (2013). *Legacy*. Hachette UK.

Lombardi, Vince (2004). *The Lombardi Rules: 25 Lessons from Vince Lombardi, the World's Greatest Coach*. McGraw Hill Professional.

López, Marcos; Besa, Ramon (2016). *Andrés Iniesta. La jugada de mi vida*. Barcelona: Malpaso Ediciones.

Marina, José Antonio (2016). *Objetivo: generar talento*. Barcelona: Penguin Random House.

Meisl, Willy (1995). *Soccer Revolution: Willy Meisl*. Phoenix Sports Books.

Michels, Rinus (2001). *Team building: The road to success*. Reedswain Inc.

Needham, Ernest (2003). *Association football*. Soccer Books.

Panzeri, Dante (2013). *Dirigentes, decencia y wines. Obra periodística*. Edición de Matías Bauso. Sudamericana.

Pasolini, Pier Paolo (2015). *Sobre el deporte*. Barcelona: Contra Ediciones.

Peucelle, Carlos (1975). *Fútbol todotiempo e historia de «la Maquina»*. Editorial Axioma.

Sciacca, Michele Federico (1958). *Historia de la filosofía*. Barcelona: Editorial Miracle.

Sennett, Richard (2009). *El artesano*. Barcelona: Anagrama.

Sérgio, Manuel (2012). *Filosofia del fútbol*. Estoril: Prime Books.

Sharpe, Ivan (1952). *40 Years in Football*. Hutchinson's Library of Sports and Pastimes.

Studd, Stephen, et al. (1958). *Herbert Chapman football emperor: a study in the origins of modern soccer*. Souvenir Press Ltd.

Taylor, Rogan; Jamrich, Klara (1998). *Puskas on Puskas: The life and times of a footballing legend.* Robson Books.

Torres, Axel; Schön, André (2014). *Franz. Jürgen. Pep.* Barcelona: Contra Ediciones.

Valdano, Jorge (2016). *El juego infinito.* Barcelona: Editorial Conecta.

Zweig, Stefan; Fortea, Carlos (2011). *Fouché: retrato de un hombre político.* Barcelona: Acantilado.

## DOCUMENTATION
(articles, research, videos, television programmes)

Aizcorbes, Aitor F; Sánchez Merino, David. 'Interview with Julio Garganta'. Fútbol holístico. https://futbolholistico.com/2016/04/06/julio-garganta-la-humanizacion-del-entrenamiento-y-la-competicion-sera-la-gran-revolucion-del-futbol/

Alarcó, Paloma. Curso monográfico. Meeting Cézanne. Cézannismo y cubismo. https://vimeo.com/91921611

Álvarez, Pilar. 'Interview with Ken Robinson'. http://elpaissemanal.elpais.com/documentos/ken-robinson/?id_externo_rsoc=TW_CC

Arte de apropiación (blog). 'Introducción al arte de apropiación y obra de Sherrie Levine'. https://b1mod.wordpress.com/2013/04/13/inicios-del-arte-de-apropiacion-y-obra-de%20sherrie-levine/

Bianca (@FCBianca1900). 'A Tribute To Pep Guardiola'. Vídeo. https://www.youtube.com/watch?v=OVXOg20rpvc

Cáceres, Javier. 'Interview with Xavi Hernández'. Suddeutsche Zeitung. http://www.sueddeutsche.de/sport/fussball-xavi-ich-glaube-dass-deutschland-jetzt-das-spiel-versteht-1.3081719

Carragher, Jamie. 'Interview with Xabi Alonso'. Daily Mail. http://www.dailymail.co.uk/sport/football/article-2844035/XABI-ALONSO-MEETS-JAMIE-CARRAGHER-devastated-miss-Liverpool-return.html

Durán, Obdulio. 'En busca de la competitividad (Estrategia, Marketing, Desarrollo Gerencial)'. Distal 1999 – Buenos Aires.

Efias (web). Lesiones en el fútbol europeo, temporada 2015-2016. www.efias.com

Hägglund, Martin; Waldén, Markus; Ekstrand, Jan. 'Risk factors for lower extremity muscle injury in professional soccer the UEFA injury study'. The American Journal of Sports Medicine (2013, vol. 41, núm. 2, págs. 327-335).

Händel, Georg F. 'Quel fior che all'alba ride, dueto para dos sopranos HWV 192'. Vídeo: https://www.youtube.com/watch?v=GSNKriIfPdI

Händel, Georg F. El Mesías. 'Coro. His yoke is easy'. Vídeo: https://www.youtube.com/watch?v=jx6PVtEZMAc

Kaiser, Joachim; Thielemann, Christian. 'Beethoven entdecken'. Programa televisión. 3sat. https://www.youtube.com/watch?v=w-npUVaJzyU

Lluch, Isaac. 'Pep pone Alemania patas arriba'. The Tactical Room (núm. 23).

Taylor, Louise. 'Interview with Jan Kirchhoff'. The Guardian. https://www.theguardian.com/football/2016/apr/08/jan-kirchhoff-pep-guardiola-sunderland-manchester-city

## INTERVIEWS AND CONVERSATIONS

- Adrià, Ferran
- Alaba, David
- Alcántara, Thiago
- Alonso, Xabi
- Benedetti, Ignacio
- Buenaventura, Lorenzo
- Coba, Rosa
- Costa, Douglas
- Del Pozo, Miquel
- Díaz Galán, Ismael
- Escher, Tobias
- Estiarte, Manel
- Grill, Roman
- Guardiola, Pep
- Guardiola, Pere
- Guardiola, Valentí
- Kälin, Herrmann
- Köhler, Uli
- Krüger, Kathleen
- Lahm, Philipp
- Lara, Juan Ramón

- Lillo, Juan Manuel
- Lluch, Isaac
- Martínez, Javi
- Müller, Thomas
- Neuer, Manuel
- Niemeyer, Stefen
- Planchart, Carles
- Pereira, Miguel
- Rafinha
- Ribéry, Franck
- Robben, Arjen
- Sanvicente, Noel
- Seirul.lo, Francisco
- Serra, Cristina
- Tapalovic, Toni
- Thielsch, Marco
- Torrent, Domènec
- Tuchel, Thomas
- Trueba, David
- Valero, Xavi

# CONTENTS

# PREFACE

Pep Guardiola didn't read *Pep Confidential: Pep Guardiola's First Season at Bayern Munich*, which was published in 2014. Nor has he read this book. He chose not to review what had been said about him before *Pep Guardiola: The Evolution* was published nor was he tempted to read it afterwards. Not even out of sheer curiosity. Back in Munich one of his friends asked him why. 'I don't want to read it,' Guardiola explained. 'At least not yet. Maybe in fifteen, twenty years I'll sit down with it and enjoy reliving my days at Bayern. But not now.'

He is an unusual man. A man who allows a writer into the intimacy of the dressing room and gives him no-holds barred access around one of the world's biggest football clubs and to the inner workings of his mind, yet shows no interest in what is being written about him.

This attitude surely explains more about his character than a thousand words ever could.

Like a teenager leaving home for the first time, Pep's experiences in Germany changed him and this book is a detailed description of that metamorphosis. It is a new, improved Pep Guardiola who takes over in Manchester, the toughest challenge of his managerial career and his third phase as a coach.

His first job as coach, his '*Azulgrana* Period', was marked by Guardiola's unique philosophy and unrelenting pursuit of excellence at Barcelona. His 'Red Period' in Munich showed us his ability to adapt to a different football culture, a process to which he brought his own challenging and, for some, disturbingly creative ideas. Now at the start of Guardiola's 'Blue Period', a blank canvas lies before City's new coach. This is a very different man from the one we watched in Barcelona and then in Munich, although he has lost nothing of his essence in the process.

I first mentioned this book to Pep in June 2016 when he had said his farewells to Bayern and had started his summer holidays immediately prior to his presentation in Manchester. As usual, he wasn't sure about my proposition.

'When I move on I like to make a clean break of it,' he said. 'I've been very happy in Munich, I've had great relationships with everyone at the club but that's all in the past now. I don't think it's worth your while to write about the last two years.'

At that point I had to tell him the truth: 'Actually Pep . . . I've already written it. I've being working on it, on and off, for the last two years.'

'Oh well, in that case, maybe all that work shouldn't go to waste . . .'

And that's how this book came to be published. I had no particular plan, the protagonist has had no interest in reading it and I wrote it without really knowing if it would ever be published.

*Pep Guardiola: The Evolution* is presented in fourteen chapters including fifty anecdotes and notes from my personal experience which develop and explain the themes I discuss.

All the chapters (except the last one) end with coverage of particular matches as well as details of tactics and other related topics. I have called these the Backstages. Readers can choose to read these as they go along or dip in to them as they see fit.

Put your work twenty times upon the anvil,
polish it ceaselessly, and polish it again.
*Nicolas Boileau*

# 1

# THE CHAMELEON

*It is ideas, not machines, which drive the world.*
*Victor Hugo*

WOODY ALLEN SMILED his iconic dry grin as he greeted Guardiola. 'Great to meet you, Pep, but you may find us boring company tonight. None of us are particularly interested in football . . .'

'No problem, Woody, I love cinema. And aren't you a basketball fan? Maybe we could talk about the Knicks instead.'

The next couple of hours flew by as the conversation and wine flowed and the New York Knicks' uphill struggles were debated back and forth. Pep, a devoted fan of Gregg Popovich, was in his element. The Catalan has a reputation for being intense, dogmatic and stubborn. In fact he's quite the reverse. A natural chameleon, Pep knows instinctively how to adapt to every situation. And this natural ability proved vital to his success in Germany where he quickly realised that, in order to impose his vision and ideas, he would have to adapt. To the club, to the players, to their opponents . . . After all, it is not the strongest or the smartest who triumph in the end but those who are willing to adapt.

In Barcelona we admired Pep's passion, ambition, talent and tenacious self-belief. Then in Germany we saw a new side to the obdurate, inflexible, relentless Spaniard as Pep's innate eclecticism and natural adaptability came to the fore.

In hindsight it's clear that only by going through this evolution could Pep remain true to himself.

'When I first arrived in Munich I thought I could more or less transfer Barça's game to Bayern but what I actually did was marry the two,' reflected Guardiola when conversation at last turned to football. 'I brought the Barça philosophy and adapted it to Bayern and the players there. And the result was fucking brilliant! It was a learning curve, though. I had to learn to adapt and there's no doubt I'm a better coach for it. It's something I am taking to my next club.'

Arguably, this versatility makes Pep more of a disciple to the principles of the late, great Johan Cruyff than ever before given that such adaptability is one of the central tenets of Dutch 'total football'. He came to Germany to play Cruyff's football at Beckenbauer's club and in the end produced a potent mix of both philosophies.

After Cruyff's death in March 2016 Pep was asked what tribute the world should make to the great man. 'Pay attention to what he taught us,' he replied. Bayern captain, Philipp Lahm, his own loyal disciple and Pep's direct representative on the pitch confirmed this. 'Cruyff's philosophy was to play football. Nothing more, nothing less. His game was not about controlling the opposition but controlling the ball and your own game. And that's what we did under Pep.' Domènec Torrent, Pep's assistant, added, 'The Pep we see today has synthesised all that he was taught by Cruyff at Barça with everything he learned at Beckenbauer's club.'

And this potent mix of football ideas has produced a unique kind of powerful, fluid, *total football*. West Ham coach Slaven Bilić predicts that 'the next revolution will be the death of the system', and Guardiola certainly appears to be in the vanguard of this revolution. 'Systems don't matter, it's ideas that count.'

Guardiola today is undoubtedly a better coach despite the fact that he was unable to lead Bayern to another treble or victory in the Champions League. Indeed, under Guardiola Bayern failed even to make it to a Champions League final. He did however win seven trophies with the Munich club, smashing all German records by conquering three successive league competitions and doing so by playing dominant, stylish and multifaceted football. He may not have left Germany the all-conquering hero fans may have wished for and, if your measure of success is limited to trophies alone, then he certainly fell short of the expectations of many. Guardiola didn't win everything in Germany. But, boy, did he transform their game. German broadcaster Uli Köhler puts it like this, 'He left us something very special – the memory of a unique brand of football. A football that Bayern will never play again and the fans will never see again.'

Guardiola has just announced that he's leaving and Bayern receives this message from fan, Marco Thielsch.

'It's desperately sad news that you're leaving although I accept that you made no promises and always said that you would only ever be a small part of the history of our club. I've been a Bayern fan for more than thirty years and can tell you that I have never enjoyed my team's football as much as I have in the last two and a half years. Stylish and entertaining. I couldn't even begin to recount all the amazing moments you and the players have given us. It's been a joy to watch my team play such exceptional football and I've been moved to tears on numerous occasions. You've said that many will consider your job half done because you didn't win the Champions League, but I can tell you that many of us see things very differently. I want to win everything. Of course I do. But I want to win playing your way. Enthralling, beautiful football. I can't really express how much I love your football. And no matter what we win, your legacy will live on in our hearts and in the memories of the wonderful times you have brought us.

'You are an absolute inspiration and I thank you from the bottom of my heart. Let's all make the most of the last six months.'

Pep was visibly moved by the message.

'This is what it's all about. If my work here has affected even one fan as much as this, then it's definitely all been worth it.'

Pep's 'unfinished symphony' in Munich has echoes in one of the biggest disappointments of Cruyff's career – his defeat at the hands of Beckenbauer's Germany in the 1974 World Cup Final. Holland lost the game that day in Munich but, in one of the strange ironies of football, emerged the victors in terms of the universal admiration they received for the way they played. Germany got the trophy but in the eyes of the world the 'Clockwork Orange' won the day.

Only time will tell whether Guardiola, Cruyff's natural heir, will see his 'unfinished symphony' become a permanent legacy, his failures transformed into lasting triumphs. Nobody can say with certainty just how far Pep's influence will impact the future evolution of German football but one thing is for sure, he has already become a significant part of Bundesliga history.

Domènec Torrent is certain that Pep has had a permanent impact on German football. 'Pep's legacy is a combination of his unique ideas about football, his talent and his versatility. Karl-Heinz Rummenigge was right when he said that as time goes on, we'll come to appreciate just how much of an impact he's made. I've lost count of the number of German coaches who've contacted us over the last few months to say just that. Pep has left a wealth of football knowledge and ideas in Germany.'

For German analyst Tobias Escher it's mostly about positional play. 'Before Guardiola arrived nobody in Germany knew anything about positional play.'

He may have won less silverware in Munich than he did in Barcelona (fourteen out of a possible nineteen at Barça, seven out of a possible fourteen at Bayern) but Guardiola believes himself to be a better coach than he was in 2012 when he left Barça for Bayern.

'I'm a better coach now because at Barça it was all about the team getting the ball to Messi so that he could score. At Bayern I had to come up with a variety of options; this player had to move into that zone, that one needed to move up behind him . . . I really had to roll up my sleeves and work out lots of alternatives and I learned a huge amount in the process.'

At Bayern, Pep had to adapt to complex and at times hostile situations. He faced endless setbacks and the kinds of difficulties he had never encountered before. Fortunately, his innate talent and natural versatility allowed him to develop and flourish and the Bundesliga wrought permanent changes in him. Fitness coach Lorenzo Buenaventura spotted it early on, just a few months into Pep's reign, 'Pep's changing Bayern but Germany's changing Pep too.'

The man who arrived in England in July 2016 was different from the guy who went to Germany in 2013. His enthusiasm and ambition remain as strong as ever but he appears more human, more flesh and blood. Manchester receives not the idealised quasi-deity of three years ago but a real human being with flaws and imperfections. His time in Germany may have exposed those flaws to the world but he is all the better for it.

You only have to compare the press photos of his arrival at Bayern in June 2013 with those taken in July 2016 in Manchester. In Munich he's wearing an impeccable grey suit, a grey tie, Italian shirt and a smart waistcoat. His shoes are shined to perfection and he's sporting a brilliant white handkerchief in his top pocket. This is style-conscious Pep, surrounded by the Bayern management team and looking for all the world like the new CEO of some massive multinational corporation. He has dressed for a photo shoot and the look is elegance, refinement, glamour, perfection.

Fast forward three years and it's a very different image Pep offers the cameras. He's dressed casually. A short-sleeved grey shirt, jeans, trainers and a sports jacket which he quickly strips off. This is a man of action. A modern man who's relaxed and comfortable in his own skin. Ready for hard work. This image is all about energy, decisiveness and focus but it also says, 'I'm a normal guy, just like you.' The fans can be reassured that he's one of them. A new era has begun.

### THANKS PEP
Munich, 22 May 2016

Bayern's players are gathered on the balcony of the Munich town hall, celebrating another double. Not only have they won their fourth Bundesliga title in a row but yesterday they won the Cup in Berlin. It was Guardiola's last match in charge. Nobody's got much sleep. Pep's wearing a white t-shirt and tracksuit trousers. The word 'Double' is emblazoned on the t-shirt. He's obviously not shaved this morning and, in the land famed for the quality of its beer, is clutching a celebratory glass of white wine. He's surrounded by staff and players, just one of the lads. This is a truly united team. He's clearly emotional, full of gratitude to and affection for the people around him. Just a normal guy. In Marienplatz, where they're celebrating the double, a senior member of a Bayern supporters' club (Club Nr. 12) has taken his shirt off so that everyone can see what's written on his chest. '*Danke* Pep' (Thanks, Pep).

Guardiola showed enormous ingenuity and resilience in his three-year tenure at Bayern. Having to cope with seemingly interminable setbacks and problems gave him a toughness that he perhaps lacked on his arrival. Managing the stress effectively was crucial and by treating each new obstacle as a learning opportunity he avoided the mental and physical exhaustion he had experienced in the past. Obviously adored by the players, club staff, the directors and fans, Guardiola left Munich relaxed and happy. As Benjamin Zander says, if you judge success by the number of tears shed at your departure then Bayern's players clearly believed their departing coach had been a major triumph and there were many, long, emotional goodbyes in the privacy of the Säbener Strasse dressing room.

On a personal level, Pep learned a great deal from his time at Munich. His new approach – *learn from your mistakes and move on* – prevented the burn-out of his fourth and final year at Barcelona as did his decision to leave Bayern after three seasons. Saying 'no' has always been difficult for Pep but this time he knew he should trust his instincts. He was then able to take on the City job without any need for a sabbatical year. A quick visit to New York with his family to see the NBA final and then straight to Manchester, refreshed and ready to go. If Pep still had much to learn when he arrived in Germany, then his time there certainly taught him some tough lessons about the realities of life at the top and helped him mature and grow as a coach.

Bayern's announcement of Pep's departure was immediately met by an outpouring of vitriol against the coach. One day the press were furious that Lewandowski wasn't playing, the next it was Müller's absence that riled them, then Götze's. Suddenly Guardiola could do nothing right and his decision to leave had turned him into the German media's whipping boy. If he would just give one media outlet a personal exclusive Pep was told, he would be protected and the critics would be silenced . . .

Of course towards the end of his time at Bayern Pep was most harshly criticised for his failure to win the Champions League. The sensationalist press were the most vociferous as was anyone who had watched Bayern's football for three years without truly 'seeing' it. To be fair, it isn't easy to grasp the complexities of the modern game. It requires a sharp, open mind and a certain amount of humility to understand exactly what's happening on the pitch whether it's the aggressive, high-tempo football of Ranieri at Leicester or Guardiola at Bayern. Otherwise, you end up with superficial impressions and sloppy analysis.

Creativity is a vital part of football. And I'm not talking just about what happens on the pitch. A modern coach has to be just as innovative and creative as any player. British educationalist Ken Robinson says, 'Creativity isn't about producing one extravagant work of art after another. Creativity is the highest form of intellectual expression.'

Some would say that football has nothing to do with the intellectual. It's about athletic prowess and technical know-how. I beg to differ. Football is all this and more. It's about ideas. New ideas from players and coaches have always been the motor that drives football and ensures its evolution.

Several months ago I read an interesting quote from Dutch fitness coach Raymond Verheijen, a man I rarely agree with but who on this occasion seemed to be talking sense. 'In football, most people prefer the status quo because they fear making a mistake. It's like a primitive sub-culture where criticism is not tolerated and people protect and defend established ideas. People in the game dislike anyone who questions them because it makes them uncomfortable and nobody enjoys being uncomfortable. In football there are many, many things we could do much better, more intelligently.'

Football can only move forward if we are prepared to embrace new ideas. As Ken Robinson says, 'Every scientific development starts with an idea. An original, creative idea born of critical understanding.'

Sadly, however, creativity remains a dirty word for many in football. People cling to obsolete ideas and attitudes, determined to stay anchored to the comfort and security of the past. The world of football has an atavistic aversion to concepts like innovation and change.

And now, with his 'unfinished symphony' behind him, Guardiola takes on the greatest challenge of his career. He has come to the birthplace of football to impose his own ideas on English football. Perhaps some see him as a kind of preaching evangelist. His right-hand man, Domènec Torrent, insists that nothing could be further from the truth. 'Let's be clear. Pep hasn't come to Manchester to revolutionise English football, nor to teach people how the game should be played. He brings his own ideas, his own approach to the game but these will develop and enhance what's already here. It's not about changing everything or teaching people how things should be done. There are a thousand different ways to play football. Pep's approach is just one way. Some people like it, some don't. It has been successful of course but nobody is claiming that this is the only way to play football. Let me say it again so that no-one's left in any doubt. Pep's not the Messiah or some kind of evangelist on a mission to change football. He's here to offer his vision of the game, learn from those who have other ideas and then create effective, entertaining football.'

It's going to be a tough job. Pep has inherited a team without any well-defined style, which seems to lack the ambition and drive he could count on at Barcelona and Bayern. He understands that he has been hired to improve how the team plays and performs, at a time when the squad needs a huge regeneration in terms of new players (half of the previous season's players were over thirty) knowing that he must compete with outstanding coaches like Antonio Conte,

José Mourinho and Jürgen Klopp as well as world-class players like Henrikh Mkhitaryan, Granit Xhaka and Zlatan Ibrahimovic.

And all of this in an idiosyncratic football environment radically different to the ones Guardiola is familiar with. It will be a greater challenge than at Barcelona in 2008, when he lacked experience but had returned to his boyhood club. Different too from Bayern in 2013 when, with an impressive track record behind him, he had expectations of a second treble to contend with. Manchester City will be a totally new experience. A club without its own developed football philosophy or brand of football. Quality of preparation and planning will be absolutely vital. As he himself puts it, 'This is the most difficult job I have ever faced.'

# BACKSTAGE 1

## TOOTH AND NAIL
### Munich, 10 September 2014

Last night Spain played France in the quarter-final of the Basketball World Cup in Madrid. The major shock is that France won 65-52. Just a week previously, the Spanish team had trounced France 88-64 as well as seeing off Senegal, Brazil and Serbia (who ended as defeated World Cup finalists). Spain reached the quarter final with six straight wins so being hammered by France was shattering. Having reflected long and hard on the defeat, Manel Estiarte, the most successful athlete in water polo history (an Olympic and world champion) and now Pep Guardiola's personal assistant at Bayern Munich, concludes, 'For a long time a worrying theme has been gnawing away at me when I analyse the patterns of elite sport. When you look at the top teams, it seems to me that their own greatness can actually become an Achilles heel. Not everyone will agree but I reckon that, having achieved so much, they can no longer even *conceive* of being beaten. I'm not saying it applies to every single great team, nor will it happen all the time, but if you look at any sport – basketball, football, handball – elite teams can become so unused to defeat that if the opposition goes ahead unexpectedly, they can be so taken aback that they fail to react. As if the idea of losing is a completely alien concept. Whether it happens because they are a little short of sharpness, because the rival's bang on their game or because the referee has had a bad night – whatever.

'Let's take football as an example. There was the Bernabéu Clásico in 2009 which Pep's team won 6-2 and then Barça beat Madrid 5-0 at the Camp Nou a year later. José Mourinho was in charge of Madrid by then and he had an outstanding team. Remember Jürgen Klopp's Borussia Dortmund beating Jupp Heynckes' Bayern in the German Cup? They won 5-2 and made Bayern look absolutely helpless. Then Heynckes' lads thrashed Barça 7-0. Messi, Xavi, Iniesta & co were completely overwhelmed. Or last year when Carlo Ancelotti's Madrid hammered us in Munich (4-0), or Germany stuffing Brazil 7-1 in their own backyard during the World Cup . . . You see it more and more often. Two elite teams go head to head, one of them scores and the other one inexplicably starts to fall apart until they lose it altogether.' In the weeks following Estiarte's comments, there were a couple of new examples when Bayern beat Roma 7-1 in Rome and Spurs whipped Mourinho's Chelsea 5-3 at White Hart Lane.

'This is my theory,' continued Estiarte. 'Successful teams are so used to winning that it becomes a habit. They go out expecting a victory and don't even consider the prospect of defeat. They don't necessarily expect an easy game – no way. But normally, if their opponent goes 1-0 up, they're confident they can turn the game around quickly. Then one day you're in the middle of a game against another strong rival and the other side takes the lead. It feels particularly bad if an apparently tight game is suddenly altered by a fluke goal or because you've screwed up or perhaps because the referee's having a bad day and influences things unfairly. All you know is they've caught you unawares and are now ahead. Subconsciously the team which has taken a "hit" finds that they're suddenly suffering from a glass jaw. Then the opposition put a second goal away and suddenly you're

2-0 down. This is a game you "should be winning". You're a "better team", results state that you're on much better form than them and you've planned this contest to the last detail.

'But here you are, on the back foot and struggling to impose yourselves. Perhaps you even deserve to be leading! But they've produced a one-two pair of blows and you're on the canvas with no idea how to get off it.

'Smaller teams are used to losing matches. They go into games mentally prepared to be battered and are used to trying to cope with that. Elite players on the other hand, never, ever expect to lose. They respect big rivals but never consider the idea that they might be dealt a knockout blow by them.

'As Joe Louis said, "Everyone's got a plan until you get punched in the mouth."*

'Suddenly you're one- or two-nil down, unexpectedly, possibly unjustly, and on the canvas without knowing why or how.

'So, instead of just hanging on to the rival, grabbing them round the neck and not letting go until you can breathe again and regain your composure, like boxers do, you carry on playing as you'd do normally and that's when they really hammer you.

'I know it's a generalisation and there are thousands of exceptions, but I believe that we've lost some of the warrior spirit of the past. I'm thinking here of the great Balkan teams, from the old Yugoslavia and around that region, I played against who, despite being technically weaker, would fight tooth and nail until the final whistle, and sometimes beyond.

'You're superior and you're leading but they cling on and won't let go – not while they've got a breath left in their lungs. Or in football, the Italian teams who, once they're a goal ahead, close down the match so that it's impossible to get past them. Or the great German sides who'd know that so long as there were two or three minutes left in a game they could draw or win no matter what the scoreboard told them. In athletics the English middle-distance runners have always shown that kind of grit and determination too. A metre or two left in the race and they could still grind their way home ahead of the leader.

'Football has to do something about this. The great teams need to work on this, to regain their toughness. Look what happened to us last season against Madrid in the Champions League. A lot was going wrong for us at the time and we were struggling with injuries and 1-0 in the first leg at the Bernabéu was not a disaster by any means. We'd played well and deserved a draw at least. We left Madrid with the feeling of having passed up a golden opportunity.

'Let me tell you, if I'm in the seventieth minute of a Champions League semi-final second leg and my team only needs to score once to force extra time I'd not be thinking that this was a terrible situation to be in.

'But, being Bayern, that wasn't good enough. We're an elite team. We demand nothing less than glory and we wanted to get after Madrid in the second leg. Which is when they sucker-punched us from a corner which we shouldn't have conceded. Madrid score.

'Now at 2-0 things look a little more complicated. Then they win a free kick which, again, we shouldn't have conceded. They score again. Another huge sucker punch. And we fall apart. A team like ours isn't accustomed to taking hits like we were suddenly receiving. In fact a side like Bayern is more used to dealing out those sucker punches. Suddenly it feels like a disaster of unheard of proportions and we're powerless to respond. So the blows become a knockout.

'I think there's a pattern through all the previous football examples and the France–Spain basketball shock. Spain came into the quarter final quite reasonably thinking that they could and would win but they were suddenly flat out on the canvas and couldn't claw their way back.

'I'm not saying that any of this is the fault of players, or coaches, or their tactics. It's just that teams nowadays have reached such an elite level that they cannot countenance failure. Great football teams these days are probably the best of all time, that's why there have been so many league records set in Europe in recent years. Records of unbeaten matches, points at the end of a season, goals scored, and fewest goals conceded . . . But the "greater" our football teams get, the less able to imagine or deal with a shock setback they become. So that when things do go wrong, they don't always have the resources to claw and fight their way back into a contest.

'Maybe I'm wrong but I really believe that we need to recuperate some of that Balkan fighting spirit. We need to plan for those times when everything seems to have gone horribly wrong and you're completely overwhelmed. You take a punch to the mouth, but you hold on. You swallow the blood, clear your head, stop thinking about how things "should be" or the pre-match plans, about whether there's been an injustice or whether the deficit is merited or not. No thinking "but we're the favorites here!" You hold on, you buy time, you keep it to 1-0 instead of letting go. Then, just maybe, you reach the last fifteen minutes and you're still in the match – and anything can happen then. If you don't get overwhelmed then just maybe you'll get a break – a bit of luck. Or perhaps they'll switch off. So then if you suddenly put one away, it's the rival who's shocked and thrown off course – and then you can go on and win a contest where you felt either on the ropes or actually on the canvas.

'Some will recognise these themes, some won't. But I think there's a central truth in all of this and that "great" coaches and players need to review differently and prepare more effectively. So that one day when a rival has us on the ropes and all the pre-match plans are in tatters we'll be able to dig deep and bring out "inner Balkan".'

*\* the quote is often mistakenly attributed to Mike Tyson*

# 2

# WHY CITY?

I would rather my mind was moved by curiosity
Than closed by conviction
*Gerry Spence*

WHY DID PEP Guardiola leave Bayern for Manchester City? Why give up a wonderful life in Munich, a legendary European club and a group of extraordinary players whom you have worked so hard to mould and develop? For a man who has spent his life in clubs steeped in history, Manchester City might indeed seem an unusual choice.

Perhaps the question answers itself. He has come from a giant of European football history and feels attracted by a club less bound by tradition and custom. In City he will hear far less of the 'but this is the way we've always done it . . .'

And we should remember: Pep's a pretty unconventional guy. Unlike most successful coaches, having completed his three-year contract at Bayern, he opted to reject the club's extremely generous contract renewal offer. His task complete, he needed something new: fresh challenges – the opportunity to grow and change.

Pep keeps his word. He'll always see his commitments through but don't expect him to stay a day longer than promised. He sees things differently from the rest of us. Why else would he leave Messi at the height of his talent and bid *adios* to the mesmerising talent of Busquets, Xavi and Iniesta and then, three years later, do the same with Neuer, Lahm and Alaba?

It's just the way he is. Having built the best team in the world at Barcelona, possibly the best ever, it was time to go. Once his players at Bayern had absorbed and perfected his brand of football, he was off.

Pep has always embraced change. For him life is about learning and growth. Catalan architect Miquel del Pozo puts it like this, 'Pep is like an artist who completes his masterpiece and then moves on. He has that same creative drive. The important thing for a true artist is the process of creating, not the finished product. He immerses himself in his work but when it's complete and ready to be presented to the world, he loses interest.'

Which may explain why he signed for just three seasons at Bayern and why he has now done the same at Manchester City. His approach calls to mind Hungarian coach Bela Guttmann who had a similarly unconventional view of life: 'Staying on for a third consecutive season at the same club usually ends in disaster.' Guttmann, who had a degree in psychology, was an outstanding coach who managed the great Honved team of Puskas and Bozsik, helped develop the spread of Brazil's 4-2-4 formation using the Hungarian tactic of the 'false 9' and who also won Benfica two consecutive European Cups (as well as then infamously cursing them, when they sacked him, and bearing a grudge which has lasted until today: 'Never again, not in a hundred years, will Benfica win another European Cup.') He was probably the first to understand that short-term contracts were preferable to the burn-out caused by years of intense, high-pressure work at the same club. Like Guardiola, the Hungarian was passionate about acquiring knowledge, getting under the skin of his players and drawing the best out of them. He adored travelling and loved discovering new ideas, new ways of doing things. For him too, football was his passion and his life.

Pep consistently flouts conventional attitudes and follows his own instincts. He has never wanted to become a permanent fixture at any club nor put down roots in one location. He craves new experiences and loves to travel and learn. Ultimately, he needs that sense of freedom.

A gruelling fourth term at Barcelona taught Guardiola that three seasons are sufficient for a group of players to learn, apply and perfect any model of play. By the end of that fourth year he also experienced the fatigue that can creep in after a sustained period of such intense and demanding work. Guardiola's brand of man management does not have a low gear and he demands the same level of hard graft and intense focus from his players as he does of himself. Xabi Alonso speaks from first-hand experience: 'Pep and his team basically put me through a fast-track Master's degree in football. Obviously the workload was incredibly tough and Pep would have us all repeating the same moves again and again until they were completely automatic. He's so pedantic about everything that he picks up on every tiny detail, when you get it right as well as when you get it wrong. It's not just about tactics either. It's much more to do with his whole philosophy. You have to be paying attention at all times and be pretty quick on the uptake. Under Pep all of us at Bayern had to develop the ability to grasp new concepts and apply them immediately.'

There's no question that this work ethic produces extraordinary results or that Guardiola's techniques create better, more skilled and accomplished footballers. But all of this comes at a cost and history shows us that the consequence of such a relentlessly demanding approach can often be exhaustion and burn-out for both the coach and his players.

## THE INFLUENCE OF TXIKI AND SORIANO

*If an idea isn't absurd to begin with*
*it's not worth anything.*
*Albert Einstein*

The presence of Txiki Begiristain and Ferran Soriano at Manchester City was another crucial factor in Pep's decision. The three men made an effective team at Barcelona and have complete confidence in each other.

Begiristain and Soriano welcomed their new coach to a club which could offer a rich history without either the restrictions of unyielding dogma and tradition or the pressures of past triumphs. Pep took on the job at City because he knew that he would be able to work without feeling that he was shattering long established customs and practices. City was a blank canvas and he would be free to create as he saw fit. In practical terms he'd be able to sign players of his choosing and hire the best technical and coaching talent available. City's generous budget also means that he can make crucial changes to the club's youth training programme.

In May 2016 City achieved the historic feat of reaching the Champions League semi-finals where they lost to Real Madrid, but few would claim that earning a place in the top four was a true reflection of their quality. There's no doubt that at least three Spanish teams (Real Madrid, Barcelona and Atlético de Madrid), two Bundesliga clubs (Bayern and Borussia Dortmund) and the champions of Italy (Juventus) were far superior. Club president Khaldoon Al Mubarak spoke to Manchester City TV about what he saw as a disappointing season: 'We owe a debt of gratitude to Manuel [Pellegrini] and his team for everything they have achieved [over the last three years]. At the same time, however, I can't deny that we are disappointed, particularly with the results of this last year. We had high hopes at the start of the season and although there's no shame in losing to Real Madrid, I expected the team to give a hundred per cent and in the end, that's not what we got.'

So let's sum up exactly why Pep left Bayern for City.

• To have new experiences and learn from another footballing culture.
• Because there would be fewer constraints and limitations at City and he would have greater freedom to create.
• Because the club had the financial clout to make the kind of changes he envisaged.
• Because he knew that Txiki and Soriano were on his wave length and would back him all the way.
• Because, by creating a new brand of City football and the language that goes with it, he could begin to build his own unique legacy.

No matter what anyone thinks about Guardiola's motives for choosing City, his decision has brought him to a critical point in his career. Although the rewards may be great, the risk he takes is equally high. This is a man who seeks change for change's sake, who chooses to leave his comfort zone in order to learn and discover. A man of courage and determination who has never craved an easy life. And for this, surely, he deserves all of our respect and admiration.

# BACKSTAGE 2

## THE PERFECT PLAN
### Rome, 21 October 2014

While Philipp Lahm and the rest of Bayern's German players returned to full fitness after enjoying a break following their triumph at the World Cup in Brazil, Pep began to think about the league games in September and October plus the matches against Manchester City, CSKA Moscow and Roma in the Champions League. He was considering using a four man defence and then adapting the shape of the rest of the team to the characteristics of their opponents. In principal he would employ a 4-2-1-3 and a 4-2-3-1, but when necessary he would switch to his much loved 4-3-3 or even 3-3-4. He knew that the key component which would allow a lightning fast change in the playing matrix was David Alaba, who would be used as what the Spaniards call a 'comodin' (what we might call a 'joker card' – a player who can be deployed wherever necessary), and could play as a central defender, left back, organising midfielder or attacking left midfielder depending on the demands of each game.

Before the game against Roma, Bayern racked up five consecutive wins, playing better each time. They had also dispatched City 1-0 in Munich on 17 September, and CSKA 1-0 in Moscow on 30 September.

The team's fluidity flowed from the centre of midfield which worked just as effectively whether the player who accompanied the duo of Xabi–Lahm (established as the axis of the team) was Götze, Højbjerg or Alaba. Pep routinely modified the attacking positions, putting Bernat, Götze or Müller on the left wing, and occasionally asking Müller to take Lewandowski's centre forward position (where even Pizarro got his chances). Robben was always a guaranteed starter when fit, unquestionably the key man, whose every action could turn a game. The Dutchman was gradually returning to the peak he had reached the previous spring when he had been one of the most dangerous attacking players in Europe, and with each match was increasingly demonstrating how vital he was to Bayern.

Pep didn't want to treat the Roma match as if it were 'just another game'. For that reason on 5 October, not long after beating Hannover 4-0 in the league, Pep, Estiarte and Michael Reschke left Bayern's partying at Munich's famous Oktoberfest and flew to Turín, where Juventus and Roma were playing a top of the table Serie A match. It was an ill-tempered game with three penalties, three red cards and a narrow win for Juventus thanks to Bonucci's shot in the final seconds. Roma played well and in patches were superior to Juve but losing damaged their morale badly. For Guardiola it was fascinating: he saw close up precisely how Rudi García's team liked to play and immediately began to plan ways to beat them. Although the pressures of the job prevent Pep from attending a lot of matches, he is a firm believer in taking any opportunity he can to see future opponents in action.

During training on Monday 20 October in Säbener Strasse, Pep explained to his players how they were going to beat Roma in the Stadio Olímpico the next day. Over and over again he made them work on how to bring the ball out from a back line of three defenders, using Xabi Alonso to drop in from central midfield to help them. It was a classic

Pep training session: a keeper, Neuer or Reina, would feed the ball to one of the three central defenders who would be pressed by teammates replicating Roma's style. The man on the ball needed to find one of his three options, the other two central defenders or Alonso to escape the pressure. Guardiola asked Pizarro to cover and press Alonso as a 'virtual Totti' imagining that the legendary Roma player would fulfil that role in the match. Pep was completely clear about how Roma would attack and was equally sure about what he wanted his team to do in reply. The match day team talk was interesting.

It was at six o'clock in Rome that Pep backed up his training ground work by showing Totti's likely position in a video prepared by Carles Planchart:

'Look lads – Totti will be covering Xabi, but he won't be able to do it for very long so Xabi, don't be too worried about it to begin with. Totti will press tight for the first ten minutes and I guarantee that he'll then stop it and leave you completely free. That's why we're able to play with a back line of three; Benatia on the right, Boateng in the middle and Alaba on the left. But David, I only want you to be a defender when they're attacking us. At that stage you'll have to cope with Gervinho's speed. But the rest of the time you must become an extra midfielder. In other words, we'll go out looking like a three man defence but the third defender will actually be Xabi even though it seems like it's Alaba. In the initial scheme Xabi and Lahm will line up like a 'doble pivote' (twin organising midfielders). Philipp, if they manage to close down Xabi then you take charge of centre midfield, you organise things, make sure the ball gets played out from the back. Robben and Bernat, you open the space by hugging the touchline. Right up and down the line. In other words, you must perform both as wing backs and wingers. Arjen, give me exactly what you gave me against Manchester United last year – you remember, don't you? Be shrewd in how you use your energy, don't burn yourselves out too soon. I want you to attack but keep an eye behind you so you can help the back three out when we're under pressure. Up top Götze will play between midfield and attack but dropping to the left to link with Lahm and Bernat. Müller and Lewandowski, I want you constantly moving because Roma's defenders hate that. Be on the go all the time, sometimes leave the centre forward position empty so they don't know who they're marking. Their central defenders are very static and traditional in their positions and they love to know exactly who their man is and where he should be. So for that reason don't help them, give them nothing to work with by switching and moving constantly. Pressurise them! Their back four absolutely hate it if they're pressed. They find it horribly difficult to bring the ball out from the back if you snap at and hassle them. So press the life out of them, don't let them draw breath! You will rob the ball from them and I promise you that will mean we score lots of goals today.'

The plan was crystal clear by now but Pep wanted to leave his men in no doubt, 'Listen up all of you. This is what's going to happen. They'll think that Totti can close down Xabi but after ten minutes he'll give up and Xabi will be bringing the ball out without a problem. Lahm will be left on his own and Alaba will be giving us superiority of numbers down the left exactly where they won't be expecting him because they'll think that the left-sided centre back in a three-man defence will never push up the pitch. But David's going to do that and help us completely overwhelm them down the left. Xabi will bring the ball out right to the centre of the pitch without any problem and we're going to create an unbelievable superiority of numbers down the left half of the pitch with Bernat, Alaba, Götze and Lewandowski at least. Müller, get away from the central defenders and link with these guys. We all know what will happen next, don't we? We'll overload them with passes down the left, their central defenders won't know what they're doing but they'll go left so we'll only have Lahm and Robben on the right – it will look as if we present no danger there. But it's exactly down the right that we'll do the damage. Overload them on the left, draw them there, then switch the ball quickly to the right. They'll be completely exposed and won't be able to cope.'

Bayern battered Roma. In less than half an hour they had ripped the home side to pieces and by the thirty-fifth minute they were 5-0 up. In their nine previous matches Roma had only conceded four goals. Now it was five in just over half an hour. As Pep had predicted, Bayern's high pressing shredded the Italians. Müller and Lewandowski tied up the entire Roma back four and Rudi García's team barely got out of their own half.

The combination of Robben's pace on the right and Totti abandoning his marking of Xabi were equally vital. Everything Pep had predicted came to pass. Bayern lined up 3-1-4-2. Alaba constantly burst into the midfield, Alonso brought the ball out from the back untroubled and Götze's movement between the lines was exceptional. Bernat consistently offered himself as the spare man down the left but the most dangerous actions flowed from the right wing where Robben waited in open space to finish Roma off. The fourth goal, scored by the Dutchman in the twenty-ninth minute, seemed straight from Pep's script at the team talk and the coach put his hands on his head in delight as Lewandowski dragged the Italian defenders away and Robben arrived on the run to put the ball away.

If a year earlier Bayern had laid down a masterpiece in Manchester City's Etihad Stadium with the apotheosis of 'rondo football' and that legendary passing sequence which lasted three and a half minutes, this was a different work of art in the historic Italian capital. Pep's team had supplied more magic for the on-line generation around the world.

Thomas Müller summed up what had taken place, 'The fact is that Guardiola showed us precisely where Roma's weaknesses were and we exploited them.'

The following day Pep was eating alone at home because his family had taken advantage of the autumn holiday in Munich to visit Barcelona and his technical staff were spending time with their families. Although he was watching the Bayer Leverkusen–Zénit game (2-0), he didn't get too involved in it because he was still mentally evaluating the 7-1 win in Rome which had stunned European football.

'I'm really happy about yesterday's game,' he said. 'We're playing much better than last season. You saw our positional play, the guys were like machines "top, top". The lads are playing brilliantly at the minute. They no longer need to think about their movements, it's all so automatic and the man on the ball always has free men to pass to. Xabi has given us new life. He's completely changed the team's outlook and it's thanks to him that we can do things like pressing so high and so ferociously up the pitch against Roma. It meant that we could exploit their weaknesses.'

Pep sips his white wine and continues, 'I love it when we can play 3-4-3. It was magic using that formation in Rome yesterday. Benatia swallowed up his winger, Alaba dealt with the other one and Boateng commanded everything at the back. Totti, as the false 9, couldn't do us any damage because Alonso was always blocking him. Lahm and Götze perpetually found free space between the Roma lines. It was such a joy to see them play like that.'

Recalling his decision to play three at the back he said, 'When we changed to play four at the back they actually made three dangerous chances against us and we lost control in the middle of the pitch. We had more security defending with three than we did with four!'

Another performance still buzzing round Guardiola's head is Alaba's: 'He's so fucking impressive. He lines up as a central defender and then, an instant later, he's brilliant as a left winger. There was a moment when his movement and pace actually made him a centre forward! But I thought to myself, 'Leave him, let him go. You never trim the wings of a player like that . . .'

# 3

# HOW GERMANY CHANGED PEP

Find what you love and let it kill you.
*Charles Bukowski*

GUARDIOLA'S TIME IN Germany helped him mature and grow both professionally and personally. Already a consummately talented man, he set about fine-tuning and extending his natural skill set. He made a quantum leap forward in terms of his professional abilities, a transformation which partly helps explain why he accepted the huge challenge offered by Manchester City.

Fundamentally Pep is the same hard-nosed, hungry competitor he ever was. A man who never lets up. Either on himself or his players. 'I don't play to produce beautiful football,' he once said, 'I play to win.'

He also retains that innate perfectionism that means he's never wholly satisfied with the work that he does. The nagging voice of his own internal critic can always find faults and mistakes, however small. There is always something he could do more of, a performance he could have bettered and every single tiny detail matters to him. He can be obsessive in this search for constant improvement and, for Pep, his best game is always yet to come. He also possesses a contradictory blend of the rational and the emotional and this presents challenges of its own. At times he can appear cold and austere, at others overly emotional and he does not always succeed in balancing the two. This paradox is present in his professional persona too and, in this respect, I would describe him as a results-driven, incurable romantic. Although pragmatism always wins the day, Pep himself is clear that passion is the motor for all that he does. 'What matters most for me is how passionate people are about the way we play.'

Interestingly, whilst at Bayern, Pep's critical self-analysis served him well in redirecting his instinctive fear of the opposition. By using his fear as an impetus for greater risk-taking he turned a potential negative into a positive. The clash of football cultures he experienced had given him a greater array of weapons and introduced him to a wealth of new concepts. He became all the more willing to gamble on the unknown.

Paco Seirul.lo, FC Barcelona's director of fitness strategy, explains why a culture shock like this is such a great learning experience. 'It can be very tough at the start of course but in the long term it's always beneficial because you're subconsciously learning patterns of interaction that are new to you. The brain has mirror neurons which allow us to copy what other people do. So that the way others behave affects how I behave. In the past we called this "learning through imitation" but nowadays we understand that it is the neurons which help us reproduce others' actions, although not necessarily immediately. If you see all your teammates immediately battering the ball forward the instant they receive it then you're going to think that the way to play football is to get the ball forward as far and as fast as you can whenever you get it. If you're watching your colleagues controlling, turning, running with the ball, passing, using just one, two or three touches in search of space and opportunities then you're not going to think that the way to play football is to launch the ball but to control it, move a couple of metres and look for the best pass to someone wearing the same colour strip as you.

'And if we continue down this route, when you see that a teammate finds a specific space on the pitch so that he draws opponents to him and you can play him the ball but he'll give it right back to you, by which time you've a much bigger space in front of you because your teammate has drawn a couple of their guys away – things are easier for you then and you've learned more about football. And while you're using interplay between teammates, passing moves which are related and linked to one another, different concepts of playing football will arise and that'll be enriching for the individual and the team.

As a result of his immersion in all things German, Pep nowadays has a far wider range of tools at his fingertips, allowing him to relish tackling the many problems that come his way. I have already talked about his great resilience as well as his newly discovered adaptability. He is more flexible now than in the past but his defining feature remains unblemished. Pep is still passion, passion, and passion.

## PASSION OR ENERGY
### Munich, 19 April 2016

Bayern have just knocked Werder Bremen out of the German Cup, thereby securing their place in the final. Pep looks exhausted.

Concerned, I decide to have a word with Estiarte, one of his closest friends. Wouldn't it be better for Guardiola to think about changing the way he approaches training and his other duties? Couldn't he conserve his energy a little more, be more restrained about how he goes about things, less obsessively hands-on in everything he does? It might just help him avoid exhaustion and allow him to keep going for longer. Estiarte dismisses my suggestion out of hand. 'In the passion and energy equation I wouldn't want him to dial down the pressure even a single notch. Yes, he can end up like this, drained and exhausted, but if he started to try to save energy he might lose some of his passion and that wouldn't be Pep. No, absolutely not. He can't and he shouldn't change.'

Here's some detail on four key characteristics Pep worked on, and updated, during his three years in Germany:
- Re-prioritising
- Ideological eclecticism
- Decision making
- The ability to innovate

# RE-PRIORITISING

*The art of leadership is knowing when to lay your baton*
*down and let the orchestra play.*
*Herbert von Karajan*

There are two things which influence Pep's attitude to his work: the way his parents brought him up and, surprisingly, his own belief that he does not in fact possess a huge amount of natural talent. He compensates for this perceived lack of innate ability by hard work and sweat.

Spanish philosopher, José Antonio Marina, agrees with Pep's view of work, 'Talent is not a gift (a thing) but a process (of learning). You don't start out with talent, it only comes through education and training.'

Or, as Guardiola puts it, 'If you don't practise, you'll forget it all.' The basis of all achievement then is training and hard work. Although he's clear that it's about quality and conceptual understanding rather than mere 'quantity'. 'The conceptual ideas are more important than the physical side of things.' The coach explains his ideas using words but the player then assimilates them through repeated practice, relying on direction and advice in a context that is as close as possible to a competitive match. 'We have to convince the players about the usefulness of the tactical concepts they are practising and they learn on their feet, playing football because that's what it's all about.'

The essential thing about transmitting concepts or playing ideas is that the player has to want to do it. It's not about mechanically repeating a series of actions but about understanding exactly why you are doing them. 'It's vital the players make their own decisions during training sessions,' explains Guardiola. 'They have to experience it before they can fully grasp what they're doing and it's not enough just to tell them. If you really want to get rid of a defect, you have to first experience the impact it can have.'

All of this demands intense planning before every training session and all elite football coaches need huge amounts of preparation time. Sadly however, time is the one resource that they desperately lack. 'There's no secret formula,' says Golden State Warriors basketball coach Steve Kerr. 'The only way to win is through concentration, effort and by paying attention to every single detail.' How then do you resolve the dilemma of having to produce meticulous work under intense time pressure? By prioritising and maximising your efforts in the shortest time possible.

Paco Seirul.lo talked me through this change in Guardiola's focus. 'In the past you played one game a week and therefore fifty a year. Now you're playing two or three per week and that can add up to seventy matches a year. It's a nightmare. So back when we were still at Barcelona we decided to re-prioritise Pep's workload so that he can combine training and preparing for matches without risking burn-out. Effectively he "disappears" during the week. He attends training without having to think deeply about what has been planned because he trusts his team (the assistant coach, fitness coach and the video analysts) to break down and apply his overall plan on a daily basis. He leads training for ninety minutes, correcting and directing the players and then he's off to start his real "brain" work: planning the next game. The day before a game and match day itself are intense and pressurised as he works with the team to analyse and prepare for the game and then directs from the touchline, but otherwise his days are spent relatively quietly, reviewing our own games and our opponents' past performances. It means that he's pacing himself and not using up all his energy on the training pitch. As I said, he started to work like this at Barça and has now perfected it at Bayern. It's the only way to do it when you have such a packed calendar.'

Guardiola continued to gradually change his working style towards the end of his time in Munich, deciding to miss three training sessions: on 3 April, before the Champions League quarter-finals against Benfica, on 20 April and finally on Sunday 1 May before meeting Atlético de Madrid in the semi-final. Given that they were all post-match recovery sessions, his presence was not absolutely essential but his decision was significant nonetheless. It was the first time in his career he had ever chosen to miss training. Domènec Torrent took charge whilst Pep worked in his Säbener Strasse office analysing their next opponents and planning his strategy: the game plan, the videos of their opponents' games and the instructions he would give to his players.

## REFINING THE ANALYSIS
### Munich, 1 May 2016

During dinner, Guardiola whispers, 'I'm completely blocked. I've been over and over how to attack and defend against Atleti and I'm totally saturated. I can't think straight. I'm going to sleep on it and hopefully wake up refreshed and clear about the two or three fundamental ideas that will help us win.'

The following morning Pep is firing on all cylinders again and feels fresh and ready for action. His son Màrius is kicking a ball about on the grass with David Trueba's son, Leo. Trueba, a novelist and film maker is also fascinated by the creative process, in whichever sphere it takes place. He knows Pep well and recounts how the Bayern coach has spent the last few days 'loading mental software', coming up with different ways of beating Atlético Madrid. He explains how Pep has managed to shake off the mental cobwebs in such a short space of time: 'As match day approaches, Pep does something very similar to the way Bob Dylan used to compose songs. He fills page after page with material and then pares it all down so that he ends up with only the key verses he wants. He makes thousands of notes and then reduces them to the bare essentials, the crux of his strategy.'

Pep's strategy planning is a solitary act of creation and by Sunday morning, two days before the Champions League semi-final, he has reduced everything to a single choice: 'Benatia or Boateng. I've decided on the other ten.'

He is also still slightly concerned about his players finding the right balance during the game. 'We just need one goal but if we ask them to be too calm and controlled from the start, it might confuse them. Then again, if we demand electric pace and high energy, we risk disaster. It's not easy to get the right balance between patient control and high-energy attacking. We'll have to find a midpoint between the two.'

Normally, training follows the same routine. Bayern's technical team make all the basic preparations. Domènec Torrent and Lorenzo Buenaventura put together a plan for the day's work based on Guardiola's strategic objectives. Carles Planchart, who is responsible for analysing opponents, has a key role in this process since each training session focuses specifically on the characteristics of the next opponent and the tactics Pep will use to neutralise them. Torrent and Buenaventura then meet with Guardiola for about an hour and a half and present their proposed plan of work for his approval or modification. Their discussion takes into account everything that could affect the smooth running of the day: the weather, the number of players with injuries or other problems, the need to re-incorporate or rotate players. They may also need to produce a personal training plan for one or more players and they'll also look at things like team spirit and morale as well as any specific issues that have come up for individual team members. At the end of the ninety minutes, the plan tweaked to his satisfaction, Guardiola leads the session. As Seirul.lo has explained, this approach means that he has only invested ninety minutes of his time in planning training and will therefore still have plenty of creative energy when he comes to tactical planning later in the day. Training ends with another meeting. This time the whole technical team get together to review the session and then discuss the plans for the next day. Pep then spends the rest of the day immersed in his other main concern: the detailed planning of the team's next game.

The need for Guardiola and his entire technical staff to conserve energy has not just been a priority in itself; working more efficiently has had the ancillary benefit of improving each man's skills. Domènec Torrent, for example, has sat beside Pep on the bench on upwards of two hundred occasions, has attended more than two hundred team talks and, with Carles Planchart, has prepared thousands of attacking and defensive set plays. Planchart himself can claim to have studied more than 1,150 matches in his quest to identify other teams' weaknesses. Over the years Lorenzo Buenaventura has come up with a host of different techno-tactical and fitness exercises for the 835 training sessions Pep has led at Bayern. All of these men recognise the positive impact that fine-tuning their working practices has had on their lives.

### RULES OF ROTATION
Munich, 14 August 2015

The number of minutes' playing time assigned to each player does not happen by chance. It is part of a carefully planned strategy which Pep explains to me over dinner one night in the Allianz Arena restaurant. It's not long after Bayern have won their first league match of the season (5-0 against Hamburg).

'My approach to Xabi will be very similar to what happened today,' he tells me. 'He'll play about sixty minutes and his job is to organise the team, set the rhythm and tire our opponents. Then he has to come off to rest. We need him fresh and in top form for April and May because we're in a different situation from last year. I also need to be careful about the Lahm–Rafinha partnership. Rafinha is vital to the team and my plan is for him to come on in the last thirty-five minutes when we play, just like he did today. When our opponents are tiring and less alert we'll be able to use his speed and intelligence to great effect. When he comes on, Lahm will just move forward a little bit, to play in attacking midfield, so between those two guys they'll do tons of damage to our rivals. Hopefully we'll already have run the other team's legs off by that time, so that when we throw Rafinha on he'll blow them away with his speed.'

Guardiola's football is played by fourteen men and nothing is left to chance. Everything, from the role of each player to the length of time they spend on the pitch, is part of Pep's minutely planned strategy.

## PREPARATION AND A PASSION FOR DETAIL

Take care of the little things.
Their presence or their absence could make all the difference
*Han Shan*

Guardiola has learned to pace himself better but that does not mean that his obsessive passion for detail has in any way diminished. What he has done is re-prioritise his weekly tasks, expending most of his energy on a dedicated and exhaustive analysis of the upcoming game. His creative instincts are obvious in his meticulous approach to planning which he treats as if it were one of Gaudi's famous trencadís (a mosaic made up of thousands of tiny pieces of ceramic tile). He can't afford to misplace a single tile because each part is essential to the beauty and artistic coherence of the finished work.

Let's look at a specific example of this fanatical attention to detail and painstaking preparation.

It's Wednesday, 18 May 2016 and the team is gathered on pitch No.1 at Säbener Strasse. Bayern are just eighty hours away from the German Cup Final in Berlin. Javi Martínez, who has just come back after surgery, trots out on to the pitch. He won't make it to the final, leaving Guardiola without his most consistent central defender on the day. Everyone else who has played a key role in Bayern's sprint to the finish line over the last few weeks is here, including Xabi Alonso and Mario Götze, both of whom have had pain killing injections after rib damage. In the meeting room inside the dressing room Guardiola has broken down what he considers to be the key factor for the final against Dortmund. He reckons Thomas Tuchel will come up with a strategy that will match man-for-man the Bayern defence with Dortmund strikers, but will only press them when Bayern's back line are high up the pitch leaving lots of space into which Dortmund's strikers can sprint. And Dortmund are definitely superior in pace.

Pep has been drip-feeding his plan to the team throughout the week and today he's focusing on something he considers crucial to their success in the final: the need to maintain numerical superiority at all times. No matter what.

Out on the training pitch, Pep explodes into action as he tries to cover every possible eventuality. He goes over how Borussia Dortmund will approach the game and outlines how he wants his men to neutralise their strengths and exploit their weaknesses. This is a closed door session and nobody has been allowed in to watch, not even the players' friends and families who are usually welcome. But they're facing a crucial match and no general risks showing his battle-plan to the enemy ahead of time. The players move through a series of short drills, lasting just ten or fifteen minutes each. Everyone's completely focused and the atmosphere is electric.

The first is a general drill in which Thiago needs to mark a 'virtual' Gonzalo Castro and Müller needs to do the same against a teammate pretending to be Julian Weigl. Two youth team players take the roles of the Dortmund footballers. Shouting continuous instructions and gesticulating wildly, Pep forces Müller to close down the space available to 'Weigl', whilst ordering Lewandowski and Douglas Costa to prevent Hummels (played by Tasci) from playing the ball long. He backs up the plan yelling instructions to Thiago: 'Thiago, close down Castro! Thiago, get right on top of Castro, don't let him turn!'

The drill is short and sharp and is a prelude to the full training session. That begins next and starts with twenty repetitions of an exercise to promote explosive strength; next there's rondos and finally a long match played across half the pitch which is alternately played by three teams of six players. At the end there's a final tactical drill, but only for those who will be part of the defence: Vidal plus the pure defenders. By now Xabi Alonso and Götze have pulled out of training and their painful expressions indicate that they won't be playing in the final.

Still hidden from prying eyes, Pep's defensive troops spend the next ten minutes focused on one more part of the strategic plan: smothering Aubameyang with markers and ensuring that, at any cost, Bayern achieve superiority of numbers in bringing the ball out from the back.

Ten impassioned minutes follow and it reveals Guardiola in his pure state. His intention is that Vidal, the most orthodox of his midfielders, somehow achieves the tactical rigour of a Busquets or an Alonso and firmly holds the organising central midfield position which he's going to have to play and around which it's likely Bayern's defensive organisation will revolve. How fully Vidal follows his instructions will, to a great extent, also dictate Bayern's success in the final.

Pep demands that the central defenders play open – something to which Boateng is accustomed, but Kimmich's still unsure. 'Josh!' cries Pep, arms flailing. 'Get wide, right to the touchline! Don't be afraid . . . split wide, right out to the line.'

Kimmich's indecision is understandable. He's a central defender yet the coach is putting him right on the touchline as if he were a right back. And, what's more, a full thirty metres higher up the pitch than Neuer and thirty-five metres to the right of the central defence position where he feels he should be.

The youngster fears that it'll be impossible to get back and cover his position in time if something happens that obliges him to do so. But there's no dissuading Guardiola, not a chance. He wants him pegged to the line, as open as a central defender can play, with Boateng similarly positioned on the left.

Not to mention that the two full backs are now situated pretty much up in midfield. In the middle of all this defensive reorganisation and risk-taking, Vidal must be the governor. The drills have two aims: Vidal's steely vigilance of Aubameyang if he drops off his centre forward position, and the speedy return of the four displaced defenders to their penalty area in the case of a Dortmund counter-attack.

To achieve what he wants to see, Pep takes Vidal's position. He takes up the role of organising midfielder (the one he once played) and talks the Chilean through every detail. How and where to move depending on what the Dortmund number 9, whose playing style is mimicked by another Bayern youth team player, tries to do. If the 'false' Aubameyang makes an outside run, Vidal's told to leave him. That'll be Kimmich or Boateng's task. But, in that case, Vidal needs to drop in and deputise for the work of the central defender who's now covering Aubameyang. 'Arturo [Vidal] move right! Don't follow Aubameyang!'

Vidal sprints and does what he's told. If Aubameyang darts down the centre then Vidal stays tight to him and leaves Kimmich and Boateng free. They go over and over it, trying out all the variants with Pep delivering a torrent of commands and instructions. He's like a man possessed, positively sparkling with the kind of special energy he seems to find at moments like this. Imagine Guardiola at his most frenzied on the touchline and then multiply by ten. The man is a bundle of volcanic energy.

Eventually he's sure his players understand the essence of his tactics for Saturday in Berlin.

Basically: Vidal needs to not drift from his position, not get pulled away from the centre of the tactical triangle where it's essential that Bayern are organised; he needs to treat Dortmund's centre forward in two diametrically opposed ways depending on which particular movements the striker comes up with; and the other four members of the defence need to open up like the petals of a rose when an attack's being initiated and close like a boxer's fist, as fast as humanly possible, if the opposition launch a counter-attack.

They'll be allowed to take as many risks on the ball and positionally as they want to, or are capable of, when building and to attack so long as they never, ever disobey one absolute non-negotiable fundamental: that Bayern must always, always have numerical superiority over their opponents when they have the ball.

This is Guardiola at his most authentic, a dynamic blur of movement and action.

He will cover the entire strategy with his players over the next few days. There will be new exercises and more explanations, team talks and videos. It all culminates on Saturday afternoon at 17.30, in Berlin's Regent Hotel when Pep will place before his men the three alternative playing schemes Borussia Dortmund are likely to use and explain how Bayern should deal with each. He doesn't know which one Dortmund will go for but that doesn't matter. They are fully prepared and know exactly how to counteract each one.

'I don't just tell them where they should be on the pitch but how, specifically, they should press and against whom. Also towards which side of the pitch I want them to push the opponents when they are trying to build from the back. How I want them to put into practice the joint movements, the support for the guy pressing the ball, the shuffling across of the team behind those who are pressing.'

These tactical set-ups are no more than a graphic realisation of all the tactical drills the team's been working on exhaustively since Tuesday. The difference is that, today, they see them all at once – in their entirety.

It's a plan which takes into account all the possible tactical variants which Tuchel might use and all the responses Pep's come up with. It's been studied, tried, taught, emphasised . . . learned.

In the event, Pep's players need almost no direction during the game. Lahm, Kimmich, Boateng and Alaba can tell immediately which system Dortmund are using and spot changes in strategy the second they happen. All it takes is a quick nod from Bayern's captain and Pep's team alter their own positions to counteract their opponents' tactics. Only Vidal needs a bit of correction from the bench as Pep screams at him to hold his position. Stick to the plan lads. No matter what.

## IDEOLOGICAL ECLECTICISM

*He who seeks only escape does not understand the labyrinth.*
*For even if he finds the way out, he will leave*
*without ever knowing where he's been*
*José Bergamín*

Having mentioned how important it has been to Guardiola to incorporate new concepts into his football bible I'd like now to examine the mental processes he has gone through to refine his ideology.

Let's go back to February 2014. I'm sitting in an office in Ehrengust Strasse, Munich, looking out at the Isar River and listening to Roman Grill, Philipp Lahm's agent. I'm not here to talk to him in his professional capacity as the Bayern captain's representative but, rather, to pick the brain of the sharpest, most lucid man I've met in German football.

It was still early in Pep's Bayern project. The team had, as yet, taken only baby steps in the direction he planned for them. But Grill demonstrated a remarkable understanding of this guy who'd only relatively recently taken charge at the club. 'I'm quite sure that Pep Guardiola doesn't go all over the world saying, "I'm going to create carbon copies of Barça everywhere I go." He's only been here a few months but it's already clear that he's in the process of analysing his team and building his strategy around the players. I think that Pep has his own career development in mind and Bayern is the first step in proving to the world how versatile he is. It's like saying, "Look at me. I can work anywhere."

'His plan will emerge over the next few years but it's not yet clear what his tactics will be. He's already experimenting from time to time and is certainly not just giving us the Barça blueprint. I'm sure he did his research before accepting Bayern's offer and concluded that this was the club that offered him the best chance of success. Even before his arrival Bayern was a talented and committed team with enormous potential. Ideal conditions for him to promote this image of himself as the kind of coach who can adapt to any situation.'

In hindsight, having watched Guardiola's trajectory at Munich, this analysis now seems remarkably prescient and for someone to have read Pep so well back in the winter of 2014 is remarkable. Back then everyone still saw Pep as a kind of football dictator, intent on imposing his philosophy and ideas wherever he went.

Guardiola's evolution may have made him more radical but it has also forced him to set aside many of his more rigid views. He still espouses the Cruyff philosophies in terms of the fundamentals of the game (possession, passing, position and attack) but has rid himself of any attachment to the restrictions and limitations of an unerring dogma.

At Bayern he's played half of his total 161 games with four or five forwards; he's mounted a defence of two, three, four and even five players; and has also tried using one, two, three or four central defenders. On one occasion his team has even played with no central defenders and on another four full backs.

Over his three years at Bayern, Pep employed twenty-three different playing models; he used five midfielders or only one; he went for symmetry one day, and the opposite the next. He's used a passing game; he's prioritised wingers going outside and crossing off their favoured foot, hoping to provide headers for the strikers. He's been both deeply Guardiola whilst at the same time breaking with the body of work he religiously developed at Barça and which, mistakenly, made people view him as some sort of High Priest of a single brand of football.

## PLAYING WITH FIVE FORWARDS
Munich, 13 March 2015

'Get me!' cried Pep, his eyes bright, a grin flashing across his face. 'The flag bearer for midfielders – playing with five strikers! My whole life defending the idea that midfield is so vital, that the key to winning football comes from the guys in the middle who control the game . . . and now I'm powering up our attack line because of how many strikers we have and need.

'But, be clear, it's not just using strikers for the sake of it. This has no relationship to the day Madrid beat us 4-0 in the semi-final. That night I used four forwards but with the full backs "open". That was where I screwed up because we were defending with two central midfielders and two central defenders which meant it was impossible to defend against Madrid's counter-attacks. This is totally different because it all hinges on the two full backs who, when possession is up the pitch, close in tight to the organising midfielder to form a line of three which protects against counters.

'With this "security system" we *can* use five forwards because they've got their backs properly covered.

'Okay, two of those five strikers are like inside forwards. The two guys who are the best at dribbling in this squad are the wingers, Robben and Ribéry. So we don't peg them to the wing, because that would leave them with no space on one side and because our opponents would double mark them with the full back and the wide midfielder. No, all they have to do is get past the other team's holding midfielder – because the other defenders are tied up by our other four forwards – and they'll be through on goal.'

'But you were the king of the midfielders,' I say. 'The guy

who said he'd like to "play a thousand men in the middle of the pitch".'

'True,' admits Pep, flashing that grin again. 'I've been like that, but this job, this squad is converting me into a coach who'll use five strikers. I know it's an unusual tactic and I owe it all to my experiences here in Germany. In fairness, if it's a big Champions League match I'll probably use five midfielders away, but five strikers at home. Away from home we try to control the game via our passing play but in Munich we'll cut loose – like the 7-0 against Shakhtar.'

'So this team which, when you got here, was going to be all about midfielders is actually all about full backs and strikers?' I ask.

'The full backs can attack, but with judgement, when the ball is moving up the pitch and especially in situations where there's little risk of us losing possession. It's ideal if they can get high up the pitch and cross it because we'll have five guys attacking that ball in and around the box. We all have to be careful about how we "name" players and their positions. Is Lahm a full back? If so, why? Why isn't he a "midfielder"? And Alaba? Rafinha? Is Robben a striker? Why not a midfielder? I'd say maybe he is!'

This rejection of dogmatism and a willingness to accept and incorporate new ideas are by far the most important changes in Pep so far. Nowadays he is much more open to alternative views, confident in his own ability to use these to enhance, rather than dilute his own core beliefs.

In 2014, Grill had already recognised this. 'Pep Guardiola produced sensational football at Barcelona. And it coincided with José Mourinho's time at Madrid. No matter where he goes – Chelsea, Inter, Porto – Mourinho's style of game is the same, authoritative football based on a meticulously organised, tactical defence. But it's impossible to define exactly what Guardiola's style is – we've yet to see it reach its apotheosis.'

In other words, more than two years ago Roman Grill had immediately seen that Guardiola would not be pigeon-holed. Far from obstinately sticking to one conception of the game, the Catalan was determined to discover and incorporate a whole range of new concepts and techniques into his already substantial back-catalogue.

Fascinated, I asked him if it was realistic for any elite football coach to embrace such an eclectic mix of playing styles and expect to continue to survive and flourish. Surely a single, consistent playing model made much more sense?

'Despite appearances Guardiola's philosophy is much less rigid than Mourinho's. People accept that he is more creative in his approach but he is also much less inhibited. He has his own set of theories of course and will always choose teams he believes will be able to adapt to his style: possession football that aims to dominate the centre of the pitch via superiority of numbers. Pep would never move to a club which expects him to change completely and although he is happy enough to adapt to established customs and long-held institutional beliefs, he will always insist on bringing his own principles and brand of football. In fact, I'd say his move to Munich is the first step in the creation of the Guardiola brand and he is clear that "control of the ball and passing" form an indelible part of that brand. That's why he sees his future with clubs who like that kind of football. This is a guy who knows exactly what he wants from his career and that's why he'll always do his research before making his next move.

'In general I think Pep is the kind of person who's very clear about his personal objectives. He wants to help his players develop professionally and will always work with them rather than against them but at the same time he has his own priorities and personal goals.'

I must confess that Roman Grill was the first person to suggest to me that Guardiola was as versatile as he has since proven. The Catalan had developed an image of an obdurate and inflexible pedant at Barcelona: the master of positional play and passing football who was only satisfied with more than 70% possession in any game. A lover of the ball whose celebrated but misnamed 'tiki-taka' quickly became the stuff of legend.

At the time Guardiola was quick to dismiss what he considered an inaccurate and reductionist term, 'Tiki-taka? Total shit. It's a meaningless concept which basically describes passing the ball for the sake of passing. Aimlessly, with no aggression or particular plan.'

At first glance his reaction seemed to be no more than that of a talented professional rejecting a term that fails to do justice to a complex playing model and which, in his view, made a mockery of the kind of football Barcelona played. But there was more to it than that. I've already said that Guardiola has an unconventional mind. Why then would he bullishly insist on his own playing model? Why would he dismiss the new ideas Germany had to offer about football? This obstinacy doesn't mesh with the image of an open-minded, curious man who is always looking for ideas he can borrow from other sports (chess, handball, rugby, the list goes on) or from the world of art and culture. If one of the motors which drives him is this need to change for change's sake then why would he reject exciting, challenging new ideas just because they are different from his own?

## EDDIE JONES AND 'TRANSITIONS'
### Munich, 19 September 2015

They had just got back from Darmstadt, where Bayern had thrashed the home side 3-0 and Estiarte had dropped Pep off at home. Within minutes he was on the phone.

'Pep, have you seen the news about Eddie Jones, and the Japan rugby team?'

'No, what's happened?'

World Cup rugby had just been rocked by the biggest

shock defeat in its history. Japan had beaten South Africa 34-32 thanks to a try in the dying moments of the game. Pep is amazed. No-one could have predicted this. Not even the most fanatical of rugby fans. The Japanese had produced a superb performance, fighting hard and never allowing the South Africans (double world champions in 1995 and 2007 and one of the great superpowers of the game) to dominate the scoreboard so that by half-time they were trailing by just two points (12-10).

Then with five minutes left the team trained by Eddie Jones (born in Tasmania to a Japanese mother and an Australian father), trailing by three points, took up residency on the South African twenty-two-metre line. Japan were awarded various penalties each of which, individually, would have tied the score and assured them of a result which would already have been historic. But, imbued with a singular spirit of competitive sporting 'honour', the Japanese chose bravery and sought glory by rejecting a draw and going for the try which would give them victory. Time and again they battered into the South Africans, hauling themselves up incessantly to create long sequences of passes by recycling the ball. Eventually, Jones' men moved the ball to the right wing before rapidly changing to the opposite side of the pitch so that Karne Hesketh could go over for the triumphant score.

Rugby lovers the world over joined the ecstatic celebrations. David had toppled Goliath.

Guardiola couldn't quite believe it.

But he knew just how significant a win it was because back in December 2014 he had spent an afternoon working with Jones. The Japan coach (now in charge of England) had come to Säbener Strasse so that the two men could chat and share experiences.

'In terms of finding space and moving the ball rugby and football are actually quite similar and I wanted to meet Pep Guardiola so that he could show me how to make my squad more flexible tactically,' said Jones. 'We need to be able to vary our tactical formation in response to the rhythm and demands of each game.' It was clearly a meeting of two great coaching minds.

When he first arrived in Munich Pep fully intended to bring Cruyff's and Barça's game to Bayern. However, almost as soon as he was established at the Bavarian club it became clear that he'd have to go another way. There were two reasons for this: he understood immediately that he lacked the right kind of players to reproduce the same playing model and the wide range of talent in the squad opened up whole new possibilities in terms of strategy and tactics.

Ferran Adrià, considered the world's best chef for many years and certainly the most creative and ground-breaking of his peers, was happy to share his observations about Guardiola. His comments about the need for personal development and education were particularly insightful. 'In my view Pep went to Bayern too soon. He would have been better taking not just one sabbatical year, but actually two or three to travel extensively and educate himself about the rest of the world. I understand a club like Bayern is hard to turn down, there aren't many clubs with such an impressive history and track record, and he really had to grab the opportunity when it came his way. I still say however that it would have been better for him to spend some time expanding his horizons. I'll explain why. Basically Pep has never developed a scientifically tested working methodology. That's why I encouraged him to visit MIT (Massachusetts Institute of Technology) during his year in New York. MIT is the most pioneering centre of innovation in the world and I wanted him to meet Israel Ruiz, its executive vice-president and see the work they're doing in their technology and design department, MediaLab. I really felt that it would help develop his own methodologies.

'It's one thing to be a football expert who has watched thousands of games but it's quite another to know how to apply scientific principles to your work. It's almost like your players are robots on whom you test your ideas. Or at least that would be the ideal scenario in a scientific context. When you talk to Pep he always says, "At Barça, my tactics consisted of getting the ball to Messi." You never really get a sense of how Pep judges his own performances. We're good friends and I think I know him pretty well but I don't see him applying any kind of tried and tested scientific approach to his work. Obviously it's a tough ask because it would involve getting away from football altogether for a couple of years. But it's the only way to get the mental space necessary to start de-codifying the game and then begin to construct the right methodology. I did it. I closed my restaurant el Bulli, put some distance between myself and my work and then started to de-codify cooking.'

Adrià gets it spot-on when he quotes Pep because the former Barça manager has often said, 'When I was at Barcelona I saw my job as making sure the team did the right things at the right time to get the ball to Messi exactly when he needed it. And then Messi would score.'

A different approach was required at Bayern. There was no Messi to work his unique brand of magic, nor a group of players who'd been trained since a young age in how to apply his philosophy on the pitch. So the coach had been obliged to construct a different circuit-board of football at Bayern, very different to that of Barcelona – most of all because he lacked a miraculous creator and taker of goals like Messi.

Adrià sees parallels with basketball. 'Phil Jackson used to say that it was what Scottie Pippen did for the Chicago Bulls that allowed Michael Jordan to be Michael Jordan – and Xavi and Iniesta were the ones at Barça who allowed Messi to be Messi.' Bayern couldn't offer Pep a Messi or a Xavi, but it was this that in the end proved the stimulus to come up with new, more imaginative ways of winning.

Adrià says that Pep's deliberate decision to test his own capabilities was the catalyst for the explosion of creativity and new-found versatility we witnessed. 'Almost immediately Pep realised that Bayern couldn't be another Barça. He had no Messi, no Xavi or Iniesta and without these three key players it would be impossible to recreate the monster he'd unleashed in the Catalan capital. So he did the smart thing and decided to rely on his own instincts and resources. He was effectively testing himself. Had his success at Barça been a flash in the pan? There was only one way to find out. And, as we know now, nothing could be further from the truth because Guardiola went on to reproduce the same basic model but with modified concepts and different interpretations at Bayern. Some concepts changed because they were inapplicable, others because there were more appropriate ways to apply them . . . Only the absence of Messi (and Xavi and Iniesta) prevented him from replicating the full glory of his Barça years and his many triumphs at Bayern prove beyond doubt that, with or without a touch of Messi magic, his model works.'

After having spent three years observing Guardiola at Bayern, I believe that this new-found eclecticism is now a central part of his character. He has successfully fused the philosophy of a radical Cruyffista (possession, passing, attack, defending high up the pitch) with the German qualities of speed and vertical play, putting the ball into spaces, crossing into the box and overloading attacks.

In reality the true measure of a coach is not so much the quality of his convictions but rather his ability to teach and embed them even in less than ideal conditions. A good coach should be constantly revising his beliefs, amending and adapting them to achieve the perfect synergy between his own philosophy and the club he represents. A belief system should never become the straitjacket of dogma and it's clear that Guardiola now sees his philosophy as just a frame of reference within which he can move and expand.

I should point out that, despite the many improvements and advances Pep made in terms of his personal playing bible as well as that of the German champions, there were one or two areas where he failed to make significant progress. I am thinking here of his planning and direction of Bayern's counter-attacking as well as his management and control of the rhythm of their games.

On the first point, even though Pep's regularly emphasised that he likes his team to counter-attack, his determination to dominate play in the opposition half makes counter-attacking almost impossible. If a team 'owns' the ball for 75% of the match and the whole objective of its game plan is to try to play right in front of the opposition penalty box as much as possible then there won't be the space necessary to generate counters. To create that space you've got to allow the other team to have the ball as a tactic to trick them into over-committing. An obvious example over the last couple of seasons has been Luis Enrique's magnificent Barcelona team which has got this tactic down to a fine art. But it's also undeniable that Barça edging away from such total domination of the ball and the game they played under Guardiola has created many more moments of defensive strain than in other eras.

Up until now Guardiola has preferred to place emphasis on dominating the play, as far away from his own goalmouth as possible, rather than creating the right conditions to manage and perfect the counter-attack ideology. He doesn't want to lose the status of being the team which dominates matches and which is regularly the least scored-against.

'What I ask my players is: "When is it more dangerous – when the ball's near our goal or when it's far away?" Of course the answer is: "When it's far away." Nobody will convince me otherwise.'

## A COUNTER-ATTACK GOAL
### Munich, 7 November 2015

Pep's in the staff dining room, delightedly reviewing the video images of six Bayern players thundering towards the

Stuttgart goalmouth to score the game's opening goal. A goal which makes the technical staff very happy for one specific reason: 'A counter-attack goal!' roars Pep, thrilled at how his players sprinted on to a successful counter.

Stuttgart have a corner in their favour but just seventeen seconds after taking it they've conceded a goal, one which Robben has glanced in off his stomach. But behind the success of the goal lies the analysis prepared by Carles Planchart. 'We studied them, we studied how to do that and it just came off perfectly.'

Torrent, responsible for planning strategic plays for upcoming matches, underlined this move in red ink when preparing his briefing notes because Stuttgart had a habit he'd spotted. Their tendency was to play corners short to allow Insúa to take a couple of touches and then cross into the goalmouth from a better angle. In doing so they took a risk however, because only Serey Die, the organising midfielder, stayed back to cover a possible counter.

In the morning match analysis Torrent had told the players that if they managed to steal the ball quickly from Insúa then it would almost certainly create a dangerous counter.

Said and done. Eleventh minute, corner to Stuttgart and they've put eight men in or around the box with Insúa waiting to receive the ball short, and only Die as the stop-gap at the back. Insúa's cross is low and weak, Vidal takes possession easily and Bayern are off on the gallop towards Tyton's goal. It's six versus one at high speed. Eight touches later during eleven seconds on the ball and Bayern score – and the coaches and technical staff feel like all their work has been worth it.

The other aspect of Bayern's game in which Pep failed to achieve total success was his management of the rhythm and tempo of games, especially in the immediate aftermath of an opposition goal. Bayern were inconsistent in this area of their game as Guardiola himself acknowledged.

'There are times in matches when we've lost control but it's really a consequence of the style of football we play. We're constantly pushing forward, pressing and pressing, hammering our opponents so they don't have time to think. It's incredibly hard to change that dynamic in the heat of a match. I've spent hours trying to solve this. How can I tell them to stop pressing, moving forward, bombarding the other team? Precisely when we need to fight back and equalise! It's so fucking hard to find the right balance. I've spent three long years telling them to go up and press, drumming it into them every second of their working day, telling them to never, ever let up. How the hell do I turn round and suddenly announce that we need more of a calm, measured response at certain key moments? It would be like suggesting to a lion that he should walk, not run.

'Too often we've not been able to instil stability once we've been hit by the sucker punch of a goal or a chance. "Stable" means being able to organise defensively as if nothing's happened, to put together twenty consecutive passes in order to calm everything down. But, no, because they feel they have to fight back immediately they're after the ball and breaking up the pitch in a disorganised way – we just run hell for leather upfield sometimes. It's because of how the team's put together – if you've five strikers on the pitch the temptation is to get the ball up to them as swiftly as we can in search of an equaliser or to get back ahead immediately. But what's really needed in moments like these is the midfielder's mentality: "win the ball, move the ball around fifty times". With that you lower the heat of the match, the team which has scored against you loses a bit of heat and energy and you can then work out how to tip the game back your way. But if you take the ball and bomb forward you'll lose it and then have to keep chasing back. If that's happening when your rival's buzzing from just having scored then there's every chance they'll catch you again. No, that's not the way. Win the ball, pass it twenty times and lower the temperature.'

And I can tell you that, to this day, this dilemma remains tucked away under 'Pending – Needs More Work' in Guardiola's mental filing cabinet.


## DOUBT AND DECISION MAKING

One can only have faith in doubt.
*Jorge Wagensberg*

A certain measure of doubt is likely to be a permanent feature of Guardiola's life but during his last year in Munich I watched as his tendency to vacillate gradually became a new-found decisiveness. Pep sees doubt as a positive quality which enhances rather than detracts from his analytical skills. Just as a chess player systematically evaluates all the possible moves available to him, Pep sees his 'doubts' as the stimulus for the forensic examination he carries out as he prepares for match day, mentally walking through his game plan in order to identify all possibilities and potential problems.

He believes that in football no strategy is foolproof and that any opponent is capable of putting his men under pressure. In the past, some have taken Guardiola's seemingly exaggeratedly high opinion of other teams' abilities as a crude attempt to play mind-games with the opposition. In fact, the truth is much simpler. Pep has never suffered any kind of superiority complex and always detects potential threats in his opponents, whoever they may be. He sees this as an essential step in exploring the range of options available to him.

Like any grandmaster, once he has completed his analysis of the opposition, he moves on to examine how to exploit their weaknesses. This will be his 'basic game plan'. The next step is working out the tactical approaches he can use to neutralise any potential threats. It's a complex, demanding process which leaves him with a long list of different playing strategies and alternative line-ups. All the options are laid out for dissection and no idea is ever dismissed out of hand, no matter how crazy it seems. This is the process after all that has given us Lahm as a right winger in a crucial Champions League match or wingers Robben and Ribéry as attacking inside-midfielders in other, admittedly less vital, matches.

This relentless, obsessive determination to study the game plan from every angle is one of Guardiola's greatest strengths. But, until his last season at Bayern, it was also his Achilles heel, at times causing the Catalan to invest far too much of his precious time in planning. Indeed, I have on occasion witnessed him furiously scribbling last-minute changes in the afternoon of a match day itself. On these occasions it seems that Guardiola's attempts to manage his doubts and identify every possible variant can also lead to unnecessary hesitation and inefficient decision making.

All of that has now changed. Gone is the hesitation. He still hypothesises, analyses and scrutinises every detail but nowadays he makes his decision and sticks with it. No second thoughts. In fact, on at least six occasions during the spring of 2016, Pep was able to describe his plan to me several days before the game, down to the last detail and the last man. And by match day, I can tell you, not a single factor had changed.

'HERE'S HOW WE'RE GOING TO PLAY . . .'
Munich, 5 April 2016

Pep is shifting up a gear as he guides his team through the quarter-finals of the Champions League. He still goes through his usual exhaustive analysis in the run-up to every match but it's obvious that he is no longer assailed by self-doubt. Bayern have just beaten Benfica 1-0 and he's already clear how they will approach the away leg. Over dinner he talks through his strategy with his dad, Valentí, and his son, Màrius.

'We'll fill the midfield with Xabi, Vidal, Thiago and Lahm. The four of them will play in a diamond shape, bringing the ball through from the back. Up front we'll play three, not four. One of the two centre forwards will be on the bench. Lewa or Müller. Two wingers, one striker, four men in midfield.

'That's the plan because against Benfica we can't allow ourselves to be stretched out too vertically or try to shell the ball to the winger to attack wide because they are extremely quick at closing wingers down with three of their players. We must play the ball to our wingers so that they can get it back into the middle of the pitch searching for an "inside" breakthrough. That someone comes up with a nice dribble to beat his man, that we create a one v one situation . . . and *then* we open up wide because once we've stretched them they won't have the time to react and cover our wingers. Goals need to come from midfield runners, arriving in the box unmarked for that cross. Rather than populate their penalty area and look to win the ball when it comes in, I want us to appear there just at the right time. That's the plan.'

Over the following seven days he studies other alternatives but he decides to go with his instincts and play with the diamond four midfield and one striker. This updated, 2016 version of Guardiola springs far fewer surprises on his technical staff.

Only time, and Pep's experiences at Manchester City, will tell us whether this new-found decisiveness is the natural consequence of the process of growth Guardiola has gone through or merely because his project at Bayern had reached its completion by the spring of 2016.

Whichever it is, I well remember Guardiola's advice to Patricio Ormazábal, former player and now 'juveniles' coach at Chile's Cruzados University. 'You have to go with your instincts no matter what. As long as you believe it can work, that it's not total nonsense, you've got to try it. If you think you've gone wrong then look at it again but if it's good, go for it. Maybe you try something – say, a new way of playing the ball out from the back – but it goes wrong; even then you shouldn't dismiss it as a dead loss – go back and re-work it. Never do what the other guy does just because he's won the clash. Follow your gut.'

I'd like at this point to say, for the record, that I've never, ever heard Pep telling anyone that his ideas are better than any other coach. He's never claimed that positional play is more effective than long ball football or defensive/counter-attacking football. Pep believes in his ideas and will always work to refine and improve them. He wants to do everything as perfectly as he can but that is a long way from believing that his is the true path and the only way of doing things. On the contrary, I have already detailed how eager he is to absorb and integrate elements of models practised by other coaches (including rivals for whom he has enormous respect, like Ranieri and Klopp).

Guardiola's admirers and detractors alike seem never to tire of pigeon-holing the coach, often labelling him a dogmatic control freak. They could not be more wrong. He is a man in constant evolution, looking for new ideas wherever he goes and moulding them to his own philosophy. If he likes an idea he makes it his own, regardless of its original source, and then works to make it work. Unfortunately, many see football through the filter of stereotypes, clichés and, far too often, abusive critique. People with limited understanding and a lack of football intelligence are quite happy to express their own misguided views and then justify them by coming up with labels. This lazy, uninformed approach then creates a belief in non-existent concepts such as *Guardiolaism* or the equally meaningless *Anti-Guardiolaism*.

In truth there is no such thing as *Guardiolaism*. Guardiola will always seek to improve and grow and I have already described the evolution he has gone through as well as his innate interest in experimentation, and he has never claimed to have created a particular ideology or set himself up as the one true light of football. He emphatically rejects all mention of *Guardiolaism* and considers many of the inaccurate claims made by his 'greatest fans' as nothing more than ridiculous and unnecessary platitudes.

## INNOVATION

To innovate is to make connections
*Jon Pascua Ibarrola*

Amongst the many possible definitions of the word 'innovation', the one offered by Ferran Adrià, whilst unusual, is probably the closest fit for what Guardiola does: 'Innovation is, and has always been about earning a living.'

But what about innovation in football?

Here the process of creation manifests itself on the pitch and it is the players who are the 'innovators'. Of course coaches innovate too, but only in the sense of managing and applying their resources in new, inventive ways. The tactical moves a coach develops are not, strictly speaking, his 'creations' but rather his attempts to come up with new ways to use the resources at his disposal.

Professor Julio Garganta explains this in musical terms: 'Music has been around for a long time and we're all familiar with the fact that there are different notes, rhythms and beats.

'None of those have really changed over time and yet every day we get new compositions, new musical interpretations. Why? Because musicians use those notes, rhythms and beats in new ways to create new combinations. It's exactly the same in football, but for innovation to take place it's necessary to know how to think and to know how to act in accordance with your ideas.'

Guardiola is not possessed of a pioneering spirit. Nor is he driven by the need to produce ground-breaking work. He innovates because his job demands it. What galvanises his creativity is his bullish determination to beat the opposition and the need to come up with new ways of doing so.

How then to describe Guardiola's ideal playing system?

In a word: change.

In this sense, his creative process is straightforward. He has a job to do, a game to win and needs to identify all potential threats and barriers. He must analyse his opponent and then devise new and better ways of using his resources (players, positions and roles) to achieve optimum results. At the end of this process he is left with the final 'product' which often, though not always, might be described as innovative.

This need to refine and improve has been the driving force behind the work of football coaches throughout history. If you look at any 'great' career, you'll see a coach who's always attempted to enhance their use of available resources and that many of the 'pioneering' tactics of the modern game have their roots in the past.

Take a look at the different 'false 9s' in football history and you will find a recurring factor in all the coaches who've played like that (Hugo Meisl, Carlos Peucelle, Gusztáv Sebes, José Villalonga Llorente, Johan Cruyff, Luciano Spalletti, and Guardiola). It's the identical idea but implemented in quite different contexts. Take a look at how Cambridge University utilised the 2-3-5 in 1880 and how Guardiola re-utilised the 'pyramid' structure in 2015 and we can see something similar. The same structure emerged from the basic wish to find new uses for the way players were usually used.

This is true of most of what we see as the advances and inventions of the modern game. They are not really 'inventions' in the true sense of the word but different ways of using the same resources.

It appears, therefore, that most coaches must regularly draw on the past for inspiration. For example, when Juanma Lillo suggested to Guardiola that he use an 'hour glass formation' in certain games it generated an intense debate between Guardiola and his assistants:

'How can we risk playing with five forwards without ending up completely annihilated?'

The answer they came up with resulted in the 2-3-5 system they used to thrash Arsenal and to fight back from a losing position against Juventus in the Champions League.

Paco Seirul.lo sheds more light on this. 'Football is less evolved than other team sports, such as basketball or handball. They have the advantage of playing in tight spaces and using their hands and that gives them more options to invent new tactics and interact in different ways. We footballers, on the other hand, use our feet and have to outsmart our opponents in a much bigger arena. So, if you want to experiment and invent, you have to improve the technical level of the players themselves. And that means that if we want football to keep evolving we must continue to develop the way we train players. The modern footballer has to accept that it's not enough knowing how to play. You have to understand the game and, unfortunately, that's what's lacking in many cases.

'Some players are intuitive and some are very talented in this area. One player will work out that it's advantageous to dribble to the right when your opponent's left foot is planted on the pitch and he's unable to react to that movement as quickly. But one of his teammates may never come to this same conclusion on his own and therefore limits himself to always passing the ball rather than taking on his man. But that happens not just because this teammate can't work it out for himself, but also because nobody's taught him.

'The truth is that individual players, regardless of where they are or who they're working for, are perfectly capable of coming up with new techniques themselves which their coaches or clubs, if they're smart, then appropriate. We then call this 'evolution'. And this is why people say that football is all about the players, which is partially true. The players are the ones who help the game develop, but I think it's more accurate to say that football is all about teams. It's the team's success that goes down in history. Look at the Marvellous Magyars, the Clockwork Orange [Holland], Sacchi's Milan, the "Pep Team" . . .'

# 'HAVE YOU EVER SEEN
# ONE OF CRUYFF'S GAMES?'
## Madrid, 9 January 2015

'I remember this time Messi, Xavi and Víctor Valdés came to one of my workshops at "el Bulli" and I asked them, "Have you ever seen the Ajax team of the '70s play? Cruyff's team?" And they said, "No,"' smiles Ferran Adrià. 'I couldn't believe it. You see footage of that team now and they look totally up-to-date. It's astonishing. If you look at Pelé's Brazil side they seem so old-fashioned. But that Ajax of the '70s . . . they were something else. Their football looks totally fresh and modern. And those three had never watched any of their games! Xavi, Messi and Valdés!

'But is it essential for the likes of Xavi, Messi and Valdés to watch Cruyff's Ajax? Probably not. They're players after all, not coaches . . .

'Now, if you want to talk about the value of innovation . . . Firstly we need to establish exactly what innovation means in football terms. At the end of the day, we measure success in goals so surely the true innovator is the guy who invents a dribble or the one who invented the lob or the overhead kick? We also need to decide where it's possible to innovate? And to do that you have to first de-codify football.

'You could believe in innovation in various areas of football, not just the work of an individual player. You could decide, for example, to make changes in the way you organise the bench, put people in different places to make some kind of impact for whatever reason. But again first we have to de-codify the methodology used.

'Pep always tells me, "Cruyff was the best. The fucking best." And I'll say, "And what about Michels?"

'So it looks like it comes down to one of two things. Either people keep inventing new techniques in football or in fact they're just re-inventing something that's already been done. However creative and stunningly innovative you may think you are, everything is based on evolving what went before.

## BARRIERS TO INNOVATION

It is one thing to know
and quite another to take advantage of what is known.
*Ricardo Olivós*

The possibility that a particular innovation becomes fashionable and is then copied is directly related, in football as in life, to how difficult it is to introduce it. For example, it's easy enough to copy a back four system (you simply have to have four players who know how to defend). In contrast, to create an organised, co-ordinated defensive structure in which all eleven players participate fluently is much more demanding. And installing a complex system of positional play, where attackers and defenders become indistinguishable and every single individual and collective movement is planned to perfection, raises the bar of difficulty much, much higher.

As such, these different levels of difficulty govern how a system can be imitated or copied. In the case of positional play, the most complex and elaborate football philosophy in existence, it's possible for a team to appear to be using it while in reality they're merely copying some identifiable parts of this style while ignoring the inherent basic concepts. They therefore only manage to produce some of the effects but none of the causes.

This is an understandable failing because the ability to implant this model of football requires certain conditions. The technical staff, particularly the coach, must have a profound understanding of positional play, its characteristics, the reasons for it and the 'why' of every position, every movement and every decision. They also need complete fluency and confidence in the enormous amount of teaching required to inculcate this particular philosophy among a squad. For the footballers, positional play demands excellent tactical comprehension and a complete willingness to learn a complex system which is difficult to dominate.

This degree of difficulty may well explain why such a small number of teams have been able to adopt and master it. Until now probably only Barcelona, Bayern and Borussia Dortmund can be placed on that list. Others who have come close include national teams like Chile, Germany, Spain, Italy and Peru, plus clubs like Hoffenheim, coached by the young Julian Nagelsmann, the Rayo Vallecano of Paco Jémez, or Quique Setien's Las Palmas. By the summer of 2016, Sevilla, coached by Jorge Sampaoli and Juanma Lillo, have also begun to completely immerse themselves in this complex tactical structure.

But perhaps there's still more, beyond the obstacles I've specified, which makes this philosophy hard to apply. Lillo is the best at explaining this: 'Those that have succeeded in playing this way have also succeeded in making most people in football fall into the easy trap of believing that to succeed with the positional system it's vital to possess truly "great" footballers. The contrary seems true to me. People are confusing the possible with the probable.

'By football's own laws, this sport allows anyone to beat anybody else and even more now that there's been the change of rule about the kick-off not needing to go forward into your opponent's half. Without crossing the halfway line you can go 1-0 ahead. That kind of concept doesn't exist in any other sport.

'The coach can train with the "probable" in mind and try to increase his team's "probabilities" of winning. But the possible? That a donkey might fly is possible but very improbable. And there are a thousand other examples of things that are possible but extremely improbable. While we're speaking I could grow and end up two metres tall. It's possible but highly improbable.'

And so I asked him, 'What positional play is trying to achieve is to greatly increase the percentage probabilities of winning specifically because of the style of play? Is that your point?'

'That's demonstrably true,' he replied, 'but not only with exceptional football teams. It also applies to much more modest sides. But given that positional play has become identified with the very best football teams like Cruyff's Dream Team or Pep's Barça, people conclude that to practise it successfully you require exceptional players. Obviously with great footballers you can, and, usually will, implement positional play successfully. And, in actual fact, some other, very different models *absolutely* depend on having brilliant players. For example, winning by playing two-touch football, where the central defender fires a long ball directly over three-quarters of the pitch to the centre forward, is really difficult. Winning when just two players take a couple of touches each is in fact far less likely than with positional play – at least unless you've got Maradona as the centre half launching the ball to Maradona as the striker. If not, then you're definitely going to struggle.'

In Lillo's opinion this explains the shortage of positional play practitioners. 'All this confusion means that instead of people preaching that with positional play you increase the probability of winning, the refrain has become that you shouldn't bother unless you possess truly great footballers. But it's just the contrary. My concept is that trying to win with only two or three players intervening in each attack, each using just two or three touches of the ball, it's a miracle if you succeed. It's possible, but it would be almost miraculous. If people tell me that there have therefore been many miracles, I'll tell them, yeah, if both teams have pinned their hopes on this "miracle" then they may achieve it.

'Anyone who claims that positional play only works if played by truly great footballers is really only interested in avoiding the difficulty of implementing this complex philosophy.'

# BACKSTAGE 3

## FIGHTING FOR 'SURVIVAL' WITH
## A 3-5-2 FORMATION
### Dortmund, 4 April 2015

It's Thursday 2 April and Pep, having checked with 'the bible', has taken the decision he'll share with his assistants first thing in the morning. Without Robben and Ribéry's anarchic skills, Alaba's unique ability to get all over the pitch or Badstuber's sense of anticipation (they're all out because of injury) things don't look good. The coach knows that Lahm and Thiago are still not fully match-sharp and that his team will be going into their next game feeling at a disadvantage. He can't just pretend that everything's fine and send his men into Dortmund's Signal Iduna Park like lambs to the slaughter, so he's decided to go for the 3-5-2 he used in the 2014 Cup Final: an extra man in defence and in the middle of the field, two less in attack. Straight from the Pep bible.

Training over the next two days focuses on practising this system. Rafinha and Bernat as wing backs need to perform like an accordion, opening and then tightening up either side of their three centre backs. Xabi Alonso will have to work really hard to ensure that there's no space between him and the centre-halves. There's to be no chance of 'handing over' that lethal zone where Dortmund's free players can do damage. Lahm and Schweinsteiger will play like inside forwards, pushing forward, pressurising and creating chances. Only one of them at a time can break away from

Alonso however, whilst the other stays tight to the Spaniard. Strikers, Müller and Lewandowski, will have the toughest task of all. Between them they have to tie down the four rival defenders playing with enough skill and aggression to prevent the opposition players moving into the midfield. They will be expected to maintain possession whilst they construct Bayern's attack, working almost completely alone. Guardiola's instructions have been clear – 'zero risks'. Lewandowski and Müller are on their own in attack.

This is the toughest stage of the season and Pep's only plan is survival.

As yet he has no idea whether or not he'll be able to move to a new game plan by late April or May. One injury after another has caused him to repeatedly revise his strategy. Having started out with a 3-4-3, Javi Martínez's knee problems forced a rethink. Then, when Xabi Alonso arrived he thought he'd be able to use a more orthodox form of his positional play only to be thwarted by Thiago's problems flaring up again as well as Lahm's injury. His third strategy, centred around five strikers, was a huge success but, just as Robben and Ribéry began to hit top form as attacking midfielders, Bayern's injury jinx struck once more and both players had to be substituted in the Champions League clash against Shakhtar Donetsk . . . Leaving Pep searching for a fourth game plan.

But it's early April and there just isn't enough time to practise and refine a completely new idea. Now every match, every three days, is like a final. With the return of Lahm and Thiago, after a combined absence of eighteen months, the option of some pure Guardiola-style football looks tempting: Alonso or Schweinsteiger as pivote helping these two returning attacking midfielders to filter the perfect 'assist' pass through to the strikers. But the reality is a little less simple.

Lahm runs on a diesel engine. He's to be relied on more than almost any other player but he needs time to regain his sharpness and they don't have a lot of time. He's been out too long. Thiago? Well, it's over a year since he played and he, like the Bayern fans, has had his confidence shaken by his constant injury problems. Can Pep really base his match strategy on two players who are so far off their best form? His answer is a reluctant 'no'. It's more important for the team to survive than for Pep to design a fourth major tactical plan.

So Bayern go into their 'clasico' against Dortmund using a 3-5-2 formation. From the start, their opponents struggle to deal with Bayern's tight, compact lines which deny them what they need most – space to run in. For the first time this season, Pep's men aren't interested in the ball, nor do they seem to want to dominate in the opposition's half.

The coach's instructions are very clear: compact lines, numerical superiority in defence and the centre of the field, minimise the amount of times you give the ball away and get the ball as often and as early as possible to the two strikers in search of a breakaway goal. Dortmund's game is as electric as ever but they're hurting and within ten minutes of the start of the match, begin to cave in. Bayern, today reminiscent of the Ancient Roman legions, stick tenaciously to their 'tortoise formation', impenetrable and protected on all sides.

The three central defenders Benatia, Boateng and Dante excel. Schweinsteiger, although the match stats seem to suggest otherwise, is more focused than ever and produces a formidable performance. As does Bernat. Müller and Lewandowski follow the instructions to perfection, tying up the back line and conjuring a goal between them.

The Pole in particular is excellent. Lewandowski not only

scores the winning goal, sharing the merit for its creation with his strike partner, but breaks a couple of Bayern records in the process, beating his opponent in thirty out of sixty-three battles for the ball, ten of which are aerial contests. On the day that Pep's team play their least recognisable football, by some distance, Müller and Lewandowski produce their best game of the season. There may be a simple explanation for this. As a rule Bayern prefer to hem in their rivals high up the pitch but today there's been lots of space to roam and both players are in their element.

Once again, Jürgen Klopp struggles to work out Bayern's game plan. It looks like the Dortmund coach was expecting business as usual from Pep's side: positional play and lots of passing around the midfield designed to drag Dortmund out of position. He and his players seem utterly confused by this compact, closed Bayern who don't seem interested in dominating in their opponents' area or in amassing vast quantities of possession. They had expected Guardiola's usual brand of explosive, dynamic football and are instead forced to contend with this cautious, measured alternative. It's not the first time Bayern have dispatched them with a compact, tight 3-5-2. Guardiola also found himself forced into emergency measures on Cup Final day.

Later on Pep says to me, 'It's great to have Thiago back. He breathes life into the team.'

The rest of his men obviously agree and Xabi Alonso sums up the feeling in the team: 'The Magician's returned.'

In the end Thiago only plays for twenty minutes, coming on for the captain, Lahm, who has once again run himself into the ground despite not being fully fit. After a year out, Thiago's first five minutes are astonishing. Apparently driven on by some internal force, the Spaniard initially seems to be playing a different sport from everyone else. He demands the ball, offers himself in the space between lines, dribbles, squirms past opponents and passes to his strikers through gaps only he can see. For five breathtaking minutes Thiago monopolises the game completely but then begins to flag as his lack of full fitness begins to show. Pep puts Götze on to give him some support but he has begun to fade and will end the encounter totally drained.

Bayern have, however, successfully outclassed Dortmund and this result is one more decisive step towards winning their third consecutive Bundesliga title and Pep's second since taking over in Munich.

Everyone's ecstatic. This is a huge boost for the team who now have two things to celebrate: their victory today plus the return of Thiago the Magician. In the dressing room his teammates cheer and chant his name, reducing the Spanish player to tears. He's had a disastrous year and the emotions of the moment are too much. He breaks down as his teammates embrace him, hugging and kissing him.

'That was a big performance for us,' says Xabi. 'Say what you want about Dortmund. They may be struggling for points, but that was a very tough game. Today was like a Champions League semi-final.'

Jürgen Klopp, as open and generous as ever, comments, 'Bayern deserved to win.'

Guardiola has now won fifty Bundesliga games out of a possible sixty-one. And he's done it faster than anyone before him. Until now Udo Lattek has held the record with fifty wins out of a possible sixty-eight. Guardiola is still setting records and he knows that this is one step closer towards his second consecutive league title but, having left the match the happiest of men, he'll end the day with a post-match analysis that will leave him frustrated and upset.

Before that however, he goes to each of his players, hugging them in delight. He's especially effusive with Lahm and Thiago and also makes a point of publicly congratulating Dante who's had a dispiriting few weeks. The coach is extremely pleased with his team and tells them proudly that they 'pulled together and played like a real team'. Everyone's proud of an achievement which has come at a particularly tough time. They may be battling injuries but Pep's men are united in their determination to overcome the setbacks and keep winning. Morale is higher than it's ever been.

Behind closed doors however, Pep's unhappy. His state of mind is at odds with his earlier displays of euphoria at the end of the match when he embraced Lahm thirty seconds before the final whistle. Pep has many reasons to be cheerful. Not least this decisive win over an opponent who, if not currently on top form, has been a colossus of the Bundesliga over the last few years. League winners on two occasions, Champions League finalists, winners of the 2012 Cup (beating Bayern 5-2), German Super Cup winners twice in a row.

'We won and we did what we had to do. I gave them the plan and the lads executed it perfectly. But my plan was total shit. An exercise in survival. We needed to get out alive so that we could keep moving forward despite all the crap we've been through.'

In this mood, he's deaf to anyone arguing how vital it was to play this way today. 'We'll get nowhere playing like that. Sure, we jump one hurdle but it's not the kind of football we should be playing.'

I mention Thiago and Lahm and point out the number of injuries he's had to cope with but he's not listening. They've won the match but he's far from satisfied. In his heart of hearts he knows that there was no other option and it was, after all, he himself who made the decision. But as soon as the victory's won his stubborn, nonconformist side asserts itself. This is a million miles away from how he wants to play. And Pep's not happy.

# 4

# WHAT MAKES HIM THE BEST?

The best teachers are those who show you where to look.
Not those who tell you what to see.
*Alexandra Trefor*

PEP'S TACTICAL EXPERTISE made a quantum leap forward in Germany precisely because he was forced to leave the comfort zone of the game he had practised at Barcelona during four outstanding years there. Having found that it was impossible to simply transfer the same system from one club to another, he realised that he would have to change and as a result developed a wealth of new approaches to the game.

Guardiola quickly grasped that, for him, survival at Bayern would mean adapting his own vision to a footballing culture that has always fundamentally favoured (despite appearances to the contrary) power and breaking at high speed without caring too much about how that leaves things at the back, or worrying about potential negative consequences. That is why Bundesliga football offers the fastest and most carefully constructed counter-attacking in Europe, although, because it is not always done with the greatest efficiency, it can at times look imprecise, hurried and uncontrolled.

Guardiola tends to have a lot to say on the dangers of long ball football and is fond of quoting Juanma Lillo on this subject: '"The faster the ball goes, the faster it comes back." It's definitely one of Lillo's best sayings and he always talks a lot of sense. I used it a lot when I worked with the players at Bayern but it took me a while to find an exact translation. I said to them, "Okay, you like long balls? No problem. But you should understand one thing – the faster the ball goes, the faster it comes back." It's just one of those bloody things you have to accept in football. In eight out of ten situations when you kick the ball long, the opposition central defender is going to get to it and win it back. You're running after it and it's already on its way back.

'They'd say: "Who cares! Get it up the pitch right away, hit the ball long." It was a fucking pain in the neck to get it over to them and I had to explain it over and over again, as no doubt I'll have to in England as well.'

Juanma Lillo has played a significant role in Guardiola's career. Johan Cruyff gave Pep his opportunity as a player and eventually promoted him to captain at Barcelona but it was Juanma Lillo who guided him through his transition from player to coach.

If Cruyff, helped by the young player's natural intuition, implanted the idea in Pep's head, it was Lillo who helped him develop a conceptual understanding of what it means in practice. Guardiola who, like Cruyff, is highly intuitive, also needed Lillo's more didactic approach to fully understand and use this model.

Hardly a day passes without Pep making reference to the ideas of one of his two great mentors and, at work, much of his conversation starts with, 'As Juanma used to say . . .'

In Pep's view Lillo's enormous talent as a coach is underrated and he himself is quite clear about where the great man's talent lies. 'When he coaches, it's all about what he does, rather than how much he says.' For Pep, Lillo's genius lies less in the words he uses but rather in his talent for teaching concepts through practical, repeated application. Essentially, he uses a 'hands-on' teaching approach around which he constructs his team's game.

I got the chance to talk to Lillo himself about this. 'If you develop your play slowly you'll be under pressure from the start, for sure. But if your football's very fast and direct you're going to have the ball thrown back at you almost immediately. In football, to get up high, you need passing movements in the main part of the pitch. There's only one thing that gives or takes away order in a game and that's the ball itself, so I like my players to be in lots of different partnerships but also strung across different areas of the field. If their passing is good, then we'll be moving our rivals all over the pitch and then you're going to find free men easily because they'll either be forced to break up playing partnerships or string themselves out across the pitch.

'If players don't take the time to construct play it will be difficult to get the ball to the right places up the pitch and then dominate the opposition. If you play the ball upfield at top speed all the time, hitting first time long balls, the ball will be back on top of you in seconds. Up and down, up and down . . . You have to pass when the moment's right, to the right player. Get that wrong and you'll be playing long balls for your opponents to gobble up and then come at you in numbers.'

I'd like to pause here and consider what the players of the past have to teach us on this point. I'm thinking specifically of Ernest Needham, a much-loved former captain of Sheffield United and one of the stars of English football at the turn of the twentieth century. In 1901 Needham wrote these words for an Association Football publication: 'Sometimes, and I'd like to emphasise this point, linking up play between defenders and midfielders is a good decision. If a defender can feed the ball to his midfielder so he can then push the play up the pitch he should do that without hesitating for a second instead of simply launching the ball long and far with a big hefty boot. This approach is much more successful than the way teams habitually play. Too many defenders, whenever they have the chance, just lump the ball as hard as they can and reckon they're pretty heroic. They're totally forgetting that nine times out of ten the ball flies over the head of their striker, landing at the feet of the rival back four who then counter-attack because you've gifted them possession.'

I think Lillo and Guardiola would have got on pretty well with Needham and indeed with Jimmy Hogan, another like-minded English coach of whom Norman Fox wrote, 'Hogan maintained that the best and safest way of playing was to bring the ball out carefully from the penalty area and move forward using short passes. Although he had nothing against long passes per se, he said that precision was essential. In fact he insisted on precision. Thumping the ball long only to end up giving it to the opponent was never part of his tactical plan.'

Before moving on from the lessons of the past, I think it's important to point out that football today does at times appear to be moving in precisely the opposite direction to the one recommended by Needham and Hogan.

## MOVING TOGETHER
### Munich, 1 February 2016

Noel Sanvicente: 'The most interesting thing about Barça was the way they always got the ball back. They were amazingly fast.'

Guardiola agrees. 'This happened because we'd move forward together as a team. There wasn't much space in between the players or the lines and when they lost the ball it was usually easy to get it back. But there's another issue here. When you attack and you've got a heap of your players in front of the ball but then you lose possession or you're robbed of the ball then you're cooked. Completely cooked. If you've two strikers high up the pitch and two very "open" wingers and then you lose the ball then none of the four can help you stem the counter or help win the ball back. Now, if the wingers are still "open" but the two strikers stay close to the ball then when you lose it you can win it back much more easily. This process of "pass-move in unison, pass-move in unison" is one where we all advance with the ball together. It makes winning it back so much more practical and straightforward.

'That Barça team had some of the smallest players in the world, Xavi and Iniesta are only about five foot four inches tall but they got the ball back easily because they moved forward as a compact unit.

'So you can go for your long balls as much as you like but when you do, ciao – they'll get it off you. It doesn't matter how big and strong you are. Not even the most physical team in the world can keep getting those balls back. It's not about brute force. It's about using space effectively. The pitch is huge. Football's huge. It's enormous and if you don't play like I'm suggesting then, ciao, you're cooked.'

## NO MORE DOGMA

Never do something you already know how to do
*Eduardo Chillida*

Throughout his time in Germany, Pep consistently looked for and applied formulas that would help his team cope with the league's high-speed rhythm. He understood that he needed to adapt to the particular demands of the Bundesliga whilst teaching his men the importance of those 'foot on the ball' moments in the middle of a fast-paced game. As a result, he succeeded in slowing down his opponents whilst allowing his own men to maintain their speed.

This kind of apparent paradox became an inherent part of Guardiola's game: his Bayern side were the best defensive team in Europe despite defending fifty metres from their goalmouth and with two young kids (Kimmich and Alaba) playing as central defenders without actually being central defenders. His players carried out between 170 and 240 sprints per game and almost always outran their opponents, yet appeared to play with calm and focus at all times. In fifty-three of their games in his final season with the club, Bayern only conceded 161 shots, an average of just three per match.

Pep defines their game like this: 'If you really want to understand what we've been doing all this time, basically we've played with Kimmich and Alaba [a central midfielder and full back] as central defenders and we've positioned them fifty metres from Neuer, allowing us to impose ourselves in our opponents' half and dominating so much that we only conceded seventeen goals in thirty-four league games. That's it in a nutshell.'

Not even Guardiola initially realised that he'd have to adapt so much. But as soon as he'd understood what kind of players he had at Bayern, he knew that they couldn't play like his Barcelona side.

Except for Thiago, who'd been through the La Masia youth training programme, none of his Bayern players had six thousand hours of training in positional play under their belts.

Pep could teach them the basics and instruct them in this playing style but couldn't make up for the years of intensive training kids at Barcelona received. If Barça was an orchestra almost entirely made up of violinists then at Bayern, whilst his musicians were less proficient in a single instrument, they could offer a greater variety of expertise.

For this reason the 'Munich Philharmonic' would interpret the same piece of music differently from the 'Barcelona Symphonic'. The Bayern players were more of a diverse mix and club directors had no interest in Pep transferring the Barça blueprint to Munich, as was evidenced by their decision to sell Toni Kroos against Guardiola's wishes.

Pep quickly understood the situation and began to revise his plans to reproduce the Barça model. He would have to go in a different direction and knew that it might take some time to achieve what he was looking for. He would not change his fundamental ideas of course: high possession, domination of matches, pace and constant attacking. He'd continue to seek to slow down the opposition, neutralise their counter-attacks and have his men move continuously across the pitch without losing their positional sense so that they'd impose themselves through confident, relentless passing. But he could no longer cling to the way he'd done things at Barça and instead created a Bayern version of positional play: high speed and played vertically.

## TWENTY-THREE DIFFERENT MODELS

Nothing gives a better sense of the huge change Pep underwent in Germany than the number of playing models he used. In Barcelona his game strategy tended to be restricted to one of two systems: 4-3-3 or 3-4-3. In contrast, his Bayern side employed a total of twenty-three different models, almost as many as the twenty-nine that Marcelo Bielsa identified as the total number of systems possible in football.

I've arranged these in three groups, according to how often and in what way Pep used them*:

- The Touchstones
- The Alternatives
- Now and Again

Touchstones
- 4-3-3
- 4-2-3-1
- 4-2-4
- 3-4-3
- 2-3-5
- 2-3-2-3

Alternatives
- 4-4-2 (with and without the diamond midfield)
- 4-1-4-1
- 4-2-2-2
- 4-2-1-3
- 4-1-1-4
- 3-5-2 (including its defensive variant of 5-3-2)
- 3-3-1-3
- 3-2-3-2
- 2-3-3-2
- 2-4-4

Now and Again
- 3-6-1
- 3-2-5
- 3-1-4-2
- 3-1-2-1-3
- 3-3-4
- 5-4-1
- 2-3-1-4

* The goalkeeper is not included.

## SWISS ARMY KNIVES

For big problems, simple solutions.
*Leontxo García*

In his first season in Munich Pep conquers the league in convincing style but screws up monumentally in the Champions League. In May 2014, having failed to achieve this crucial objective, he tells me: 'I need more time to be sure that the team is mine. Just a little more time. We've won and we've won the league convincingly so of course we're delighted. When you keep winning it buys you time to do even more. More trophies mean more time to build and plan for the future. But real satisfaction only comes when you feel that the team is yours and is playing the way you want it to. And that takes time. This team isn't mine yet. Not completely. Why do I say that? Because what I'm suggesting to them is at odds with the football culture they're used to. Don't forget they've just won the treble playing the way they're accustomed to and with basically the same group of players. It's my job to sell my ideas to them although obviously it cuts both ways, "You meet me half-way and I'll do the same." We just have to find that midpoint and for that to happen I have to find a way to convince them.'

In his second season the speed of change steps up a gear although it isn't immediately obvious in Bayern's results.

With Xabi Alonso at the tiller he manages to blend Bayern's predilection for a 'vertical' axis with the 'Pep' passing and possession, the 'pausa' of Spanish football (expressed as 'foot on the ball' intelligence and 'thinking-time' in England), plus the compact space between his team's three lines. If Lahm is the fundamental piece of the first season's jigsaw, that title is earned by Alonso in the second term.

This season a plague of injuries prevent Bayern reaching their full potential and, once again they fall at the last hurdle, in the Champions League semi-finals.

It finally all comes together in Pep's third season when no one player really stands out because the whole group is on fire. The team's matured and grown into its new playing style and is now capable of interpreting different formations according to the occasion and the rival they're facing. Guardiola has become a chameleon, as have his men. This is an eclectic mix of talent, capable of alternating between two, three or four different game plans in the same match and moving between them all seamlessly, almost without any need of guidance or instruction.

The players have mastered several different positions: Javi Martínez plays as a centre half or inside left; Alonso as the 'pivote' midfielder or central defender. Douglas Costa is as effective as outside left or inside right. Kimmich is a left back, centre half or right winger . . . In Barcelona Pep wanted every player to have the capacity to play in three different positions and in Munich he's gone one better. Rafinha's moving between five different positions, David Alaba excels in any one of six and Joshua Kimmich and Philipp Lahm can be used confidently in an astonishing eight different positions.

They've learned how to play every instrument in the orchestra and the result is beyond even Guardiola's wildest dreams. The world has always seen his style of football as one which demands specialist players but at Bayern his players have become multi-functional. Every one of them is like a Swiss army knife and can be used in a number of ways without losing any of their specialist talents. The transformation's taken time and patience on the part of the coach and his men have shown intelligence, commitment and the determination they needed to achieve the coach's goals.

In his Bayern picture book Pep has smudged the lines between images – he's blurred almost all the delineations between 'set' positions or roles. If, in the past, his game was considered only suitable for *Guardiolista* footballers like Lahm and Kimmich, he's proven that it can be played by the likes of Vidal and Robben, whose profiles, theoretically at least, are incompatible with their coach's style.

The coach ends his tenure at Bayern having established the key distinguishing markers of his playing style: dominant possession, positional attack, meticulous organisation, plus a high defensive line (his team is always the most attacking but the least scored-against), pressing and constantly altering permutations . . . But Pep's Bayern have also used many non-Guardiola-like tactics: vertical football, high pace (not just in the circulation of the ball as in his previous work but the players too), the long pass into space, placing high priority on wingers, training his players to arrive in and around the opposition penalty area en masse in order to take advantage of cutbacks or crosses and score and even shooting from distance.

'I've actually learned much more than I would've if I'd not been forced to adapt,' he reflected. 'It's been a fucking brilliant experience. I've learnt so much here.'


## ADAPTING AND LEARNING

Continuing one's education is the only antidote to old age
*Howard Gardner*

When Pep talked about change, he was imagining a joint process of adaptation: him to the players and vice versa. In practice however, the reality was quite different.

As coach, Pep gradually modified his ideas to fit his squad but found that for his players it was more about understanding and learning. The conductor had to adapt to a new group of musicians and instruments whilst the musicians worked to master an unfamiliar composition. The fact that each was prepared to put their trust in new ideas does credit to both parties although possibly more to the players themselves, as German football writer Ronald Reng remarked: 'The Bayern players really surprised me. Even more than Pep. They showed such humility and a real willingness to learn. It was quite astonishing.'

Hungarian psychiatrist Thomas Szasz explains that 'each conscious act of learning requires the willingness to damage one's own self-esteem.' That Bayern's players, led by Lahm, Neuer, Alaba and Boateng were prepared to take this risk says a great deal about their generosity of spirit. In fact, the group's attitude is probably one of the most open and generous I've witnessed in modern football. That these elite champions, who had just won everything it's possible to win, were humble enough to take on board someone else's idea of how to play football, is impressive. Indeed, they threw themselves into the process, stoically enduring the inevitable setbacks, including, presumably, the knock to their own self-esteem that Szasz describes. And their coach found that he too was a beneficiary of this process as he watched his own knowledge and skill-set expand. Perhaps it's true after all that the best way of deepening your knowledge is to teach others what you know.

Domènec Torrent shares his memories of this process: 'The players were used to treating rondos as a bit of fun but Pep told them from the start how crucially important they would become. In fact what happened with the rondos is probably the best example of the process of adaptation they all went through. The players started out seeing them as a bit of a laugh, a good way to start and end the warm-ups when the ball could end up ten metres outside the perimeter of the rondo circle without it ever having touched the ground. But from day one Pep insisted that they pay attention to how they positioned themselves, how they received the ball, whether they controlled it with the left or the right foot . . . For him, this exercise is crucial to any player's development. It allows him to position himself correctly in relation to the others around him, maintain possession, receive the ball efficiently and increase his speed on the ball.

'The Bayern players grasped his point very quickly. It made sense to them and, as a result, their progress was more or less immediate. I remember one day comparing the rondos of the early days with what they had become by the end. It was amazing. Like looking at two entirely different exercises. By the end of our time there, that ball was flying.'

As well as the new, improved rondos, Pep had to teach positional play. 'Yes, he had to cover that too because they'd never played like that before and had no real understanding of what it meant. For Pep and Barça it became a habit but in Munich they still believed that it was a style of play used to maintain high possession. Rubbish! It's a game of position, not possession! It's about how you place yourself in relation to the others on the field when you have the ball and where you should be so that you can continue pressing when you lose it. In training terms it's a tactical exercise which has a physical component. In fact, Lorenzo Buenaventura would often check the players' pulse rates afterwards and they were always racing. It's a very complete training exercise – essential from Pep's point of view, because of the speed at which the players and their minds are forced to work.'

His players quickly realised that it wasn't about holding on to the ball but about how to play it and how to be aware of the position of everyone around them. 'They really had no problem getting to grips with it and Philipp Lahm in particular loved it. He used to complain if we'd left it off the training schedule!

'Manu Neuer was another devotee. He found it helped him improve his technique controlling the ball with his foot and always asked to join in our practice sessions, even on his rest days. They all came to realise that practising positional play made them better players. It made sense of everything else we did and meant that things went more smoothly on match day.

'Positional play definitely symbolises all that Guardiola achieved at Bayern and, despite the rubbish reported by the local media, the players bought into it immediately. They were enthusiastic about all of Pep's ideas and keen to incorporate them into their own game. Many people argue that a more direct style is always more effective but both Barça and Bayern have proved that positional play can be just as successful. The German players were actually quite surprised by the intensity of this kind of work, how much physical effort is required. They also came to see that positional play is more or less the essence of football; you lose the ball, you press, you get it back, you begin to open up the play again and you're in control again . . . There was a bit of a culture shock involved but it was felt by the press and some sections of the fan base, not by the players who were more than willing to follow Pep's directions.

'By our third month they were already saying that they'd never been so dominant in the Bundesliga. They told us that even during their glorious treble winning year, they often only edged ahead in the dying minutes of a game through sheer guts, determination and skill.'

Now Pep has taken a similar approach at Manchester City with the rondos as a first step followed by positional play as the second rung of this new process of teaching and learning.

It's important to point out that this is an ongoing process whose ultimate objective is the pupil developing complete mastery of the concepts, much like a master craftsman who prepares his student to carry his teachings on independently after a long apprenticeship. In football terms, the aim is for the team to be able to 'think' for itself, without relying on instructions from the coach and the learning process therefore has to be long and exhaustive. The end result should be that every player is able to perform at his full potential without having to think about each movement or decision because they become automatic.

Let's turn now to a concrete example of this process, specifically as it relates to Joshua Kimmich's transformation from organising midfielder to central defender.

# KIMMICH AS CENTRE HALF
# – LUCK, INTUITION AND GUTS

In the end every action is a gamble
And in every action you reveal your true nature.
*Howard Zinn*

Benatia's out, then it's Boateng. Five days later Javi Martínez joins the list of Bayern's walking wounded and then it's Holger Badstuber's turn.

Guardiola's 2016 kicks off with all his central defenders missing and it looks like he's going to have to improvise. Again. His response is immediate, 'We'll use Kimmich at centre half.'

Pep instructs Domènec Torrent to give the orange bib to Joshua Kimmich, who will now have to change sides. He came to training expecting to play as a central midfielder for the red team but instead he'll be the orange team's centre half – working on a particular strategy for helping Lahm bring the ball out from the back. Pep's made his decision on the hoof. Martínez is out and the team needs to practise playing the ball out from the defence. He's about to take a risk but knows that it might well pay off.

Under Cruyff Guardiola learned that a high quality 'pivote' midfielder should be able to switch relatively easily to playing as a central defender. In his playing days Pep occasionally found himself deployed as an emergency centre half and, on one memorable occasion in 1996, actually took on the role against Bayern in Munich.

As a coach he's also resorted to using his organising midfielder as a centre-back on several occasions: notably, Yaya Touré in the 2009 Champions League Final and Javier Mascherano in the 2011 Wembley final. So, today he doesn't need to think about it too much. He trusts his instincts and calls Kimmich over.

It's 28 January 2016. Martínez is out after the Basque informs the coach that he can no longer bear the pain in his knee. He's going back to Barcelona for surgery and, although it's not a big operation and he should be back in a couple of months, his absence will open up a crater-sized hole in Bayern's defence.

Kimmich takes up a position in the backline with Lahm and Bernat at full back and Badstuber beside him. Over and over again they practise playing the ball out from the back: Lahm repositions himself around the centre circle, tucked in beside Alonso, and the three at the back exchange a series of quick, short passes to move possession up, passing as often as is needed, until there's five of them ready to cross the halfway line, still using rapid first-time passes.

Bayern's coach has decided that the last phase of the season is going to be heavily reliant on them playing three at the back. The basic logic of his decision is that this will give 'guaranteed' security as the three of them inter-pass while moving possession upfield.

'With only two centre backs the passes between them sometimes have to be over a large area of the pitch because the two of them are split and there's a fair distance between them. In contrast with three players [the two centre-halves and the left back once Lahm's moved into midfield] the passes are shorter, across less space and therefore much more likely to be accurate no matter how rapid they are. It gives us precision and security but I'm only going to do it like this if Lahm moves forward, next to Xabi. I want a significant change from the last couple of seasons – I always want us to play out with three defenders trying to break the opposition's first line of press – and with Lahm as the second organising midfielder alongside Xabi.'

Pep has had his men practise ten different ways to use the 3+2 structure to bring the ball out. This is a key part of the coach's strategy because, for him, the construction of the entire game depends on the way it starts from the back. It's similar to chess where the way you start your game is crucially important (albeit that in football we don't have technical terms for different tactical variants when playing out from the back).

Bringing the ball out cleanly and smoothly is an essential part of positional play as Juanma Lillo explains: 'If the basic idea is to set up camp in the opposition's half then the fundamental thing is to play the ball out from the back in a manner which takes advantage of, and is inherently linked to, the talents and culture of your team. Only if you achieve this clinically and intelligently can you drop anchor in the opponents' half. Without best practice this just isn't possible or practical.'

The training match includes two halves of twelve minutes each and Pep doesn't leave Kimmich's side for a second. The youngster's struggling to cope with Müller and Coman's attacks and the scene reminds onlookers of the efforts of another Bayern player, Javi Martínez back in 2013.

Pep's even shouting the same instructions, 'Hold the line Josh, hold that line. Stay in line with the other two Josh, don't drop off, push up, push up tight . . . On the move Josh KEEP the line!'

As each team fights for supremacy (a Robben goal gives the Oranges victory in the end), Pep only has eyes for Kimmich. 'Push on up to the striker Josh . . . Not like that Josh, not there . . . Look at Badstu, LOOK at Badstu and where he is!'

Badstuber sets the defensive line and Kimmich is often disorientated about where he should be. He's trying to follow the instructions being bellowed at him as he fends off Müller and Coman who are confusing the hell out of him as they dance around. He's still getting used to his new role and looks like he's missing the guiding presence of Lahm on the other side of him. Still, Pep and his staff are satisfied with the experiment.

'I reckon he'll get it after about four days' practice,' comments Domènec Torrent who then calls a controversial offside which Müller protests vehemently. 'Look at how well he's getting the ball out,' says Carles Planchart. 'The boy's got talent. He'll definitely pick it up,' agrees Lorenzo Buenaventura. 'He's certainly got guts,' adds Manel Estiarte.

The four judges are on the touchline . . . watching Pep run alongside Kimmich. He's become the player's shadow and is scrutinising his every move, making corrections, helping him refine his movements and giving him endless tips on the role of a central defender. The young player is evidently expected to take it all in as he moves across the training ground at high speed.

When the game ends, Pep's technical team surround him. They're ready to share their verdicts. 'Yeah, I really think he can do it,' says Pep, scratching his head. 'It won't be easy. He'll have to learn the discipline of holding the line but he's more than capable. It's too early to make a final decision though. It's one thing to have a kick-about with this lot and quite another to cope with a competitive match. This is a tough league and we could do the kid a lot of harm if we throw him in at the deep end like that.'

This is what he says . . . but Pep's tone of voice suggests quite the opposite and his listeners suspect that what he really means is, 'The kid can definitely hack it and I'll make sure that he does.'

There's an unavoidable comparison with Javier Mascherano, the Argentinian midfielder whom Guardiola converted to a central defender at Barcelona. Kimmich is the same height as Mascherano (5ft 9in), he's fast, turns easily and heads the ball well. Essentially, he's a mini-Mascherano. Pep spots the similarity immediately and believes that Kimmich may even have some advantages over the Barcelona player, 'He's young and a quick learner with amazing panoramic vision. He uses his feet well and could bring the ball out brilliantly for us. He'll have to put the work in though. We'll do special individual training sessions with him, hammering it all home. He'll need total concentration to hold the right line with Badstuber and Bernat and to learn everything else a central defender needs to do. He's quick, disciplined and very good in the air. Because he's a top midfielder he's good on the ball. What he's got to learn is when and how to drop back into the defensive line of three. We need to let him have a go, at the very least.'

Domènec Torrent explains, 'In Pep's game, a good midfielder playing as a defender can bring the ball out with force, like a catapult, and that gives tremendous impetus to the rest of the team. Obviously, the boy'll have to learn to defend first . . .'

Over the next few days the young German receives a masterclass in defending from the coaching staff. He practises on the pitch and watches endless video footage. It's a steep learning curve and he spends an intense week taking in an extraordinary amount of information about movements and concepts. (When Javi Martínez was at the same stage he had to watch more than two hundred different videos with Pep.) By the end of it all Kimmich's head is bursting. In true Guardiola fashion, the coach has felt the need to cover every aspect of the new position with his usual forensic attention to detail.

In five days Kimmich will line up as a central defender in the league match against Hoffenheim, in what will be his seventh position in just six months. The young player does well and Pep begins to seriously consider using him this way again over the next few weeks. And not just as an emergency measure. 'We need to try him out in a harder game than today's – maybe in Leverkusen against Kiessling – but I liked the way he performed today. He knows how to hold the ball if there's a problem, he's fearless about dribbling past the first line of press – if he's part of the three bringing the ball out he gives us a lot of security. I really think that he could be the perfect central defender for us. He has no fear of going forward. None at all.'

Kimmich performs well in all of the next seven games. After one rest day he returns and is in the line-up for most of the important games at the end of the season facing, amongst others, Juventus, Borussia Dortmund plus Benfica and giving a good performance in the Cup Final. His contribution exceeds all expectations and it's enough to earn him a starting place for Germany during the European Championships in the summer, and, although his success is obviously due to the hours of intense work put in by player and coach, his smooth transition to the new position owes as much to the sheer courage and determination of both men. Guardiola has taken a gamble on the youngster by trusting him in such a risky situation and Kimmich himself has shown tremendous guts in sticking with his new position, on the good days and the bad. In this case, their willingness to gamble on a high-risk strategy has proved as important as the quality of the learning process itself. Once again, life has handed Pep a lemon and he's made lemonade.

# TACTICS

> 99% of all statistics only tell 49% of the story.
> *Ron DeLegge II*

In *Pep Confidential* I outlined the major strategic changes Guardiola made during his first year at Bayern as well as detailing the systems and tactics he used: the high line of defence; moving forward jointly so the ball is brought out in a coordinated manner; making sure the passing moves give order to the team; numerical superiority in midfield; full backs as attacking midfielders; the disappearance of the 'false 9'.

Two years on, it's interesting to examine the type of football Bayern were playing at the end of 2015/16:

### • Keeping possession

In Guardiola's 161 games in charge, Bayern averaged a possession rate of 70.47% per match (the highest in Europe). This represented a significant increase on their stats for possession under Jupp Heynckes (2012/13), when they averaged 61.35%.

### • Moving forward as a compact unit by passing the ball

Over his three years at Bayern, Pep's team averaged 726 passes per game, 159 more than under Heynckes (567). Along with the change in position of the defensive line, this was probably one of the most emblematic parts of Pep's impact on Bayern.

### • Precision passing

Guardiola's Bayern achieved the second highest rate of pass completion in Europe (87.9% against Paris Saint-Germain's 88.7%), despite being the team with the highest passing rate out of all the big European leagues (726 to PSG's 686). The regular players who produced the best stats in this respect were: Alaba (91.31%), Lahm (91.04%) and Alonso (90.59%). In Alaba's case this was all the more impressive when you consider how much his stats improved each year from 2013 to 2016: 89.35%, 91.65% and 92.48% respectively. The two players with the least accurate passing were Lewandowski (77.97%) and Müller (70.1%).

• **Players high up the pitch**
Under Guardiola, eight of his team would always have their average pitch position in the opposition half. The other two (setting aside the keeper) would average more time in the centre circle than in defence. The epicentre of Pep's team would be 58.3 metres higher up the pitch than Manuel Neuer. The average distance between the lines was 29.3 metres.

• **Defence high up the pitch**
In order to have the whole team much higher up the pitch, Guardiola had to move his defensive line. Under Heynckes the line tended to be around 36.1 metres from goal but in his first year Guardiola had already moved them 43.5 metres away and by his third season had positioned his defenders even further away from the goalkeeper at a distance of 48.5 metres. Despite this, Bayern's opponents had fewer chances on goal (only three per game) than in the five previous years and in 2016 the Munich club beat Bundesliga records by conceding just seventeen goals in thirty-four games. The total number of goals they conceded also dropped with each consecutive season: forty-four, thirty-six and thirty-one respectively.

• **The lack of space making counter-attacks impossible**
Having the team play so high up the pitch unfortunately meant that counter-attacking was almost impossible for Bayern. Ironically their dominant position robbed them of the necessary space and the team only managed around thirty counter-attacks plus an average of 3 such goals per season . . . (Against Heynckes' 7.5 per season).

## • Shooting at goal

Pep's brand of football increased the number of shots on goal with respect to the stats under Heynckes: 986 compared to 908. The increment was more significant in terms of shots on goal from within the penalty area (631 over 571) but Pep's Bayern also shot more from outside the box too (355 v 337). The total number of shots, both on and off target, grew to 2,914.

## • Zonal defending

Using zonal defending for corners and free kicks ended with a balance of just fourteen goals conceded this way in 161 matches. Three seasons at Bayern saw seven goals conceded from 470 corners [one every 67]. Zonal defending at corners was updated a little as the seasons went by – modifying the two lines of defence depending on the type of rival and by adding specific 'blocks'. Domènec Torrent's work to improve this area was so effective that the number of goals lost at corners went down each season from five to two and then zero in year three.

## • Tactical variations

Guardiola used ten different strategies in terms of bringing the ball out from the back and twenty-three different playing formations . . .

*[Source of data: OPTA]*

## TRIANGLES AND PERMUTATIONS
### Wolfsburg, 27 October 2015

All teams go through continuous change and the 'inner life' of the group has a significant impact on its daily evolution.

Nobody is indispensable and today Robben is substituted in a Cup match.

The relationships that develop within the group affect everything it does. Each player is influenced by those around him and the synergy this creates can drive the whole team on to new and greater heights. All of this of course weighs heavily on any coach as he plans his line-up in preparation for match day.

Today in Wolfsburg, Bayern have produced a resounding victory (1-3), but it's also clear that there's been a shift in the way the players interact on the pitch and something very exciting is happening. When Alaba pushes up into the left wing position, Thiago becomes left back. He's a 'false' left back as he uses the position simply to cover and then to view the rest of the pitch so that he can make the most intelligent decisions.

How has all this come about? Domènec Torrent fills us in, 'Pep insists that we create triangles of passing options on the left. On the other wing we don't emphasise it so much because there it's easy to play the ball out via Jérôme, Phillip and Xabi. But on the left we're looking to be more aggressive. The emphasis is on combinations between Alaba and Coman and the third part of the triangle will be Thiago when he drops in a little bit and plays like a "false" left back. He's not only the base of that three player triangle, he's also getting a huge benefit which is that he can see the whole game in front of him and it's much more easy to make the right decisions when he passes. The dynamic is that Coman and Alaba attack constantly, interchanging who's inside and who's outside, and Thiago's job is to guard their backs and use his space to initiate the play again as if he were the left back. He's comfortable in this role and so are his teammates. Between the three of them there's a passing triangle forming quite happily . . . in fact their attacking power is peerless.'

Unsurprisingly the 'master and his apprentices' relationship between Pep and his players was at its most productive in their third season together. The team was firing on all cylinders and the results were better than ever. Sadly, Bayern's elimination in the Champions League semi-final crushed hopes of a more glorious end to the relationship and many in Germany began to refer to Guardiola's tenure at the Munich club as 'unfinished'. Pep's incomplete masterpiece lacked that vital final flourish that the Champions League trophy would have bestowed.

As German journalist, Uli Köhler, says, 'He said he would change some tiny details here and there and then he changed everything. He revolutionised the team and got them playing football. He brought their game to a whole new level, right at the top of the elite. Playing like that, with your defensive line almost in the opponents' half, is very, very dangerous and I don't believe we'll ever see football like it again. It's been a total triumph. He improved the team and its players but he also made the whole of the Bundesliga sit up and take notice. Other teams could see the new ideas he was introducing and knew that they too would need to up their games. Guardiola won a great deal here and he left us something very special too: unforgettable football. A style of game Bayern will never play again and that the fans will never see again. It's just a shame he didn't manage to win the Champions League. That would have been the icing on the cake for him.'

Guardiola's great achievement in Munich was to show his players that they could and should become more flexible, more multi-faceted. The deep bond he developed with his team meant many found inner resources they'd no idea they possessed. Of course this is the job of every good coach; to identify and nurture his players' innate talent so that they develop all their skills, including those previously undiscovered. Lahm's skills in attacking midfield, Kimmich's new-found abilities as a central defender, Boateng's exquisite passing and the astonishing eruption of Douglas Costa are all Guardiola 'discoveries'. Although, in essence of course, what he did was create the conditions that allowed his men to express themselves freely and fully in the work they were doing. In a complex, varied, non-linear sport like football this is one of the most important qualities any coach can have: the ability to facilitate and develop all his players' talent, much of which often lies dormant beneath the surface.

PEP GUARDIOLA'S STATS AT FC BAYERN
(2013–16)

161 games
121 wins (75.16%)
21 draws
19 defeats

396 goals in favour (2.46 per game)
111 goals against (0.69 goals/game)
7 titles (3 Bundesligas, 2 Cup titles, 1 World Cup of Clubs, 1 European Supercup)

Average passes per game: 726
Short passes: 644 (88.7%)
Long passes: 63 (8.6%)
Crosses: 17.3
Average completed passes: 87.9%
Average shots per game: 18.1
Average dribbles per game: 16.6
Average possession: 70.47%

BUNDESLIGA
102 games
82 wins (80.39%)
11 draws
9 defeats
254 goals in favour (2.49 goals/game)
58 goals against (0.57 goals/game)

## COPA DE ALEMANIA
17 games
14 wins (82.35%)
3 draws
0 defeats
45 goals in favour (2.65 goals/game)
7 goals against (0.41 goals/game)

## CHAMPIONS LEAGUE
36 games
23 wins (63.89%)
5 draws
8 defeats
87 goals in favour (2.42 goals/game)
37 goals against (1.03 goals/game)

## OTHER COMPETITIONS
6 games
2 wins (33.33%)
2 draws
2 defeats
10 goals in favour (1.66 goals/game)
9 goals against (1.50 goals/game)

## PEP'S RULES

We play the same way we live.
*Xabier Azkargorta*

So just what do the Manchester City fans expect from Guardiola?

Something familiar and in keeping with what they know about the coach. He produced two different kinds of football in Barcelona and Bayern, but in each the style was unmistakably his own, much like a musician whose songs will always be recognisable no matter how much his influences change.

Guardiola will encounter new influences and experience many more evolutions along his journey, but, like all true artists, he'll remain true to his inner values and beliefs. His football will always be unique, distinctive and instantly recognisable.

In Munich he used the full backs like 'false' inside midfielders and the wingers as midfielders, he changed systems like someone turning the pages of a book, he recuperated the 'pyramid' system (the 2-3-5 model) and, depending on circumstances, played with either five defenders, or five strikers, five midfielders . . . or just one. His personal database of football knowledge has expanded but that doesn't mean that he's going to do the same things at City. One should never confuse ideology with the correct strategic response to a specific situation.

The fundamental principles of Pep's ideology are the same as ever. They were the same at Barcelona, then in Munich and they remain unchanged now as he starts his tenure at Manchester City. These are the immutable beliefs that he will never abandon, wherever he goes: take the initiative, dominate, attack, use the ball as a tool, build the game from the back.

He's unwavering in terms of the fundamentals of his game but that's not to say that he isn't prepared to change almost all of the details. In Germany Pep demonstrated his willingness to challenge the established credos, he introduced new ways of doing things and re-modelled positions and moves. In fact, he changed so much of his game that at times it appeared as if his entire playing model had been transformed – but the essence was identical.

And this is a crucial point to make when we talk about Pep's transformation in Germany. Yes, he evolved but he conserved the essence of who he is as a man and as a coach. He may have fine-tuned thousands of details but he emerged with his fundamental ideas intact. And if we only see the obvious modifications and tactical changes, we risk missing the point completely. Despite his transformation, Guardiola remains the same man he ever was.

The same beliefs underpin everything he does: the idea of bringing the ball out from the back upon which he builds his game of position; a high defensive line (governed by the position of the ball and two basic tenets: pressing the opponents and covering your teammates); the sequence of fifteen first passes which helps you make the transition from attack to defence; establishing superiority (numerically or positionally) in midfield; passing movements as a deliberate means to disorganise the opposition; establishing and passing to free men in the space between opposition pressing lines; the patient forbearance of his strikers who mustn't go and look for the ball but rather trust that their teammates will get it to them at the right time; and the control of free opposition players who will try to counter-attack.

Now let's examine in greater detail four fundamental elements of Guardiola's football at Bayern:
- Taking the initiative
- Players who complement each other's style
- Speed and 'pausa' (foot on the ball)
- Pinning them back and opening them up

## TAKING THE INITIATIVE (BY KASPÁROV)

There is no such thing as a good or a bad coach.
There are only coaches with courage and those without
*Juanma Lillo*

The importance of taking the initiative is one of the basic pillars of Guardiola's philosophy. His ideal is possession-based football executed as part of united, cohesive attacking (as Juanma Lillo describes it: 'Travel together but not just on the same train – in the same carriage.')

He expects his men to use their passing as a means both of organising themselves and confusing their opponents. He wants them winning the ball back aggressively as well as monopolising the other team's area as they push forward in a relentless, overwhelming block.

'My football vision is pretty simple: I like to attack, attack, attack.'

Pep spent some time last winter reading *How Life Imitates Chess*, by his great friend, Garry Kaspárov and made copious notes on what the grandmaster had to say about the need to dominate and control from the start. He was fascinated by the ideas expressed in the book: 'I've already mentioned this idea of taking the initiative as a vital part of any successful attack. If we're the ones initiating the action, as opposed to simply reacting, then we'll be able to control the flow of the game. The opponents then have to react to what we do, which automatically means a limited choice of options. It makes them more predictable. Now we're in the driving seat and can anticipate what's going to happen next and can go on controlling the action. As long as we continue to create lots of danger we'll retain the upper hand and in chess at least this means that your opponent will have no way of countering your attack. Taking the initiative is a useful strategy in other spheres too; in business it gives you a competitive edge, in negotiations it'll probably get you a better deal and in politics it's going to get more voters putting a cross against your name. It's a cycle: you take control, show that you have the upper hand and then you slam home your advantage, getting both tangible and intangible results. This is what it means to eclipse the opposition.'

Kaspárov explains that it's not enough just to take control early on, you must dominate throughout the game.

'Once you've taken the initiative you have to exploit and sustain your position. Wilhelm Steinitz [first ever world chess champion who repeatedly won this honour between 1886 and 1894] always said that the player with the advantage must attack, otherwise he'll lose control of the play and squander his advantage. Domination of a game can be lost in an instant so you MUST keep attacking. You'll win more chess pieces or it may end up with your opponent giving up, unable to cope with your continued dominance and the pace of your game.

'This doesn't necessarily mean that you should concentrate all your efforts on one particular tactic, no matter how clever you think it is. That approach might work occasionally but, in reality, there's no one tactic that will guarantee you complete domination. This isn't Star Wars and none of us comes to a competition with a Death Star up their sleeve. So when our competitors react to our attack and launch their defence, we must use all our creativity and skill to maintain the initiative. We also need to be clear about how we define the term "success". An attack doesn't need to be all or nothing or breathtakingly fast. Sustained pressure can be just as effective if we use it to chip away at our opponents' weaknesses little by little until they eventually collapse. One of the key qualities of a successful attack is to get the most out of any situation without attempting to achieve the impossible.'

The title of the relevant chapter in Kaspárov's book is 'Initiative rarely knocks twice' and his comments echo much of what Guardiola has said about what he calls the fundamentals of positional play: crowding your men into certain zones in order to trick the opposition and the need for fifteen passes before you attack so that your rivals lose their organisation.

For Pep, football is a process, 'I'm a big fan of wingers and we have some outstanding exponents of that art at Bayern. They make all the difference to our game but before they can get on and do their thing, we need to bring the ball out from the back, passing the ball and building the game as we go . . . And that's not easy – it's long and complicated.'

Kaspárov defines chess in a similar way:

'Each move is intended to unbalance our rivals allowing us to change tactic and move in a way which exposes their weaknesses. They then have to plug the holes as best they can whilst trying to resist this constant pressure. And that quickly turns into mission impossible. They block us on one side and another gap opens up elsewhere until the whole edifice collapses and we can push through their defences. In chess we have the "principle of two weaknesses". It's very rare to beat a strong opponent using just one attack point so, instead of focusing on a single weakness, we exert more pressure so that weaknesses are exposed.

'The "tools" we use are mobility, flexibility and distraction. If we build our armies and then use them to attack a single point, we limit our options as much as our enemy's. Even D-Day [Operation Overlord, the largest sea invasion in history] involved a host of different distraction tactics to prevent the Nazis from anticipating the Allies' plans and mounting a counter-attack. Allied commanders used traditional military tactics as well as other less conventional approaches such as the creation of a fictitious army, made up of props including dummy tanks and trucks. Just like a Hollywood set! The idea was to trick the enemy into believing that they were facing double the number of Allied troops.'

There is a direct link between this idea of establishing supremacy early and the ideology of a coach and his players. The history of football is in essence the history of different ideologies and of the innovators who developed and applied them. Over dinner in Munich one evening Guardiola chatted about the concept of football ideology with Noel Sanvicente, ex-coach of Venezuela.

'You know Pep, there's nothing new under the sun and everything we do in football today has some link with the past. We think we're the true innovators whereas, in reality, it's all happened before in a different form. What's actually happening is that we are adapting old concepts to new circumstances. The thing that changes is what's happening in the moment, the circumstances I find myself in, the players I have . . . But I'm still applying a system, a model or a position that somebody somewhere has used in the past.'

Pep agrees, 'Yes, there's definitely a thread running through history that connects to all playing models today. Take "catenaccio", for example. Mourinho used it in the Camp Nou in 2010 and you can trace it right back to Nereo Rocco. In football you have to decide what you want to do and be. The basis of my game is, for example, all about the defence. My defensive strategies have always worked brilliantly for me and we concede fewer goals than everyone else in the league. Every single year.'

'So basically football is a debate about different ideologies and therefore the important thing is not whether we win or lose but how and why we choose one playing style over another. It is this constant exchange of ideas that gives football its richness and depth.'

'I definitely tend to adapt to the circumstances,' says Guardiola. 'For me it's impossible not to change. Here in Germany I've changed the way I attack (although not my defensive strategy, that never changes) because I've had to adapt to the players in the team. So if, for example, your wing back isn't up to running eighty metres up and down the park non-stop, you have to accept that and adapt the plan. If I put my winger inside and leave my full back to make the runs forward and he just can't produce the kind of speed I need, up and down, up and down those eighty metres without stopping, then I need to adapt. If I put the winger "inside" then the full back will push up – okay.

'But if the full back just isn't capable of getting up and overlapping giving us a two v one option with his winger inside him then I've got to leave the winger wide and move the full back inside. Because successful attacking high up the pitch is impossible if you're lacking width. Completely impossible. And you have to adapt your strategy to be fully aware of this absolute reality.

'By the same logic, if my wing back is super athletic and can go non-stop, up-down, up-down, then of course it's different again. But I really believe and I'm only talking about positional play here, not any other playing model, that there are less and less of those kinds of players. The beasts who can go all season charging up and down, eighty metres at a time. I definitely think it's the way football's going. There won't be guys who can sustain it, or, if they do manage it for a season, they'll be suffering the next year and on their knees by the third.'

Seeking to dominate will always be a high-risk strategy in football, as the history of the sport confirms. Many a team has gambled on this tactic and payed a heavy price, defeated by teams skilled in reactive, counter-attack football. Obviously there's no strategy so foolproof that it eliminates all possible risks. Take Bayern's last Champions League semi-final game against Atlético de Madrid. The team hammered away at Atlético until they were practically crushed up against their own goal. Bayern dominated from start to finish, making constant attacks and playing with pace, aggression and determination. They had at least fifty-three chances on goal in 180 minutes (a Champions League record) but it took just one misplaced pass from Boateng followed immediately by a poor decision to rush into a press on the Atleti ball carrier, then a moment's indecision from Alonso and a weak touch from Alaba for Atlético to grab a hugely damaging away goal and Pep's team was out. It felt that everything they had worked so hard to build throughout the year had come to naught and Guardiola then had to deal with widespread and vocal condemnation for his failure to lead his team to the final. A high-risk strategy indeed.

Anyone who is prepared to be unconventional and creative in any walk of life takes this kind of risk. It may well turn out fine but if it doesn't then the consequences can be dire. But you can no more ask life's risk-takers to play it safe than you can tell a lion to go chase butterflies.

None of which means to imply that Guardiola doesn't make a great deal of effort to weigh up the risks in advance and protect his players as much as possible. 'What I try to do is teach them all the elements of my style of game, at the same time ensuring that I reduce the risks to the minimum and help them exploit their skills to the maximum.'

Pep's teams, Barça in Spain and Bayern in Germany, have always conceded the fewest goals. On the only occasion he failed to win the league (in 2011/12 when Mourinho's Real Madrid bested him) Barcelona still emerged as the team with fewest conceded goals. He improved all of his stats in his last season in Munich, conceding an average of 0.5 goals per game against 0.68 of the first year and 0.53 of the second. And all this during the most difficult stage of the season when he had to use the Kimmich–Alaba partnership in central defence.

Ernesto Valverde, Athletic Club coach and a good friend of Guardiola, tells me what he sees as Pep's greatest virtue. 'What Pep achieved at Barça and Bayern was to teach his teams how to organise an almost impenetrable defence. People tend to think that his greatest skill's in attack but I don't agree. His positional play resulted in superb attacking but his real genius lay in the way he created and managed his defensive line.'

Guardiola would love to achieve even more dominance. 'My dream is to shut our eleven opponents up in their area and prevent them from crossing the halfway line. To do that you'd have to be absolutely meticulous about your defensive play. Marcelo [Bielsa] got it spot-on when he said, "Everyone defends tight spaces and attacks wide open spaces. What I like to do is press forward into small spaces and defend the wide spaces." Obviously if even one or two of your players can't handle it, then forget it. But if they're all willing and able then I'd love to force the other team back into their area and not give them even a sniff of the ball for the whole ninety minutes. I started to play with this idea after a chat with Marcelo. We met up in Buenos Aires to talk football. It's important to spend time with people who talk so much sense. For all of this to work you need players with talent and patience who understand that they're not helping if they jump the gun and get involved in the action too early. That's what's so difficult in elite teams, getting the players to understand that by hanging back they're doing exactly the right thing. Because it means than when the ball comes to you you'll just be facing one opponent or you might even find yourself completely unmarked. It's a tough thing for players of this calibre to accept. Bide your time till the ball comes to you.'

Obviously, taking this approach opens the team up to the possibility of sudden counter-attacks. We've seen it a thousand times. A carefully constructed attack traps the opposition in their own area and they're fighting for their lives, but you slip, suddenly they've got the ball and they're off. They breach your lines, DISASTER, the ball's in the back of the net. The threat of a counter-attack is always going to be there. But we've also seen the opposite happen time and time again. A team pushed back into their own area who are then pounded with goals by a dominant opponent.

Guardiola's teams will always produce dominant, attacking, high-risk football but he can't conceive of any other kind. And what is football after all, if not a game of high-stakes risk and rich rewards?

## POSITIONAL PLAY, 'DISPOSITIONAL' PLAY

> We've implemented positional play perfectly.
> It's got Pep's touch all over it.
> *Philipp Lahm*

A belief in the importance of seizing the initiative lies at the very heart of positional play because it encapsulates the entire philosophy of its practitioners. And this is not new. In 1952, footballer and writer Ivan Sharpe wrote about his concerns regarding the direction of English football, using the term 'positional play' to describe the more sophisticated game being produced in other, more advanced footballing nations. (A year later Hungary would thrash England 3-6 at Wembley.)

'Other countries are now way ahead of us in terms of the football they play,' wrote Sharpe. 'Foreigners have picked up on our core ideas and the Scottish passing game has now been adopted overseas. We've let them see all our tricks and then forgotten how to use them ourselves. The tense atmosphere at English stadiums nowadays plus the endless promotions and demotions have made our football messy and disorganised. Running about like a mad thing isn't football and other nations have developed a much more scientific approach to their game. Positional play is a more highly developed style of game because of how many passing movements it is based on. If we're talking solely in terms of style and methodology we can no longer consider ourselves in the top three of world football and the fact that, in almost every other country, they've started to train their youngsters to play this way, presents us with a real threat. We need to seriously rethink the way we play football.'

Almost sixty-five years have passed since Sharpe penned these words and positional play has evolved into a more sophisticated version of itself, both in practical and theoretical terms. One of its principal exponents and a man who has also given much time to the analysis of all things football, Juanma Lillo, looks at the terminology we use to describe this style of game. 'We call it positional play but, if you think about it, it's a pretty imprecise term. Can you be well positioned in the wrong place? Or badly positioned in the right place? Of course you can. Why? Well, if you look at the dictionary definition you'll see that "position" is related to posture whilst the roots of the word "situation" are to do with "site" or "place". So you could therefore have perfect posture (position) but be in the wrong place, or you could be in exactly the right place but have the wrong posture. It has to do with what has just happened and with what you intend to do in order to continue to construct the game.

'That's why words like "position" and "situation" don't really help to define this playing model and terms like "location" and "disposition" more accurately encapsulate both the exact meaning and the inherent idea of intentionality. We should therefore all be talking about "dispositional play" – the tendency of something to act in a certain manner under given circumstances.'

At first glance all of this may appear to be nothing more than the intricate musings of a brilliant mind but in fact Lillo's thinking goes far beyond mere semantics. The new interpretation he suggests could have far-reaching consequences in terms of our understanding of the internal logic of any game. This is not just theorising and the practical application of 'dispositional play' could help us make new connections in terms of how we train, bringing new ideas, developing our players and enhancing our collective use of this model. I'm really talking about using language in a very precise way so that it actually helps in the development and improvement of the way we train and play. Words matter and we should never underestimate the importance of using accurate terms for the things we do. Lillo has always been a fan of Ludwig Wittgenstein's thinking and the Austrian philosopher's belief that 'we are nothing more than words' is particularly pertinent here. Words after all help us to make the world smaller whilst allowing our intellect to expand exponentially.

Osho (Bhagwan Shri Rashnish) said that human beings 'invented language because they had no idea how to communicate' and in football the process of defining and redefining the terms we use can only help the relationships we develop in the continuous cycle of coming together and separating.

This is why Lillo suggests reviewing the terminology we use (although he in no way seeks to set himself up as the new guru of the football lexicon), 'I always say that there's only one guide to training and tactics: the laws of the game. We need to be very careful about how we use words and I really think that "dispositional play" would help coaches communicate exactly what they mean. I'm NOT suggesting that my suggestion is adopted universally. In fact I agree with Krishnamurti when he says that while words are a necessary part of communication, they are not the important thing. In the same way, as coaches we shouldn't just be thinking about how to win a match, but about how we communicate so that our players understand what they have to do.'


## COMPLEMENTARY PLAYERS

*The most important measure of how good a game I'd played was how much better I'd made my teammates play.*
*Bill Russell*

The people responsible for taking control of the match are the players themselves and one of Pep's rules is that his players should have complementary playing styles. When Dutchman Frank Rijkaard chose to play Xavi and Iniesta together the critics in Barcelona rounded on him. The men were considered too similar in style, almost identical types of player and when the team's performance dipped Spanish journalists concluded that 'Xavi and Iniesta can never be played together.' Then Guardiola arrived, put them together and the rest is history.

'People got it so, so wrong back then,' says Seirul.lo. 'Everyone was saying, "But Xavi and Iniesta do exactly the same thing.' Nonsense! They are completely different. Complementary, certainly, but completely different. Each has his own distinct style. The same thing happens with many of the concepts we work with in football. Take concepts like "order" and "balance". Order and balance co-exist. That's why we talk about situations and organisation. Organisation is a dynamic phenomenon, whilst balance is static.'

It's essential to have players who complement each other in any team and not just for technical reasons, because of their different tactical or physical abilities but also crucially for their distinct personality traits. During a sponsorship event Guardiola went into some detail on this subject.

'There are players who think about what the team needs, what the best solution would be for the whole group. Players like Bastian Schweinsteiger who control the game. He's a good example of someone who thinks about the whole team as he's playing. This type of footballer is intelligent and tends to have the kind of global vision we need. That's why you have some players who control the game. They do exactly what the coach wants and what the team needs. Then there are others who basically create chaos. Players like Arjen Robben who think, "Right, I'm going to move inside because I want the ball passed to me so that I can dribble a bit and score." These guys rely on their talent and play on instinct. Their heads are somewhere above what's actually happening on the ground and sometimes they don't get involved in the construction of the game. But we need them for those crucial last fifteen or twenty metres. They can end up making it up as they go along and the coach can do nothing to stop them. You can't control that kind of player. So basically, you have chaos or control and we actually need a bit of both. They're both part of what we do. We need players who can analyse the game and decide what needs to happen next and others who have the freedom to get on and do what they're so good at. If you manage to get a mix of both types in a team then it gives you a real advantage.'

This need to combine different personalities, abilities and styles can also lead to new roles within the team.

By January 2015 Guardiola had already developed his plan to make the full backs perform as inside midfielders on either side of the pivote. Lahm and Alaba (plus Rafinha and Bernat) had been trained in the new roles and the coach told me, 'My understanding of the role of full backs has changed in Germany. I no longer think of them as overlapping wing backs but as inside midfielders. And this will let me develop an inside midfielder who's very different to the players I have used in the past [Xavi, Iniesta and Thiago]. Now I can go out and sign another midfielder who's brilliant at arriving in the penalty area to score or make goals because these guys will be covering his back.'

Sure enough, five months later, Bayern signed Arturo Vidal, a significantly different kind of midfielder to the others in Pep's squad.

In fact, the truth is that most of the players who work with Guardiola are not what they seem, it's just that most of the football world loves stereotypes. Joshua Kimmich explains it brilliantly, 'Here at Bayern, we have our own way of interpreting the game so that, for us, a full back is almost the same thing as a midfielder.'

Spanish coach Ismael Díaz Galán expands on this, 'This is exactly what we've been saying for years: a defender isn't really defined by his position but by what's happening at the time. The rules concerning offside were changed a long time ago and players at the back no longer have a uniquely defensive function. The Clockwork Orange team of the 70s which inspired geniuses like Pep, worked on the principle that everyone should defend when you don't have the ball and everyone should attack when you do, regardless of the position you play in. A good coach must identify the skills of each of his players so that he can exploit those skills at different times throughout the match, as the game flows and the situation changes. In doing so he ensures that his players interact at the right moments to maximise the impact of the whole team.'

Ismael Díaz Galán, like many before him, has used the term 'genius' to refer to Guardiola and I'd like to take a moment here to reflect on this term. I've now written two books dedicated to Guardiola (*Pep Confidential* and this one) and have chosen not to refer to him as a genius because I'm not entirely sure exactly what the term means. As part of my research I've read a great deal of documentation about people who are considered to be geniuses and they tend to have a number of characteristics in common. On the whole they're analytical, impulsive, self-taught, highly self-critical, methodical, passionate. Guardiola certainly possesses many of these traits but this doesn't automatically mean he's a genius. Does his success give him this status? No, he's successful because he's a born winner with an innovative and bold approach to football. Above all, I see him as someone who works tirelessly to achieve his aims and meet his commitments and perhaps it will be many years from now, once Pep has retired, that we can look back at his coaching career in its entirety. Only then will we be able to say for sure whether or not his has been the work of a genius.

## SPEED AND 'PAUSA'

Football has become more and more like a game of chess
and if you lose even a second's concentration in chess, you're dead.
*Sir Alex Ferguson*

'The key to success is speed,' says Guardiola. 'If you want to win in sport you need to be just a little bit faster than all the rest. It's not so much about strength and power. It's about speed.'

However, the word 'speed' has different connotations in football than in, say, athletics. In football 'speed' is:

- Always in the context of the game and the ball
- To do with thought processes: split second decisions and anticipation give you a huge advantage
- About deliberate, strategic choices: whilst you're constructing your game, you need moderate speed to allow the group to advance as a unit whereas once you get to a more decisive stage, an elevated pace will give you the advantage
- About precision. Dashing about the pitch makes no sense if you're passing and receiving the ball sloppily and with no particular plan. Precision play makes you faster and more effective
- Used intelligently: the ability to rapidly anticipate and intuit play is vital for both exploiting your advantages as well as compensating for any weaknesses. Choosing to slow the game down at key moments will prevent the ball moving wildly from one half to the other. 'The faster the ball moves forward, the faster it comes back the other way.'

According to Lorenzo Buenaventura, Guardiola's fitness coach, the term 'speed' can be 'defined in several different ways but I suppose the three most obvious (although there are many more) are:

- Pure, athletic speed: basically who runs the fastest
- Applied speed: if our players intuit and anticipate what's going to happen they can neutralise any athletic advantage the opposition may possess by moving a split second before them
- Modulated speed: let's say our striker is a bit slower than the defender marking him. He's not going to try to outsprint him but will instead confuse him with sudden, dramatic changes in pace. An explosive burst of speed followed by a dead stop, then, when the marker brakes too, our man surges forward again . . .

With this approach, although the whole thing takes more time, you actually reach your end goal much faster.'

This third point is a fundamental part of why 'slow' players like Iniesta or Lahm are constantly able to beat faster, more athletic opponents. This 'modulated' or 'intelligent' speed is not only a fundamental part of the game but without it, it would be impossible for any team to dominate a match.

In his book, *The Infinite Game*, Jorge Valdano explains it like this: 'There are three kinds of speed in football: movement or how long it takes to run a certain distance, so, for example, Usain Bolt's times in the Olympics; speed of thought (making split second decisions) which is the ability of players to process information and select the right response even before they get the ball and is a crucial part of the modern game; and technical speed, what we call "precision". This is the most important of the three at both an individual and a collective level. If I can control the ball with just one touch, I'll be faster. If I pass after just one touch, the whole team will be faster. All of this isn't really about numbers, it's about critical understanding.'

Let's take Lahm's passing for example. It's so precise and clean that it's like he's gifting the receiver extra time or more space, or both. And not only does he pass brilliantly, he reads the game so well that, as he's passing the ball, he knows exactly how he'll follow up his teammate's next move. All this makes him look super-fast when he's actually relatively slow compared to most of his regular opponents. It's his speed of thought that's so fast. He's making decisions about his next move as he passes the ball to his teammate and that means that he's exactly where he ought to be when he's needed, whether it's in a supporting role, or in a one-on-one battle for the ball, or simply to dribble the ball forward. Physically, Lahm may be slower than others but mentally he's lightning fast, which is why he'll almost always get to the ball first.

## LAHM – SHARP AS A TACK
### Munich, 12 December 2015

Guardiola: 'Philipp knows how to play. He knows how to do everything. And that has made all the difference in his career. If you're a veteran and you really know how to play you can extend your career for as long as you want. A player who doesn't really know how to play is over the hill at thirty but someone like Lahm could go on till he's forty because he understands the game. And the same goes for Xabi Alonso.'

## PINNING THE OPPOSITION
## AND THEN OPENING THEM UP

*All tactical actions should be based on the principle of using the least energy to cause the maximum fatigue in the enemy*
*Sepp Herberger*

'What's the most defining characteristic of the All Blacks?' asks Guardiola.

'They pin the opposition back and open them up.'

'You see! That's what I do. I pin them back and open them up. I attack through the centre and open up on the wing. I push my men forward as a unit, at the same time opening up on the wing. That's the best kind of attacking, what they do in rugby. I attack and divide, attack and divide, attack and divide. They're obliged to pass backwards so the receiver is always facing the game. There's really no better way to attack! In rugby it's against the rules to pass the ball forward. They're forced to put it back so they're always facing the way they're going. I move up through the centre, drawing our opponents in so that the guys who are free on the wings can go forward and finish them off. What happens in rugby, that's exactly how to attack.'

The New Zealand 'All Blacks' are the most successful sports team in the world, in any discipline, ever, with a win-rate of over 79% set between 1903 and 2016; in November 2015 they became the first team to win back-to-back World Cups, dominating the competition from start to finish and seem to be pushing on to even greater heights. In the rugby world, they are head and shoulders above every other nation on the planet.

They are also world leaders in a particular tactical idea: that it isn't only the ball carrier who is part of the attack. It's also the guys who are positioned high up in the opposition half.

'So someone who's in the opposition half without the ball is attacking?' demands Guardiola.

'Yes, even though he doesn't have the ball, if he's high up the pitch then he's nearer to the team's objective.'

Pep's curious: 'And the All Blacks press high?'

'Of course they do. Now and again in a match they'll decide: "We've been stuck attacking the opposition by pinning them back and opening them up for too long without success. It's time to change." So they thump a long kick as near to the opposition try line as possible and send the other fourteen players bombing after it. Now the opposition has the ball but, crucially, it's in the part of the pitch where the All Blacks want to be – the opposition try zone. The New Zealanders don't care that the other team is starting to build their passes, they're going to pressurise them, tackle and block them until they win the ball from them. And then they'll just be a few metres away from scoring a try. Then the All Blacks will say, "NOW we'll go back to our usual attacking style, pinning the opposition down and opening them up." It doesn't matter if they have to go through twenty-five phases because eventually the other team won't be able to sustain their marking. Basically, the All Blacks have achieved a perfect harmony between their specific players, speed and a playing philosophy.'

'It sounds like "total rugby",' muses Pep. 'These guys could certainly teach us a thing or two . . .'

## BACKSTAGE 4

## WE MUST FIRST LOSE IN ORDER TO WIN
### Munich, 18 September 2015

Just a year ago France beat Spain in Spain. Yesterday it was Spain's turn to thrash France on their home ground. We're talking of course about last year's basketball World Cup and the current European championships. Manel Estiarte has watched the game with Pep, another great basketball fan, and he reflects on the significance of the result.

'It was a brilliant game and I'm not just saying that because Spain won. I would still have been impressed if France had beaten us. They both deserved to win today and it was fantastic to see such intensity, these guys don't let up for a minute. In the end the pressure of playing at home got to France, who are actually a better team, and they failed to give the performance everyone was expecting. And although Spain aren't as good a team, you could see their heads go up and their confidence grow as the minutes passed. Another unforgettable game. Just like last year's but for different reasons.

'Last year we watched a team in a state of grace who managed to grab control of the game and prevent the Spanish team from reacting. The Spaniards had sailed through the competition unbeaten up to that point and looked like they were unstoppable but when things went against them they had no response.

'Today's match has been very different. The Spanish had to field a weaker team than last year because of injuries but the guys who did play grabbed every chance and clung on till they won the match. They refused to let up even for a second, not even when things were going badly and they looked like they were going to lose. Today it was all about fighting, fighting, fighting.

'I think we can all learn something from the Spaniards' performance: you have to lose if you want to win. In a competition like this, which has lots of games and then knock-out rounds, a bit like the Champions League, you have to take a few knocks along the way. It's only by having your wings clipped that you become stronger. Sure, it's great if you keep winning and you feel unstoppable, like nobody's ever going to beat you. It's a great feeling, you're on cloud nine but maybe, just maybe, that success is going to end up causing your downfall.

'Because it stands to reason that you're messing up in some aspect of your game. It might be insignificant things, stuff that won't stop you winning a game but which are there nonetheless. But nobody's paying attention to those things, not even the coach. So you go on winning and you're over the moon, having a ball and celebrating your victories. You may even be tempted to laugh at your opponents. "We whipped them out there today," you say as you toast your success and you completely forget those little black marks in your own performance. And therein lies the danger!

'Of course, if the opposite happens and you take a hit on day one and you're down but not yet out, it may turn out to be the best thing that could've happened. Because that's when the alarm bells start ringing. Where did we go wrong? What are our weaknesses? Where is our game lacking? How are we messing up? And that's what you're all focused on: the coach, the players, the technical staff, the analysts, everyone. Nobody's having a celebratory drink or jumping with joy or having a laugh at anybody's expense. Suddenly the red light's flashing. We're in trouble, lads. But it's as if all your senses are suddenly on red alert and you're seeing clearly at last. You see every last flaw AND you know how to fix them.

'Obviously no coach is going to tell a champion team to stop winning and go for a defeat in the next game. That would be ridiculous and it's certainly not what I'm suggesting. If you're on the crest of a wave, then of course you must keep riding it. No way should you ever go out to lose. All I'm saying is that sometimes you will get beaten. You're riding that wave when you suddenly crash into the water. But that crash can at times be the impetus you need because it unites you as a group. You're all in this together and you have to solve it together. You have to work on your weaknesses and re-assert your goals: "We're rubbish. They wiped the floor with us, we're a hair's breadth from elimination. We were the favourites and look at us now. On our knees." These are the thoughts that go through your mind. You're at your lowest point but that's exactly what could save you if you are able, as a group, to pull together and convert the despair into positive energy.

'A year ago Spain looked like (and almost certainly were) a much stronger team than France. They'd proven their superior quality at the early stages of the competition but that had made them cocky and when the time came to grit their teeth and fight for survival, they were completely nonplussed. Today the opposite happened. They'd been hammered by Italy and had a hard time with the rest of their opponents. They'd put on a very average, rather sluggish performance so far and the Italy game had really shaken them up. But they responded heroically, digging deep and finding the will to fight on. The Spain team that won today came out, not to win, but to do battle. Everything was against them: their own results, twenty-seven thousand Frenchmen and the evidence of their own eyes. The French were a better side but today they were also the complacent, self-assured, know-it-alls and Spain were the bare-knuckle fighters. They won because they had been ripped to shreds by Italy (98-105). Because that defeat left them bruised and bloodied and they needed to get back in the fight. They needed to find all their black marks, all their faults and failings and they needed to believe. Believe that they could do it, fight tooth and nail for every ball as if their lives depended on it.

'Perhaps I've got it wrong but it definitely makes sense to me. I was right last year when I told you that champion teams who get too full of themselves can lack the warrior spirit that makes you grab even the flimsiest of chances and battle on. It's the fighting spirit of the Balkans I talked about. And I really believe I've got it right again. In order to win, you need first to lose because sometimes it's only in bloody defeat that you find the warrior within you and the will to fight on.'

# 5

# PEP'S INFLUENCE ON
# GERMAN FOOTBALL

*If you want the rainbow, you've gotta put up with the rain.*
*Dolly Parton*

WE'VE ALREADY SEEN the changes Germany brought about in Guardiola, but let's now look at his influence on German football, starting with the impact he made at Bayern Munich.

Despite having failed to secure ultimate victory in the Champions League during his time there, the transformation in Bayern's game nonetheless exceeded all expectations. During his three years in Munich, the team became the unrivalled master-practitioners of positional play, moving forward vertically in a style reminiscent of the Barcelona of 2008/09 but quite different from the Barcelona of 2010–12.

Bayern's defining characteristics were: consistency of performance; match domination, whatever the circumstances; and painstakingly constructed attacks which kept them in the opposition half as much as possible.

Their stats (2.46 average goals per match with only 0.69 conceded) proved beyond doubt the efficacy of their offensive play and the control they commanded over their rivals' attacks. Neuer kept a clean sheet in 81 out of 154 games (52.6%).

Throughout Pep's tenure Bayern always achieved higher possession rates than their opponents and spent more time in their rival's half than their own. Their record for total possession in any one game was the 82.7% they managed in March 2016 against Werder Bremen (5-0), a game in which they also achieved 993 passes with a 92% success rate. 72% of their goals came after sustained, carefully constructed and co-ordinated actions which involved five players or more.

This uncompromising control and complete domination became one of their distinguishing characteristics and encapsulated the three most important components of their game: possession, space and rhythm. In fact it's easier to list the games they failed to dominate than the ones where their control was almost absolute: the first twelve minutes against Arsenal in 2014; the catastrophic defeat by Real Madrid; being beaten by VfL Wolfsburg in January 2015; the fourteen minutes in the Camp Nou when they watched as an acceptable 0-0 became a disastrous 3-0, with Messi in the role of lead executioner; the thirty minutes of hysteria away to Mönchengladbach at the end of 2015; and the first fifteen minutes against Atlético de Madrid in the Champions League semi-finals.

In truth, Bayern were rather more accustomed to delivering resounding victories, accumulating silverware and producing multi-goal extravaganzas. They also gave us astounding moments of collective genius: the ninety-four consecutive passes against Manchester City; their routing of Roma in the Stadio Olimpico; their exhibitions of explosive, attacking football which left Arsenal, Porto and Shakhtar in shreds; and the endless clashes with Borussia Dortmund, Wolfsburg, Bayer Leverkusen and the other, less significant Bundesliga sides.

Arguably, Bayern's game under Guardiola reached its zenith in three games played in the last months of his tenure there: the first hour against Juve in Turin, their epic comeback against the same side a few weeks later; and the semi-final against Atlético de Madrid in the Allianz Arena.

At an individual level, the most impressive performance was undoubtedly Robert Lewandowski's in September 2015, when he scored five goals against Wolfsburg in only nine minutes.

Under Guardiola, the team's performances became increasingly consistent and for the first time in the club's history they won four consecutive league titles – three under Pep after Heynckes' treble winning season. As Ottmar Hitzfeld says, 'Guardiola hasn't been given the recognition he deserves and anyone who fails to value all that he achieved, is completely deluded. Most treble winning teams usually crash and burn the season following their big success but Pep made Bayern even more ambitious than ever.'

Historically, Bayern had never managed to win the league after a German World Cup victory and Pep overturned this jinx in typically accomplished style. His team only dropped its competitive level once the Bundesliga was already won – something that was very evident in 2014, significantly less so in 2015 and then avoided completely in 2016. As long as a trophy was up for grabs the team played with a single-minded, ruthless determination to win. They conquered the league in the shortest time ever in March 2014 (after only twenty-seven league games); achieved nineteen consecutive league wins (ten of which were away from home); emerged unbeaten from the first half of season 2014/15, in which they conceded only four goals in seventeen matches, leaving thirteen games with no goals at all against them; and consistently notched up outrageous goal tallies, scoring four or more in 25% of their games (38 out of a total 161); on seventeen occasions they won by a difference of four goals, on nine by five, on three by six, twice by seven and on one occasion put eight goals away against HSV Hamburg in February 2015 (8-0).

Although there were other impressive score-lines in Bundesliga games, (0-7 against Werder Bremen, 1-6 against Wolfsburg and 5-1 against Borussia Dortmund) they achieved their most astounding victories in the Champions League: 5-1 against Arsenal, 6-1 against Porto, 7-0 against Shakhtar and 1-7 away to Roma. If we consider these stats alongside their conceded goals tally (111 in 161 games) we can have no doubt of the effectiveness of Guardiola's strategy at Bayern; confident, determined, offensive football; meticulous defensive organisation to prevent successful counter-attacks; the need for control at all times (they only lost this on a few, memorable and painful occasions); and the expectation of aggressive, competitive football at all times.

The Bayern Guardiola passed on to Carlo Ancelotti was different from the team he had inherited from Jupp Heynckes. In terms of results, Pep failed to match his predecessor's treble but he did leave behind a more than respectable legacy of two double winning seasons as well as a team with as much aggression and competitive drive as ever which had achieved a superior degree of stability and consistency in terms of results. As regards their playing style, however, the team had assumed a new personality and, although they retained many of the characteristics of Heynckes' game (verticality, speed and energy), their total immersion in Pep's positional play meant that in his last season there (2015/16) they became the most proficient practitioners of this style of game ever, matched only by the Barcelona of 2011 and the Ajax team of 1996.

And Guardiola's impact extended far beyond the dressing room. He persuaded the club to introduce a range of improvements: state-of-the-art equipment for more effective injury prevention and rehabilitation; the extension and modernisation of the gymnasiums; the reduction of time spent away from home in hotels to the absolute minimum; up-to-date and clear rules about nutrition and healthy living; a large team of analysts who delivered high level, detailed information about the opposition; plus details of all his training methods including every drill and exercise used. Journalist Stefen Niemeyer is clear about the impact the coach made: 'Pep and his assistants have helped the club take a significant step forward in terms of our development. We've achieved a higher level of efficiency and proficiency than ever before and, for me, it's a great example of how the cross fertilisation of skills and ideas across Europe can make us all stronger and more successful.'

Ancelotti is the ideal successor to Guardiola and his appointment is likely to ensure the continuity of the football ideas Pep introduced. Although an excellent coach in his own right, the Italian's skill lies in his ability and willingness to work within and adapt to the technical and tactical framework already established at a club rather than set about imposing his own ideology. The fact that there is no distinguishable 'Ancelotti brand' means that he's the perfect fit for the current Bayern team which still bears the indelible mark of Guardiola's philosophy and he is likely to continue with the same, or similar, playing model as well as understanding exactly how to support the players in managing the pressures of competition.

The fact that Ancelotti immediately scrapped the use of rondos as a training technique may be seen by some as a deliberate attempt to break with his predecessor's ideology but is possibly nothing more than a practical decision based on his years of experience using different training methods. Only time will tell which interpretation is the more accurate.

Arrigo Sacchi, the Italian coach, has his own views on the situation facing Ancelotti. 'Any coach who takes over from Guardiola has a problem because it will be impossible for anyone to do better. But he will have one advantage: the key's in the ignition and the engine's running.'

## WHAT PEP GAVE TO THE BUNDESLIGA

If you do not fight for an ideal
or to make things better, then you are lost.
*Norman Foster*

Competitive drive and a new football ideology. These were Guardiola's main gifts to the Bundesliga.

In the three years prior to his arrival in Germany, Bayern had produced inconsistent results. Although they won the treble in 2013 under Heynckes, in the two previous seasons the only major title they had managed was the 2012 German Super Cup. Clearly, Jupp Heynckes' work brought about a transformation in the club's relative status in German football and Guardiola succeeded in maintaining this advantage and preventing a sudden downturn in their fortunes. In fact the board of directors' greatest fear was a possible crash after the treble in 2013 followed by Germany's triumph in the 2014 World Cup.

The Catalan coach ensured that none of his players became complacent after the treble and achieved three consecutive league titles (adding to Heynckes' 2013 Bundesliga title) whilst smashing records in almost every aspect of the game. He also insisted that his men bring the same aggression and competitive drive to every competition. They produced glorious results in the league and the Cup (two titles and two doubles) but were left bitterly disappointed in the Champions League where they were eliminated in three consecutive semi-finals, hammered in the first, beaten by the better side in the second and leaving the third feeling utterly dejected after a brilliant performance was thwarted by a cruel turn of fate.

Many have claimed that this competitive drive made little difference because of the superior quality of the Bayern squad relative to other German clubs. This is true, to an extent. Even before Pep arrived Bayern already boasted an outstanding group of players who were also the heart and soul of the national team and, during his time there, players like Douglas Costa, Xabi Alonso, Lewandowski, Thiago, Vidal, Kimmich and Coman added more talent to an already superbly gifted squad. Surely then the obvious question is: what on earth were their opponents doing all this time?

If we analyse Guardiola's first two seasons (which is when these claims were made) we see that, during this time, Bayern made a net investment (signings minus sales) of 20.4 million euros. How much did 2011 and 2012 league champions Borussia Dortmund invest? 66.7 million, more than triple that amount. And VfL Wolfsburg? A whopping 73.5 million, almost four times as much as Bayern. Let's look now at the relative classifications of these teams. Wolfsburg finished thirty and then ten points behind Bayern over the two seasons with Dortmund trailing the leaders by nineteen and thirty-three points in the same period.

It's therefore interesting that in Guardiola's third and last season in charge, Bayern spent 33 million net whilst each of the other teams made a net gain. (Dortmund, 22.5 million and Wolfsburg 46.6 million thanks to Kevin de Bruyne's transfer to Manchester City.) In the league table, BVB ended ten points behind Bayern and Wolfsburg, thirty-three.

Here's what the figures look like over the three seasons:

• Bayern invested 53.4 million net and won three league titles.
• Borussia Dortmund invested 44.15 million net and trailed Bayern by a total of sixty-two points.
• Wolfsburg invested 27 million net and trailed Bayern by a total of seventy-three points.

The difference in the amount invested by the three clubs is not sufficient to explain the huge gap between the champions and their two main rivals although of course net investment is not the only relevant factor and the size of salaries must also be taken into account (Bayern pays its players more than any other German club although substantially less than its great European rivals). We should also consider the fact that Bayern's signing of Götze and Lewandowski was a major blow to BVB's ambitions. But does all this fully explain the yawning chasm between Bayern and its opponents? Surely BVB's own performance under Tuchel last season shows that other things matter just as much as money. Things like competitive spirit and the quality of the game a coach gets from his team.

The other contribution Guardiola made to the Bundesliga was the quality and quantity of his ideas about the game. Guardiola's ideas enriched German football, at the same time emphasising the contradiction implicit in the changes the nation made at the turn of the century.

The German football authorities didn't make these changes because of the results of the national team or individual clubs (who sometimes managed to cover up defects by pulling off a shock win), but because they believed that their game and ideologies were obsolete. From 2000 on German football's governing bodies worked to introduce sweeping changes in all levels of club life, from the training of coaches, to scouting, youth training schemes and the young talent they fostered, as well as introducing procedures to ensure financial stability at club level. Journalist Raphael Honigstein gives a wonderful account of the reasons for this renovation and the parameters within which it took place in his book, *Das Reboot*. By 2006, the year the World Cup took place in Germany, the impact of the changes was already beginning to be felt and over the next few years the results of the national team plus club sides like Bayern and Borussia Dortmund took a quantum leap forward.

What do I mean then by the implicit 'contradiction'? What possible contradiction could exist in such an exemplary process? Well, it's the contradiction inherent in the fact that the German game is currently played according to three great footballing ideologies:

1. The traditions dating back to the 70s
2. The culture of *Gegenpressing* popularised by Klopp
3. The game of position advocated by Guardiola

This clash of ideologies is a fascinating study in its own right but to describe it fully would require a substantial body of work which would distract us from our present purpose. I'll therefore restrict myself to some short reflections. At the moment German football (both at club and national level) is firmly rooted in a playing model which was hugely successful in the 70s and 80s whilst at the same time coaches are being trained in the 'vertical, front-foot' football exemplified by Jürgen Klopp's *Gegenpressing* and continued by the likes of Roger Schmidt and Ralph Hasenhüttl. The latter, a playing model which demands that players run for ninety minutes, fight tooth and nail for every ball and are prepared to die for the cause, captures the essence of the Teutonic character and holds a special place in the hearts and minds of German football fans. It's not for nothing that the Bundesliga leads the table in terms of the kilometres run by its players as well as the speeds they attain.

Tobias Escher, one of the most informed commentators in German football, examined these themes in his book: *From the Liberal to the Double Pivot: A Tactical History of German Football,* and I asked him to share his views on this conflict of ideologies. He confirmed something that you and I already know: anything we haven't yet 'discovered' or 'recognised' usually ends up being considered an 'abstract' phenomenon.

Escher: 'Before Guardiola came to Germany nobody here knew anything about positional play because it was never part of our football culture like it was in Cataluña and Holland. In Germany the term, "*taktik*" (tactic) is often used as a synonym for "defence" and a "tactical" game is therefore a defensive game where both sides essentially "park the bus". With this playing model, tactics become something you use as part of your defensive play but you don't need them for your attacks. I think that this was one of the challenges Pep faced when he first arrived because everyone, fans, journalists and coaches couldn't see that if we want our players to score goals, we need to give them tactical instructions regarding how they position themselves, how they interact with each other etc. A lot of people here genuinely believe that the best way of scoring goals is to leave it entirely in the players' hands. Or, in Beckenbauer's words in 1990: "*Fußball de Geht raus und de spielt!*" ("You just need to go out there and play some football!") So there was no awareness or understanding about what Guardiola was doing from a tactical point of view. For Germans, attacking is all about speed and Guardiola wasn't particularly interested in speed. He preferred to use a system people didn't really "get". And all of that resulted in this monumental clash of ideologies that we're seeing at the moment.'

## TUCHEL, PEP'S POSSIBLE HEIR

There are no infallible coaches, we are all the sum
of our experiences . . . Of our victories and defeats. What matters is
that they give us more joy than sorrow
*Jesús Candelas*

Many German coaches are fascinated by the exciting, trophy-winning football Barcelona play and have spent time studying and adapting it to their own game, with Germany coach Joachim Löw as perhaps the manager who has invested most in this process.

Guardiola injected a host of new ideas to Bayern's game and these generated intense debate and discussion as the rest of the country watched, learned and, in many cases, began to imitate. Respected men like Julian Nagelsmann, André Schubert and Thomas Tuchel in particular have made significant changes to their own brand of football, adapting to a style which Guardiola describes as 'counter-cultural', given the evident mismatch with the traditional German game of continuous counter-pressing. It may surprise, given its recent success, that German football is currently involved in an internal struggle between proponents of different ideologies and as yet nobody is clear how the situation will be resolved. Guardiola made a significant contribution by demonstrating a level of tactical versatility which forced other teams to come up with strategic responses.

Their strategies covered the whole gamut of possibilities: from sweeping changes in defensive organisation (the defensive formation 6-3-1 is no longer an unusual choice and has become almost commonplace) to the use of intense pressing to prevent Bayern bringing the ball out from the back. Other Bundesliga clubs produced a vast range of tactics in the search for an antidote to Pep's ideas. Inevitably, their efforts only drove the Bayern coach to seek more innovation and invention. Now, one man has emerged as Guardiola's possible successor in Germany: Borussia Dortmund's Thomas Tuchel, a passionate believer in positional play who has now adopted this playing model.

Without losing any of the intense, direct and aggressive football Klopp established at Dortmund, Tuchel has introduced a variety of tactics which have helped the team develop their own version of positional play. In fact, this was one of the main reasons for Dortmund's collapse in the last few months of Klopp's tenure, when their opponents consistently allowed them to have the ball and then dropped back to deny them space to run into. Tuchel's strategic intelligence makes him the most interesting German coach to emerge over the last few years and we've yet to see the best of him. He proved his worth at Mainz 05 and is now doing it again at Dortmund. Under his guidance, Dortmund has gone from being a team which runs a great deal, to a team which runs with a great deal of purpose.

## LET'S HAVE DINNER
### Munich, 6 November 2015

As they say their goodbyes in the corridor outside the Allianz Arena's dressing room, Tuchel asks, 'What's next week like for you Pep? Can we have dinner one day?'

'Sure, Tuesday's good for me. Give me a call and we'll fix something up.'

Bayern have just thrashed Dortmund 5-1, but in the post-match press conference Guardiola is fulsome in his praise for their opponents' game. And he means every word.

He says it all again later to Domènec Torrent and Manel Estiarte. He feels genuine admiration for how much Tuchel had achieved in such a short time.

Klopp turned Dortmund into a formidable fighting machine but the team had begun to play poor, inconsistent football towards the end of his tenure. Tuchel had then come in and turned the team around, taking his players to a new level of total domination over every aspect of their game. If they've failed to perform at their best this evening in the Allianz Arena, the defeat has done nothing to detract from the success of the evolution that's going on within the club.

Guardiola and Tuchel clicked almost as soon as they met, back in the early days of Pep's first season in Germany when Tuchel was in charge of Mainz 05. Pep had been instantly impressed by the other coach's aggressive, clever football on both the occasions the teams met. The two men had been keen to maintain the relationship and had decided to meet up during Tuchel's sabbatical year after leaving Mainz. They had lunch together in Schumann's Bar where other diners looked on in amusement as they turned their table into a mini football pitch, using salt cellars and glasses to represent the players and moving them around to imitate the tactics they were discussing. The fact that Tuchel then became Pep's main rival when he took the helm at Dortmund did nothing to affect the bond the two men had developed, which is why on Tuesday night, just forty-eight hours after clashing in the league, they've met up to talk football over dinner.

Tuchel's keen to learn about the mental processes Pep went through as he prepared for the match. The Dortmund coach accepts that his own strategy was unorthodox given that he changed the roles and positions of no less than six of his key players. Overkill perhaps? He's determined to go back over Sunday's game and establish just how Pep had come up with a plan that made such quick work of a team which until then had been a model of organisation and inventiveness.

Guardiola's also enthusiastic about getting this chance to talk. He wants to know why Tuchel went for so many changes and to get an idea of what his rival might be planning for future clashes. The two men are dining alone, intent on having a serious, detailed exchange of ideas and reactions, much like two rival chess players who sit down after a tournament to discuss the game. Neither Pep nor Tuchel have any reservations about speaking openly and Pep shares some of their discussion with me the following day.

'I told him that he's the one who's going to have to take positional play forward in Germany.'

I later discuss this same subject with Swiss coach Hermann Kälin, who himself is the product of a range of different football influences having trained in Germany, applied his theories in Mexico and perfected his game with Paco Seirul. lo in Barcelona.

'Tuchel's Borussia Dortmund's definitely going to be the one to watch in the future and not just in the Bundesliga, but in Europe too. He's far and away the most promising coach Germany's produced in the last thirty years – and I should know. He arrived at Dortmund and almost immediately transformed the model Klopp had established. Now the players run an average of 10 km less per match, are more intense and produce better results because they have more possession. There's been a huge rise in pass completion and he's found a way to get the very best out of each of his men. They're running less but that makes them much more effective. If Pep was German football's sheriff then maybe it's time for Tuchel to pin that star on his chest.'

But Tuchel's challenge is a daunting one. After a brilliant first season in which he returned Dortmund to their blistering best, he failed to win a trophy, ironically enough losing out to Guardiola in the Cup and to Klopp in the Europa League. He then lost three key men during the summer transfer window, Hummels to Bayern, Gündogan to Manchester City and Mkhitaryan to Manchester United, losses which forced him to overhaul his entire team, rejuvenating it with players like Merino, Dembélé, Mor, Rode, Schürrle, Guerreiro, Bartra and Götze. Just as Guardiola is facing the challenge of a lifetime in Manchester, 2016/17 will be a serious test of Tuchel's skills and character. By the end of the season we will no doubt be clear about whether or not he is Pep's true heir in Germany.

# HIS IMPACT ON THE NATIONAL TEAM

*The problem with the world is that the idiots and fanatics
are completely sure of themselves
whilst the smart guys are assailed by doubts*
*Bertrand Russell*

It's difficult to accurately judge the impact any one club coach makes on a national team. It's impossible to say for example how much Guardiola's Barça influenced Spain's success. There's no doubt that almost by a process of osmosis the Spain team adopted much of the Catalan club's playing model with coach Vicente Del Bosque adding his own clever additions and adaptations (Xabi Alonso as double *pivote* beside Busquets is one of the best known). Guardiola's Barcelona players also made up the nucleus of the Spain team and they undoubtedly brought with them many of the disciplines inculcated by Pep, thereby ensuring an extensive run of success for the national team.

The same can be said for the Germany team which won the 2014 World Cup with a core group of Bayern players in the ranks. The *Mannschaft* benefited from the improved performances of individual players such as Boateng, Kroos, Neuer and Lahm plus the application of Bayern's playing model which Löw adapted as he saw fit (for example, having Khedira play as an inside forward and asking Lahm to take an organising role despite using him on the right touchline).

Even if we accept that Guardiola had a significant influence on both these countries' national sides (their success coincided with his tenures at Barça and Bayern) because his men formed the bulk of the squads and were performing better than ever, we must also factor in the wisdom and tactical intelligence of Del Bosque and Löw. What we end up with then is the product of the synergy between smart, progressive, like-minded professionals, without any possibility of quantifying exactly the contribution of each man. It would be just as ridiculous to attribute two World Cup trophies to Guardiola (which many of his devotees insist on doing) as it would be to blame him for

Germany and Spain's eliminations in the recent Euros competition (an accusation often levelled by his detractors).

## HIS PLAYERS' PROGRESS

*What you do every day is like the work of a master craftsman*
*Roberto Olabe*

There is one area where there's absolutely no doubt about the significant, long term impact of Pep's work: his players. One of the people who has most influenced Pep is Argentinian volleyball coach Julio Velasco who has this to say: 'A coach should approach his work like a craftsman, not like a shop steward. That's where the real joy is. We are the artisans of the training and formation of sportsmen and should be more concerned with the progress they make rather than the results they achieve. It is the process that matters, not the victories. That's where the joy and satisfaction comes from. Our first priority is to ensure that our players develop and after that we think about how to win.'

Velasco's words sum up perfectly Guardiola's relationship with his players. 'Usually in life, you can work out who's who. You know exactly who really cares about the team and who's just in it for themselves. Similarly, amongst all the players I have I know exactly which ones I've helped a lot, which ones I've made a small difference to and which ones I've made almost no lasting impact on. In terms of the last group, it's never about any kind of ill-feeling, it's simply because my playing model doesn't suit them.'

Pep's objective is to help his men develop and this is more important to him even than winning. Ironically, it's precisely his failure to help midfielder Mario Götze succeed at Bayern that demonstrates just how deeply he cares. Never before had Guardiola dedicated so much effort and so many hours of video, analysis and explanations to one player. He had never demonstrated such patience, nor given so many opportunities, nor tried so many different approaches. And all to no avail. This failure may well be due to the excessively high expectations people had of Götze who, as an eighteen-year-old, was proclaimed the 'German Messi' when in reality his talents were far inferior to the Argentinian prodigy. Perhaps he may be one of those sportsmen who, for some reason, fail to manifest their full talent. What's certain is that both coach and player made a concerted, dedicated effort for thirty-six long months without ever really enjoying the rewards of their labour.

In contrast, the list of Pep's triumphs in this respect is a long one. Under his tutelage Lahm went from being a brilliant full back to a deadly midfielder, the brains of the team out on the pitch no matter where he was, a superb passer of the ball and a player capable of setting the rhythm of play and bringing confidence and security to his team. Pep also immediately spotted Boateng's huge potential and worked with him until he reached a level beyond even the player's wildest dreams. Today Boateng is a gifted and at times almost clairvoyant central defender with a superior passing ability. Neuer, too, flourished under Guardiola: already a superb goalkeeper with phenomenal levels of concentration he quickly adapted to his new role as sweeper-keeper, adding continuity to Bayern's game and demonstrating the same level of short-passing ability as his outfield teammates.

## NEUER: TOTAL FOCUS
### Munich, 5 November 2014

It's been a curious game. Bayern's dominated throughout, shooting at goal twenty-four times with Roma only putting two shots on target. Each arrives in the eighty-third minute when Neuer manages to block two brilliant consecutive efforts from Gervinho and Nainggolan. What's so impressive is Neuer's ability to remain totally focused even late in a game, after eighty-three minutes of having more or less nothing to do.

I mention this to Bayern's goalkeeping coach, Toni Tapalovic. 'You shouldn't be surprised by today's display,' he replied. 'Manu is always totally focused. He never, ever gets distracted. He's as much a part of the action as the rest even when he's not physically playing. He's mentally involved in the game for every second of every minute.'

Joshua Kimmich was another footballer whose latent talent was immediately obvious to the coach. 'Sooner or later, Kimmich will be an international. He's got everything it takes to make a great player,' he said in September 2015. And Kimmich turned out to be everything one could wish for in a pupil. With courage and determination the young German worked to master new and unfamiliar roles under the constant supervision of the coach who tested, nagged and corrected him until he became the exceptional international footballer he is today.

## KIMMICH, THE GREAT HOPE
### Munich, 10 August 2014

It's searingly hot in Munich when Estiarte's siesta is interrupted by a phone call. It's Pep. 'Get up! We have to go to the Allianz! I'll come and get you in ten minutes!'

Michael Reschke, head of scouting, is waiting for them at the stadium where it's not Bayern who're playing but their city rivals, second division TSV. They're facing RB Leipzig, who have Joshua Kimmich, one of the jewels of German football, in their line-up. Only ten days ago Kimmich became European champion with the U-19 *Mannschaf.* Guardiola and Estiarte arrive at 15.30, just in time for kick-off and then sit through what turns out to be a dreadful game. The play is mind-numbingly sluggish and the ball is thumped from one half to another without ever really stopping in midfield. It's appalling football and the lack of tactical ability is quite depressing. Kimmich only gets about thirty-three touches.

Seven days later Guardiola's on the phone again and this time he sounds even more excited. 'Manel, Manel, I'm in the car. I'll be with you in two minutes. You've got to see Kimmich! The guy's a machine!'

Pep's decided to give the kid a second chance and is brimming with enthusiasm about what he sees: the player's ability to bring the ball out, his understanding of the game and its rhythm, his technical skills and body position when he receives the ball, taking it with one foot and passing with the other, his instinctive sense of when and where to mark and what to do next. Pep believes he's spotted a great talent and he wants him signed. Now.

Douglas Costa arrived at Munich under a question mark, Pep having had to fight for the club to sign him. 'Who the hell is this?' demanded journalists, fans and the odd Bayern director alike. Within months the player had become not just *the* discovery of the Bundesliga but the player who, regardless of position, ensured unity in how the team constructed their play.

Kingsley Coman arrived at Bayern having had almost no playing time at Juventus but rapidly became a key part of the team and, ironically, one of the main protagonists of Bayern's extraordinary comeback win over the Italian club. As Guardiola commented, 'If you're willing to base your midfield around a kid of nineteen, then he's either going to make you look like a genius or a complete idiot.'

Toni Kroos too was an excellent player who Pep taught the fundamentals of organising the midfield and the positional sense to help get his team in the opposition half by knowing exactly when and where to move the ball. Pep's work (which was then developed further by Ancelotti at Madrid) helped convert Kroos into a midfield maestro.

Full back David Alaba was a high-speed, virtually unstoppable force when Guardiola arrived. His three years under the Catalan master transformed a player who was already the most athletic man in the squad into the complete footballer: he played as a central defender in the decisive spells of the third season, an improvised attacking midfielder, a winger, and even a centre forward. He accomplished all this without losing an iota of his natural ability although he tended to make faster progress when given clear tactical instructions rather than being allowed to float free.

Mavericks Lewandowski and Müller presented Guardiola with a tricky problem which he successfully resolved by creating tiny 'ecosystems' in his game plan, allowing them to express their considerable, if anarchic talents. The solution worked brilliantly and both players smashed their already impressive goal-scoring records. Lewandowski scored forty-four goals, an increase of 50% on his performance over the three previous seasons and Müller managed thirty-two, an increase of 39% over the same period.

Xabi Alonso summed up the secret of Pep's success. 'Under Pep you work on every last detail. It's not luck or him standing on the side-line shouting instructions that gets the results, it's sheer hard graft. With Pep, you work, and work and then you work some more.' Undoubtedly the fact that he was able to develop so many players was the biggest source of satisfaction to Pep as he said his goodbyes to Munich. 'This is the greatest contribution we can make as coaches. A coach came to see us the other day and told us, "You've no idea how highly Toni Kroos thinks about you and all your technical staff." He keeps saying, "The staff there knew our opponents inside out and could tell us exactly what they'd do in any game. And they were always right!" If he's saying things like that then that's it for me. My work here is done and I'm completely satisfied. It's not about methodologies and all that stuff. It's about teaching your players and them understanding what you've given them. If you know you've helped a player understand the game more or play better then, that's it, mission accomplished.'

# BACKSTAGE 5

## LEWANDOWSKI – IN THE ZONE
### Munich, 22 September 2015

'We'll get four today . . .'

The man making the prediction is Juanma Lillo, one of Guardiola's life-long friends and mentors (along with Johan Cruyff). The two are on the phone, discussing today's Wolfsburg match and reviewing last Saturday's performance away to Darmstadt 98. They do this every week.

Today they're feeling very positive. Last weekend's match was a 0-3 routing of the home side with Rode and Coman in particular turning in dazzling performances.

'Have you noticed how much less running they're doing now?'

Pep's question is rhetorical. He already knows that his men are running less but playing more effectively. Both Guardiola and Lillo believe that the ball should come to the player, not the other way about. Run, for sure, but do it with purpose. Run a lot even, but with a lot of purpose. It's not about sprinting up and down the park to impress the spectators or about launching yourself after every ball. It's about everyone being in the right position at all times so that the ball can move quickly between players. And, yes, you'll need to do a lot of running but only to press your opponents, to make it to your position in time, to attack hard and high and to get back fast to your own half when they counter-attack . . . Of course Pep needs his men to do a lot of running ('Run like bastards!' he often cries) but always, always with a clear sense of purpose and never just for the sake of it.

Sometimes his players run 'too much'. Without any real purpose or need. Like Arturo Vidal who's worked hard on this area of his game and got the balance absolutely right in Darmstadt last week. Lillo points out how far the player's come and Pep agrees. He's delighted with the way the Chilean midfielder has adapted.

The coach wants to talk about Joshua Kimmich, the young player who bowled him over a year ago and who also excelled in the Darmstadt game (his full Bundesliga debut). Pep reckons that Germany has the two finest central midfielders in the world at the moment: Kimmich and Borussia Dortmund's Julian Weigl. (Gündogan is another superb midfielder who's also capable of covering any position in the middle of the park.) In action Kimmich bears a remarkable resemblance to the playing style of a young Guardiola, Weigl is reminiscent of Sergio Busquets and Gündogan possesses a superb ability to circulate the ball. Germany's midfield is going to be secure for a long time to come.

Now Guardiola turns to Wolfsburg, Bayern's great rival last season who beat the Munich side in the Super Cup just a few weeks ago. They come to the Allianz Arena today, undefeated in the league this season. A dangerous opponent.

'Don't worry Pep. We'll get four.'

In the event they get five. Five glorious goals which come, one after another, in almost nine minutes of pure, unadulterated ecstasy. Lewandowski's in the zone.

'It was crazy,' he explains later, 'I was banging them

in, one after the other. Totally caught up in the moment, oblivious to everything else around me.'

In just eight minutes and fifty-seven seconds Lewandowski only touches the ball nine times, hitting the post once and netting five stunning, magical goals.

This is no longer about stats or breaking a few records. This is the stuff of fantasy and the Allianz Arena erupts. No-one can believe it. Nine minutes of total rapture and Lewandowski is a new man. He's had a hard time of late, struggling with self-doubt in front of goal and a nagging fear of failure but this is his moment. He's focused, energised, a goal-scoring machine. In the zone.

The entire football world is stunned. Television pundits scream like madmen whilst the fans leap up in euphoric wonder as each goal crashes into the net. One after the other they fly past Diego Benaglio who can do nothing but look on in shock and take his beating like a man. Lewandowski's in a state of trance, repeatedly attacking the goal as if propelled by some inner force. The spell holds as Wolfsburg, compact and solid in the first half, collapse and everything Bayern's men do suddenly turns to gold. As if by magic, huge corridors of space open up for Vidal, Müller's tying the opposition up in knots and Costa seems to be speeding along twice as fast as usual. Götze is a blur of movement, sending three perfect assists into the path of the evening's hero. The young midfielder, perhaps more than anyone else, understands that tonight Bayern is making history.

Of all the astonishing spectacles football has brought us down the years this one surely eclipses anything that's gone before. In less than nine minutes a single player has achieved a feat of cosmic dimensions, confounding all expectations and stunning the world. Nobody reflects the shock and surprise of it all better than Guardiola himself. The awe everyone's feeling is written all over his face as he stands, his hands on his head and his mouth open. He's in a state of shock and obviously close to tears. Pep's usually our point of reference for what's happening on the pitch but right now he looks as bewildered as the rest of us. What the hell's just happened?

'No idea! I can't explain it. It was totally magical,' he'll tell me later.

Magic. Nine wonderful minutes for Lewandowski to find his mojo and make the impossible possible.

Today Bayern have come out to dominate as usual but Wolfsburg have not only managed to slow them down but are leading 1-0 at half-time. Their first half has been a bravura performance, the twelfth time this year that Hecking's team have scored with their first shot on target.

Bayern are struggling to find solutions when, thirty minutes in, Guardiola tells Javi Martínez and Robert Lewandowski to start warming up. At half-time he makes his changes, knowing that when things look bad, his men need tactics, not a ticking off. Bernat and Thiago are out, and Javi Martínez comes on to neutralise Bas Dost, which he does with consummate ease, beating him in the air no less than seven times and allowing Boateng as left-sided centre back to ignore the bemused Dutchman and begin to re-organise how the home side play out from the back.

Now the wingers join the fray. Each of them is playing on their preferred side: Götze on the right and Costa on the left and they set about demolishing Hecking's carefully planned defensive structure. Alaba's playing high up the pitch as left back, drawing a marker away from Douglas Costa and Müller is now behind Lewandowski. The changes plus the 4-2-4 formation they're using mean that Bayern's midfield are completely protected. The scene is set for the magic that's about to unfold.

Step forward Mario Götze. He passes to Arturo Vidal as the Chilean sprints from midfield into the box. Vidal taps the ball back to Müller and the rebound off Dante sends the ball straight to Lewandowski's feet. He scores.

Götze, who's still a question mark for Pep, is on a roll. The catalyst for Bayern's first goal, he continues to serve his striker with a series of sensational passes. His assists provide the third and fifth goals and he's moving constantly, dribbling round the opposition and snatching the ball back whenever they get possession. He's finally the Caped Crusader everyone hoped for, emerging from the shadows whilst he works to create the miracle that's unfolding. Quietly, carefully, Götze lays the dynamite, strikes the match . . . and Lewandowski explodes.

None of this surprises anyone who's watched Götze over the last few years. Despite the fact that he has never (and will never) hit his peak under Guardiola, the young midfielder is certainly amongst the most underrated of Bayern's squad. An outstanding footballer, who has wrongly been declared the 'New Messi', the young German has suffered under the crushing weight of people's wildly unrealistic expectations.

But something else has happened here tonight, and not for the first time, although it's probably slipped under most people's radar. Half-time: Bayern 0 Wolfsburg 1, full time: Bayern 5 Wolfsburg 1. If we analyse the results of this season's matches so far, we'll see something important is happening in terms of when Bayern concede and score goals. These are the stats:

First halves:     four scored          three conceded
Second halves:  sixteen scored      zero conceded

I mention this to Pep after the Wolfsburg match, telling him that stats like these can't be a fluke. 16-0 doesn't happen by accident.

'Go speak to Dome [Torrent]. He'll talk you through it.'

The assistant coach is only too willing to explain. 'It all comes down to the kind of game Pep plays. We know that people still don't entirely understand what we do but it's all planned down to the last detail. We take control, maintain possession and run our opponents into the ground. Nowadays our players have no problem adapting to mid-match switches so Pep can alter tactics when and how he sees fit. And then we wait . . . Sooner or later the opposition begin to slow down, they're pressing less and failing to close down the space. And that's when we pounce. It's as simple as that.'

# 6

# STRATEGIC PLANNING

Thinking strategically involves applying
a single question to all accepted hypotheses: why?
*Kenichi Ohmae*

HOPEFULLY EVERYTHING I'VE written so far goes a long way
to explaining Guardiola's personality, what he achieved at Bayern, the
changes he made, the football he tried to produce and this tendency
to become completely absorbed in his own learning process. However,
this is only half the picture. It's time for a forensic examination of his
work, looking at it from a wider perspective: his 'strategic plan'.

At the start of a new project Pep prepares a strategic plan. This will
be his guide as he works to provide his team with the knowledge and
tools they need to develop the kind of football he wants. The plan takes
into account the competitive context around him plus the specific skills
and profiles of the men in his squad. This is what he did at Bayern and,
having used this approach successfully for his seven years at the top,
he'll do it again at Manchester City. The plan deals with the following
elements:

- The playing model
- The basics of his game
- Training methodology
- Match planning
- Tactics
- Perfecting the technical/tactical balance
- Analysing opponents and the competitive context

It also includes several non-football related elements. These deal with
all aspects of man management:

- Nutrition
- Injury prevention
- Rehabilitation
- Recuperation
- Psychological preparation
- The culture of the team

Clearly, any strategic plan must be more comprehensive than the playing model or the specific systems and tactics used for each match. It's the framework for Guardiola's work over three years during which time he'll develop his ideas and help his players achieve their potential.

The concepts behind his tactical decisions change continuously in response to all the different elements of competition: who his opponents are; what's happening in his own squad; squad morale (individual and group); his team's physical fitness; their tactical ability; the endless demands of the football calendar. His ideas are living things, going through constant transformation as the years pass and his strategic plan unfolds.

If we think of the strategic plan as the frame which holds the canvas in place, then his tactics are the brush strokes and artistic flourishes with which he'll create his art.

Although the terms are often used indistinguishably tactics emerge once the strategy is in place. Strategy's about 'what' and 'why'. Tactics tell you 'how' and 'when'. Strategy tells us where we're going; tactics, how we're going to get there.

WHAT ARE TACTICS, PEP?
Barcelona, 27 June 2016

'Tactics are about ensuring that every player knows exactly what he should be doing at all times and in every position he occupies during a match.'

'Do you have to adapt your tactics to whoever you're playing?'

'Of course we do. We're not playing in a vacuum. We're playing against opponents who have their own skills and talents and we have to know them inside out. We have to scan them thoroughly, get to know their strengths and weaknesses, and then adapt to them. It's our responsibility to know exactly who we're up against and change our tactics accordingly. And each of our players must know their rival too and understand exactly what to do in every situation.'

'So what happens if your opponents don't play their usual game or suddenly switch the game plan mid-match?'

'We'll have worked out in advance how to deal with that. And when I say "we" I mean we, as a team. Every single man needs to know exactly how to react if the team has to respond to a change in our opponents' tactics. It doesn't matter if it happens at the start and they come out to defend with five men, instead of their usual four or if it's a mid-match tactical shift. We have to go through any and all possibilities at training so the players understand them and can cope with them instantaneously if they occur.'

'So this kind of knowledge and preparation is more important than the model you're using or your starting formation?'

'Definitely. Tactical prowess isn't about producing lots of numbers, it's about knowing what to do at all times.'

Guardiola's always been more of a tactician than a strategist. His forte is preparing for battle and he excels at drawing up exactly the right tactical plan for each game. When he arrived in Germany his strategic thinking was less fully developed and during his time there, he worked hard to develop this aspect of the job. He's now a considerably more able strategist and takes this stage of planning more seriously. Unfortunately the downside of this is the personal frustration and disappointment he can feel despite repeated victory. The team may be winning but if they're not on the right path, it can feel even worse than defeat. Short term results must always be measured in the context of the long term objectives.

Press and fans alike can be left shocked and confused by an apparently sulking Pep after his team has just pulled off a fantastic win but this is just his way of protecting himself and he's often more reticent in victory than in defeat. The growth and development of a football team is not just a product of the number of triumphs they rack up, it's driven by their ability to learn. From both victory and defeat.

A result may provoke joy or misery but these are emotional reactions, not rational judgements. Marcelo Bielsa has called success 'the imposter' and Garry Kaspárov too has often warned of its danger: 'I call it the threat of success. When you win you create the illusion that everything's fine and there's an enormous temptation to focus solely on the positive result rather than all the things that went wrong (or could have gone wrong). We all want to celebrate a victory, not analyse it. We go over and over that moment of triumph until we start thinking it was inevitable . . . Complacency is a dangerous foe and can lead to you dropping your guard, missing opportunities and making mistakes. It's a kind of paradox. Success and satisfaction are our ultimate objectives but in the short term they can create negative patterns of behaviour that destroy our chance of great success and deep satisfaction.'

Forearmed by this advice from people he likes and trusts, Guardiola continues to place victory over any other objective but, once he's secured that victory, he is very, very careful about how he manages its effects.

Let's look at specific aspects of his strategy. In *Pep Confidential* I provided details of his work at Bayern Munich: training methods; the rondos and games of position; the physical fitness preparation; his focus on nutrition and the psychological well-being of his players; plus the importance he placed on the analysis of opponents. This time, let's put the tactics he's used under the microscope, focusing on three specific aspects of his strategy:

- The playing model
- The game plans
- The culture of the team

## THE PLAYING MODEL

*A playing model is only as strong as its weakest link.*
*Fran Cervera*

The playing model is developed by the coach for his team and reflects his ideology and beliefs. It's as if he hands each of his men a toolbox containing everything they need to do the job. And they must be the right tools. You wouldn't give a plumber a surgeon's scalpel, or a joiner a policeman's truncheon. A good coach selects the tools that match the characteristics and abilities of his players, whether these are already well developed or yet to be discovered. The better his judgement in this, the greater harmony, cohesion and football efficiency there will be.

There's no doubt Guardiola established a distinctive football model at Bayern – based around positional play.

But what happened on the pitch was dependent on which players he chose to put into midfield. The brand of football he got with Lahm, Kroos and Thiago in the middle was distinct from what Alonso, Vidal and Müller produced.

The individual characteristics of the players you use has a decisive impact on the team's football and, as such, can offer a distorted impression of the model the coach prefers.

Let's look again at the main pillars of Guardiola's playing philosophy:

- Possession: possession is a tool, nothing more. It's not a playing model nor is it the philosophy behind it.
- Numerical superiority in defence plus positional or numerical superiority in the centre of the pitch.
- Playing as wide and as high as possible using passing sequences to pull opponents around, confuse them and leave attacking players more likely to be left with a one v one situation.
- Structured positioning of your players so that they can bring the ball out and advance as a compact unit.
- Seeking the 'third man' at each stage of the build-up play plus using the 'free men' between the lines of your opponent's pressing. (Third man = creating a free man via passing triangles.)
- Using high possession as part of the defensive strategy (Pep: 'The best way to cool a highly charged atmosphere is to keep hold of the ball') and intelligent pressing if the ball is lost.
- Varying the players' positions and prioritising passing the ball to the right man at the right time. Players must NEVER drop out of position to come looking for the ball – the ball must be delivered to them, quickly and accurately.
- Technical excellence: good body position in receiving the ball and short, accurate passes which improve the receiver's position.
- Playing with 'intensity' (total concentration) for the duration of each game.
- Dominating the game high up the pitch (symbolised by the daringly high back line) and the team's attacking mentality.

Having understood the complexity of this playing model, it's surely impossible for anyone to perpetuate the fallacy of 'Pep Guardiola – master of tiquitaca'. Anyone who insists on sticking rigidly to this perception of the man has clearly understood nothing of his eight years as a coach.

It also goes without saying that the application of this model will change depending on the team in question. The 'positional play' of Busquets, Xavi and Iniesta looked very different from the game Pep produced at Bayern. Pep's Barcelona used slow, short passes to advance up the pitch in horizontal attack followed by an explosive finale, usually provided by Messi, in the final third. At Bayern, the players' characteristics inevitably meant that their game was faster and more vertical. The emphasis was on diagonal passes to the wingers who played a more pivotal role than their Barça counterparts. There was also more collective responsibility for taking chances in the penalty box.

At City, it's likely to be Fernandinho, Gündogan and Silva in the middle of the pitch and we'll therefore see new patterns of play emerge there too.

Has Guardiola changed his playing model? Well, if we consider the way he's continually adapted his game to new ideas and to the characteristics of his available players, adding important nuances and tweaking it here and there, it's safe to say that 'Yes, he's definitely changed his playing model.' And he's done so, not just as part of the transition from one club to the next but during every single season and even from game to game. Each match isn't simply about competition and survival. It's a small part of the 'grand plan' to execute his methodology. He's not discarded a single essential of his fundamental beliefs, only enriched them by learning to apply his playing model to defeat his rivals.

Positional football possesses two stand-out qualities. It's a structured, well defined model used best by a dynamic footballer who understands the use of space. Through training, technical staff provide each player with a GPS to help him traverse the detailed landscape of the game and move into the right space at the right time. Although this may appear contradictory, given my earlier comments, I'd say that positional play is also an open, 'evolving' system, ideally suited to the complexities of football. An astute coach can improve and advance the model, modifying any weaknesses that emerge and adapting it to match precisely the needs and abilities of his squad.

We can compare this playing model to the sheet music of an orchestral piece. Guardiola has his score but each orchestra he conducts will add their own specific nuances to the music. Every so often the conductor will introduce new notes depending on how the orchestra sounds, how the musicians feel and what the acoustics are like. It's a 'living' score continually evolving during its three-year life. The music sounds pretty similar but if you compare the original version to the final symphony you'll pick up notable differences in rhythm, harmony and interpretation.

## A TEAM IS LIKE AN ORCHESTRA
### Barcelona, 1 July 2015

A football team is like a symphony orchestra.

Paco Seirul.lo agrees but adds an interesting qualification, 'You can say a team is like an orchestra if your vision of football is linear. The defence destroys, the midfield constructs, the attackers tuck the ball away while the coach conducts with his baton. So we say a team's an orchestra. But what's the sheet music? It's the history of football. If this metaphor were really close to the reality of football it would imply that the trombonist could instantly change instrument and play the violin. As could each of the instrumentalists. Now of course we know that doesn't happen in an orchestra but it does in football.'

The high priest of this type of football philosophy, Juanma Lillo adds, 'There's another important thing here: in football you always have an opponent. I don't know if a team is an orchestra or not but if it were it would need to have a rival orchestra right in front of it playing their music at exactly the same time . . .'

In the end, a playing model is both fixed and completely fluid. It's a composition modified every day by a coach as he assesses his opponents, experiments with new ideas and continues the process of his own and his team's evolution.

# GAME PLANS

The battle begins in a conventional fashion
But only surprise tactics ensure ultimate victory,
Surprise and convention are cyclical
*Sun Tzu*

The unique nature of German football forced Guardiola to develop a completely different range of game plans. This was a new, unfamiliar league and the strategies he'd used at Barcelona weren't going to fit the bill. At Barça he had practised a distinct kind of football: on-pitch dominance with one principal formation (4-3-3 which could change to a 3-4-3) against opponents whose strategies tended to be about defending en masse either around the midfield or deeper.

His Bundesliga rivals, however, used a variety of tactics to counteract Bayern's attacking style and Guardiola began to innovate. As his opponents continued to evolve their own playing strategies, so Bayern's tactical plans had to change and Pep found that producing his game plans became a more time-consuming and challenging part of his job than ever before.

But what exactly do we mean by the term 'game plan'? It is, in essence, the strategic scenario for planning a particular match including: the system or playing model; the starters and substitutes; the tactics to be employed depending on the characteristics of our opponent (which positions to cover, particular movements which divisions of the team may need to make, special instructions concerning man marking); defensive and offensive set play strategies; and the match tempo we want.

The process requires the coach not only to plan his tactics down to the last detail before the match but to read the game as it happens and adapt as necessary.

As such, the game plan is more comprehensive than, say, the playing formation. Back in Germany, whenever Guardiola was asked about the number of formations he'd employed in a single match, he'd respond, 'It's not the systems that matter. It's the ideas behind them.' In this instance, when Pep referred to 'ideas' he was really talking about his game plan.

Any game plan is like a military strategy in the sense that it involves evaluating your best chances of victory in a 'battle' between two opposing forces.

These are the four stages of planning used by Guardiola:

- The strategic plan: the global framework covering the duration of Guardiola's tenure (usually three years)
- The playing model: the tool box the coach provides for his players
- The game plan: the tactical decisions as well as the dynamics of his team's play
- The playing system (or model): the spatial-distribution of the players at any given moment in the match

Guardiola's game plans evolved greatly during his time at Bayern. In his first season there, his plans were more or less linear with relatively few variables. They tended to focus on Bayern imposing their own game whilst wearing opponents down with constant passing. Patience and a total belief in their own playing style were an essential part of Bayern's game and both were in evidence during the Manchester City match in October 2013 (1-3) when the Etihad Stadium bore witness to a performance of positional play *par excellence* with Bayern at one stage producing an astonishing ninety-four consecutive passes in just three and a half minutes (essentially a giant rondo).

The antithesis of this was played out against Real Madrid in Munich (0-4) when patience, passing and unified progression were forgotten and Pep's men, exposed and unprotected, launched a suicidal attack that eventually ended in humiliating defeat.

During his second season Pep expanded his arsenal of tactical weapons. By this time, his players could confidently and ably apply a wide range of tactics, were adept at switching between systems and had a much greater understanding of the need to combine different rhythms. This allowed Guardiola to introduce greater complexity. Take for example the plan he used in October 2014 against Roma in the Stadio Olimpico (1-7) where the home side were thwarted by a sophisticated and ruthless Bayern. Pep made a number of unexpected tactical decisions that day: a three-man defence; Xabi Alonso positioned so that he ended up more or less unmarked ('Xabi, don't worry. Totti will only manage to stay on top of you for the first ten minutes'); immense superiority of numbers in attack down the left (including central defender Alaba) 'overloading' which gave Bayern unstoppable power on that touchline; the use of full backs as traditional wingers ; Robben reserved almost exclusively for one v one situations . . . Thirty minutes in and Roma were already trailing 0-5 with things about to get even worse. After the game Thomas Müller explained the key to Bayern's triumph: 'Guardiola basically told us exactly what Roma's weaknesses were and how to exploit them.'

Things took a different turn for Bayern during another match in Pep's second season. This time they were facing Barça at the Camp Nou. Bayern (decimated by injuries) had again fielded a three-man defence with Rafinha as a left-sided centre back. Pre-match, it felt like the right way to go because the same approach had worked brilliantly a few days previously against Borussia Dortmund. 'I wanted an extra man in the middle of the field so that we could dominate. Risking the loss of a defender would be compensated by greater control in the centre. But Messi and Suárez knew what we were up to and began to outmanoeuvre us so I was forced to switch back to a four-man defence.'

In the end, Bayern lost the match, not because of Pep's tactical decisions, but as a result of Messi's clinical finishing and the visitors' loss of tactical discipline in the dying minutes.

In his third year, Guardiola's plans became still more sophisticated as he employed an impressive array of new moves and tactics. At the start of the season, with his men yet to hit peak form, Guardiola asked them to use their passing play in the first half to tire their opponents so that, having weakened them sufficiently, they could then finish them off in the second half. The stats reflect this. In the first ten games of the season (nine wins and a draw) Bayern scored thirty goals (twenty-three in the second half) and conceded five (only one in the second half).

Later in the season, when Guardiola felt that his team was at last firing on all cylinders, he decided to make some drastic changes. Juanma Lillo had often suggested experimenting with an hourglass shape and Pep began to seriously consider it. He'd gone as far as he could with many of his ideas. It was time for something new.

As Kaspárov says, 'We must never stop questioning the status quo, especially when things are going well.'

Life works in cycles (learning and discovery, growth and development and, finally, decline) and if we try to avoid change and growth, we'll almost inevitably hasten our own decline. The only antidote to this is to embrace change and alter the way we do things, before it's too late.

There was also a compelling practical reason for Pep to modify his plans. Increasingly, Bayern's opponents were fielding five or even six defenders as well as a second line of four midfielders who also took on a defensive role. His team now tended to be facing a solid wall of defenders every weekend and Pep responded by switching to four, and then, five Bayern strikers, initially using the WM (Herbert Chapman's 3-2-2-3) and later the pyramid formation (2-3-5) initiated by Cambridge University in 1880. Both choices were inspired by Lillo's 'hourglass' suggestion.

He unveils his new tactics on 24 October 2015 against FC Köln and Bayern erupt into the match with a massive show of strength and power aimed at eviscerating their rival in as short a time as possible. This is very different from Bayern's usual game given that it involves an all-out devastating attack on their opponents in order to establish a significant early lead. It's then possible to re-organise and revert to a more traditional approach with the midfielders slowing down the game as the whole team moves calmly into 'possession mode'. The plan works so well that Pep uses it again in other Bundesliga games as well as against Arsenal (5-1) in the Champions League. It also comes in handy as an emergency measure for the fightback against Juventus after the Italians go ahead in the Champions League quarter-final (4-2).

## OPERATION BLITZKRIEG
### Wolfsburg, 27 February 2016

Today the plan's simple. It's an all-out *Blitzkrieg* using five strikers. Pep's piling on his forwards so they can do maximum damage in the shortest possible time. They won't all be staying on for the whole ninety minutes and it's basically a 'shock and awe' operation to ensure Bayern an early and significant lead. He's re-using the 2-3-5 formation and tells his forwards to 'fire at will' until they have subdued the enemy. Douglas Costa lines up on the inside and Coman on the wing. Not everything has changed however and Pep maintains his three phases of play (starting – constructive build-up – finish) but today the rhythm is very different: faster, more direct and much more aggressive. They want goals. And lots of them.

According to the plan, once Bayern take an early lead, they'll move to Phase Two: one less striker and an extra man in midfield so that Bayern can begin to construct their usual intricate passing game and, hopefully, confuse and exhaust their embattled opponents. In the event that their full-on assault fails to achieve the desired results, the coach will still move to Phase Two. Lightning strikes, by definition, don't last long and at any rate, Pep knows that his strategy increases the risk of lethal counter-attacks. So the more conventional Phase Two is an essential part of the game plan.

Things don't go entirely to plan today in the Volkswagen Arena, where in the first thirty minutes the mighty Bayern miss six clear chances on goal. In contrast, Wolfsburg are managing to repel the attack and they make frequent assaults on Neuer's goal. Time to move to Phase Two. Thiago comes on for Costa and suddenly it's 'business as usual'. Bayern assume possession of the ball and, although Max Kruse manages a couple of excellent shots on goal for Wolfsburg, the Bavarians seal the deal with goals from Coman and Lewandowski. It's Bayern Munich's 116th anniversary and the team has just secured its twentieth league victory in twenty-three games.

Pep's happy with their performance. This is one more step towards the league title, his third in a row. He's about to take his place amongst the legends of German football, Udo Lattek and Ottmar Hitzfeld. It will also be Bayern's fourth consecutive league win, another 'first' in Bundesliga history. Just eleven games stand between him and the prize. He's delighted that his players were able to switch mid-match from full-frontal attack to a more conservative system without losing their aggression and strike power. Operation Blitzkrieg has gone well today and he'll use it again soon, against Juventus.

Perhaps the greatest testament to the sheer variety of Pep's game plans is his last match with Bayern: the Cup Final in Berlin on 21 May 2016 against Borussia Dortmund.* Pep prepares three alternative plans for this match. 'Dortmund will use any of three different systems and we've no way of knowing which one it's going to be. Nor do we know when or what they'll change mid-match,' Carles Planchart tells me.

In recent months Thomas Tuchel's Borussia Dortmund have alternated between a 5-3-2, a 5-2-2-1 and a 4-2-3-1. Guardiola reckons that his own team will need at least three systems too and his men prepare all week until they know exactly what to do in every eventuality. The final becomes the stage for the Bayern players to prove beyond any doubt just how far they've developed. They put Dortmund off their game by pressing high up the pitch and closing down their passing lines, Pep bases his defence (Kimmich and Boateng) near the centre of the pitch and they pressurise Hummels and co into launching random long balls into space. Tuchel's men are on the run and the team begins to resemble the Dortmund of his predecessor, managing a paltry 30% possession (their average this season has been 61%).

It's thirty minutes before kick-off and Pep and his men are gathered in front of the whiteboard in their dressing room. The coach talks them through the three alternative game plans that they've practised all week. Every time Dortmund switch from one system to another, Pep's men must immediately change their defensive organisation. The plan is to keep on top of their opponents until they're worn down. Bayern's captain, Lahm, will be taking the decisions without reference to Guardiola on the side-line.

And here's how it looks in action. Dortmund starts the game with a 5-3-2 and Bayern field a three-man defence plus Lahm in the centre of the field. Dortmund then change to a 4-2-3-1 and Lahm moves back to the right back position, triggering a ripple effect through the rest of the team as players automatically move into their new positions. Some time later Dortmund change shape again, moving to a 5-2-2-1 (a 3-4-2-1 with the ball). Lahm and Alaba are on it. They move closer to Vidal in the midfield and Bayern switch to a two-man defence.

Lahm has been the key tonight. He's followed his instructions to the letter, leading his team through each stage of Pep's plan. It's worked to perfection because they've all understood and committed. It's taken a week of solid work but tonight's result makes it all worthwhile.

*\* Please see chapter three for a detailed description of how Bayern prepared tactically for this game.*

# TEAM CULTURE

No achievement is mine alone;
all of us have done the work.
*Maori Proverb*

All great teams start with an idea. An idea that inspires and moves key people to dedicate their energies to building their dream. Great teams are also born of failure. Crushing, sickening failure from which seeds future greatness. If the idea is the foundation and failure the cement, then team culture is the edifice that arises from them.

Team culture is the strategic framework within which the emotional life of and the relationships within the group are managed. As a rule, football teams don't set about planning their 'culture' in any strategic, systematic way. It tends to develop spontaneously. One good example of what happens if you do decide to 'create' a specific culture is the All Blacks rugby team who did exactly that after a particularly catastrophic defeat (they were beaten in the quarter-finals of the 2007 World Cup).

So, is team culture all about showing motivational videos or coming up with slogans? Does it include rituals and rules and language? It is, in fact, all this and more. It's the conduct and behaviour of everyone involved, it's working together towards shared objectives and, as such, is an immediately identifiable part of the group's identity. All Black coach Wayne Smith spoke to James Kerr for his book, *Legacy*: 'We must do things correctly and not leave them to other people. Nobody should be doing our jobs for us. The All Blacks should be looking after themselves . . . We must never consider ourselves too important to do the little jobs, whether it's mopping out the shower or sweeping the floor.'

Guardiola didn't fully develop a clear, identifiable group culture at Bayern, probably because he felt that his time was best spent on the already complex and high-risk task of transforming their playing model. He did, nonetheless, sow the seeds for the future. During his third year at Bayern he banned visitors (including friends, relations and club directors) from the dressing room. Only the players and board members were allowed access. For the coach, professional behaviour was a matter of trust. 'At work we basically have four rules. Outside Säbener Strasse do what you want. You're all adults.' He expected his players to respect the rules as well as adhering to established disciplines (good nutrition, enough rest, adequate rehabilitation).

He often showed the team footage of random moments in which he felt they showed the right kind of team spirit: an injured David Alaba cheering the team on from the stands; Alonso racing up the pitch for a counter-attack immediately after defending a corner; Thomas Müller saluting to thank Robben for an assist. Domènec Torrent and Carles Planchart would capture these moments whenever possible so that they could be used by Pep as examples of the sportsmanship and unity he wanted to see.

When the players arrived at the training ground in July 2015, there was a surprise waiting: the number four (this year they'd be competing for their fourth consecutive league title) had been painted in red on every wall in the building. Some walls had a single gigantic number four, others also bore the legend 'Jeder Für's Team' (Every man for the team) but the majority declared 'Champions 4 ever'. The offices used by Pep and his technical team had all the titles Bayern had won so far inscribed in black whilst this season's objective was emblazoned in large red figures. Just in case it slipped anybody's mind . . .

I was often pleasantly surprised by how spick and span the team's dressing room always was after a match. Once the players had gone, if you looked really carefully you might find a tiny bit of grass or some torn tape on the floor. There might even be the odd empty glass on a table. Otherwise, however, the place would be sparkling. The players always cleaned up after themselves and ensured that the dressing room was left spotless. ('We must never consider ourselves too important to do the little jobs.')

One important part of team culture at Bayern was the need to balance the mental and physical demands of training with the freedom Guardiola allowed in terms of rules and behaviour. Let's look at a specific example.

One of the things I shared in *Pep Confidential* was Pep's policy NOT to go into the dressing room before a match to give a last minute team talk. He believes that three tactical talks is sufficient (one the day before and two on match day itself) and none of them take place in the dressing room, nor are any of them the rousing call to arms that you and I might imagine. There may be some subtle motivational content in the third talk, which he does in the hotel a couple of hours before the game, but its main purpose it to announce the line-up and run through the game plan one last time. Making sure that his men understand the plan is the coach's priority and he'll spend as much time as necessary until he's sure they've got it. For his first match in charge at Manchester City (a friendly away to Bayern Munich) Pep gave his new players so much tactical information that they arrived at the stadium just forty-five minutes before kick-off.

At Barcelona the pre-match talk was occasionally a rallying cry and before playing the Champions League Final against Manchester United in Rome in 2009, Pep showed his squad a motivational video which had been meticulously prepared by his assistants. The film, set to a soundtrack from the movie *Gladiator* was intensely moving and Pep's players were visibly affected. His troops sprinted out on to the pitch, raring to go, but then produced a disastrous first few minutes. After the game Pep conceded that stirring up his team in this way was not, after all, conducive to good football. As basketball legend Phil Jackson said: 'I knew that whenever I was too worked up mentally, it had a negative effect on my ability to stay focused under pressure. So I went in the opposite direction and instead of rousing speeches I developed strategies to calm their minds and keep them in the moment.'

When he arrived at Bayern Guardiola requested that the club convert a small storage room outside the dressing room into his office. He was determined to stay out of the dressing room before games and believes that the coach should never 'disturb' his men as they mentally prepare for the game ahead. He's already given them his instructions at training and during the team talks and considers them perfectly capable of managing their own mental and emotional states without his assistance.

He was also happy to allow the players to add their own exercises to the warm-up routines. Boateng, for example, always headed back early to the dressing room where he ran through a range of lumbar/pelvic stretching exercises. Neuer too had his pre-match routine and restricted himself to practising between six and eight catches during the warm-up session. In Pep's third season at Bayern, Müller and Lewandowski asked Lahm to help them practise heading at goal and they would do this a dozen times. Lorenzo Buenaventura supervised these warm-ups, under strict orders from Pep to allow the players freedom to make these kinds of decisions. Warm-up complete, the players would then trot back into the dressing room to prepare themselves mentally for the upcoming clash.

## SKY BLUE SPIRIT

*The key to continued success is constant growth.*
*Winning means embracing the unknown*
*and creating something new.*
*Phil Jackson*

At City he decided to use the word 'spirit' rather than culture because Pep felt it was more easily comprehensible to everyone . . . and less pompous too. Guardiola was presented to the Manchester City fans on 3 July 2016 and he immediately told them, 'what we want is to build strong team spirit as soon as possible'. Prioritising that in public, ahead of the actual playing model, was significant as far as his intentions for City were concerned. First? Team spirit. Second? Play well.

'The key thing,' he continued, 'is to make people proud of the football we play.' He then promised, in third place, to 'try to win our first game. And our second. And every one after that . . .'

Gaël Clichy spoke for those players who'd grasped the message: 'Pep wants us to be proud of the jersey we're wearing. He also wants us to earn the right to wear it.'

Already it's clear that Pep sees team 'culture' or 'spirit' as the foundation for everything he plans to do at City. If his strategy works and he manages to develop a strong team spirit, then it will be easier to impose his playing model, which in turn will ensure better football and therefore, greater success. The task ahead of him is a formidable one for he must create a distinct, unique identity composed of all the factors I've previously mentioned: professional conduct on and off the pitch, mentality, the type of player who forms the team, language/communication, rituals, rules, attitudes. It's through these that the team's 'identity' will be formed.

Clearly, this won't be straightforward. There will be mistakes, stumbling blocks and inconsistencies, all of which will have to be tackled as they arise. And that process is already underway. When two players turned up for the pre-season noticeably overweight, the coach immediately ordered them to follow a separate training programme and informed them that they would not join the rest of the squad until they had achieved minimum fitness levels. Pep's message was clear: nobody's above the rules and everyone has to earn their place. He also defines training as a prize to be earned on merit, not simply because of a contract with the club.

Building the kind of team spirit he wants will be long and complicated. It will require time, patience and the full allegiance of his players who must be prepared to commit to the plans he lays down for them.

## HIS ALLIES, THE PLAYERS

A team is like a good watch.
If you lose one of its parts, it still looks good.
It just doesn't work as well.
*Ruud Gullit*

Guardiola has always tried to maintain a certain distance from his players. It's an attempt at self-protection. 'I try not to get too close to them because I don't want them to think that the relationship influences whether or not they play. I'm the one who has to make that decision and I don't want emotions getting in the way.'

In Munich however, the barriers came down and, by the end of his time there, Pep had developed a strong bond of mutual trust and open affection with his men. From his first day at the club he was impressed by the players' determination to work hard and learn from him as well as their willingness to adapt to the changes he proposed. The strong foundation he laid down in that first year paid off in his second season when, instead of destroying morale, an epidemic of injuries resulted in an even stronger sense of unity. It was already clear that an unbreakable bond had formed between the coach and his men.

## LADS, WE'RE FUCKED
### Dortmund, 4 April 2015

The technical team is no longer struggling with doubts over exactly which strikers and which midfielders should be in the line-up for the big games. This was the problem they were facing in March. Now the choices are so much easier. Whoever's fit will play.

It's not going to be the same without Robben and Ribéry. The stats speak for themselves. Up till now Bayern have won 85% of their games if the two strikers have played but only 60% if not. They're about to play Borussia Dortmund and things don't look good. Pep gets straight to the point. 'Basically lads, we're fucked. This is our big moment and we're in deep shit. But if we pull together we can do it. Everyone who's still fit and able to play just has to move up a gear. We need to up our game lads, you and I both.'

After a hard fought victory against Klopp's Dortmund in April 2015, the league title was almost in the bag and Pep was beaming with pride. 'Whatever happens these players are my heroes and always will be. Things have been really tough and they've handled it brilliantly.'

By his third season at Bayern Pep was in no doubt about his team's high regard for him and the feeling was entirely mutual. Everyone could see the huge change that had taken place in the previously reserved Catalan and, in the face of repeated attacks from the media, his players demonstrated their affection and loyalty by forming a solid protective wall around him. They would go to any lengths to defend their coach.

Immediately after the Real Madrid defeat, Bayern's lowest point in three years, captain Philipp Lahm spoke on behalf of the team. 'We're all behind you Pep. All the way.' Lahm and goalkeeper Manuel Neuer had been a huge source of support to Pep from the outset and both men had played a fundamental role in helping Pep adapt to his players. They couldn't change him completely and Pep remains the same demanding perfectionist he ever was but, with their guidance and support, the coach was able to open up to his players. He took time to get to know his men, taking particular care with the least confident members of the squad and, as the relationship grew, lost much of his natural reserve and became increasingly close to them all.

Guardiola earned his players' trust and affection not just because of his brilliant tactical planning and in-depth knowledge, nor because he helped them play better, more effective football. No, they loved him for his loyalty. At times Pep would make preposterous claims to the press, such as 'I'd love to have a thousand Dantes in my team.' His intention was to give the Brazilian a boost at a particularly difficult time and his players were impressed. They appreciated their manager's willingness to risk criticism and ridicule to defend one of his men. But more than that, they understood that this was a man who would always support them, through thick and thin. And that mattered. A lot.

'Love' seems too strong a word to use to describe a professional relationship but it's how Guardiola and his players have described their mutual bond and I personally witnessed Pep yelling 'I love you

Philipp. I love you!' on numerous occasions, as he hugged the captain or planted a couple of kisses on his cheeks.

So we should assume then that everything was rosy from the start? Not exactly. Croatian Mario Mandzukic packed his bags soon after Guardiola's arrival after waging war with his manager over football-related, as opposed to personal, disagreements. Guardiola also battled Müller's anarchic ways for two long years until they eventually agreed to meet halfway and, happily, by the end of his third year at Bayern the two men were on excellent terms. Thiago, Pep's surrogate 'son', probably came under the most sustained pressure of any of the Bayern players and had to put up with constant criticism from his coach. Guardiola also invested enormous time and energy (more than any other Bayern player) in Götze, trying, unsuccessfully, to draw out the explosive ability that lay beneath the surface.

Guardiola also failed to nurture the talents of teenager Pierre-Emile Højbjerg and, despite the coach's almost fatherly interest and concern for the player, the young Dane never settled and eventually left the club. Sadly Bastian Schweinsteiger was one of the big name Bayern players who found himself repeatedly falling short of Pep's expectations and eventually he too had to accept defeat and move on.

## XABI AND BASTIAN DON'T PLAY WELL TOGETHER
### Stuttgart, 13 September 2014

Pep uses every trick in the book in Stuttgart, where they win by 0-2. He has had to be inventive with his tactical changes because the team aren't playing fluidly today. During the ninety minutes he changes the formation several times: from 3-4-3; to 4-3-3; and then 3-2-3-2, using Alonso and Schweinsteiger as the 'double pivot'. It feels like he's tried everything but for some reason it's not working.

There's something worrying him. Why do the team play better with one midfielder and five strikers? Or, to put it another way, it has become pretty obvious that Alonso and Schweinsteiger don't play well together.

Football is, amongst other things, the product of the chemistry between players. I'm not talking here about friendship and affection but something much deeper: professional empathy. The synergy between two players can have startling results just as any failure to gel can spell disaster. It's all about chemistry, although of course other factors (the opposition, the unity and synergy of the whole team, how well they follow instructions etc) have an impact. But it's chemistry that can make or break a playing partnership.

For years the Barcelona press had claimed that Xavi and Iniesta couldn't play together until Guardiola partnered them to amazing effect. But sometimes players just don't click. Alonso has produced fantastic performance alongside guys like Busquets and Khedira, two very different players, but, for some reason, it isn't working with Schweinsteiger. For his part, the German has had brilliant partnerships with Javi Martínez and Toni Kroos and in theory he should be a perfect match for Alonso but on the pitch they're a disaster. Both try their best to make it work but the chemistry's not right and over the next few weeks it becomes more and more obvious. Off the pitch, they're great mates who understand the game in a similar way and there's plenty of mutual empathy. Off the pitch. But play them together and they seem to cancel each other out. It's not good news for Bayern or Bastian.

Pep himself has a strong personality and having to manage twenty-five professional footballers, each of them with his own ego and distinct character traits was a constant challenge. Of course there was the occasional disagreement but overall, the relationship was extremely good and the bond of loyalty and trust between players and coach, unbreakable.

'The atmosphere in this team is fucking brilliant,' said Pep in February 2016 just after being hit with a barrage of criticism from the German press. 'We've got no moaners, no loners and we've all got exactly the same priorities. I've been so lucky with these lads. They're superb people, amazing players and it's been a joy to work with them.'

The coach's emotions finally betrayed him just after winning the Cup Final in Berlin's Olympic Stadium in May 2014. He broke down in tears and, fittingly, almost symbolically, his players rushed to comfort him. As he sobbed in their arms, Lahm pointed to the trophy, 'Pep, you take the Cup.'

'No, no Philipp. It's yours. Yours and the team's.'

'It belongs to all of us Pep. You take it.'

Lahm had always been Pep's main support at the club. He helped him implant his ideas and adapt them whenever necessary, encouraged him to rethink his decisions at difficult times and provided reassurance and comfort. At all times he showed integrity, self-control and solidarity as well as profound loyalty and intelligence. In December 2015 Lahm sought Guardiola out in his office and, on behalf of the whole squad, asked him to renew his contract. Guardiola had won his players' hearts and minds. They wanted him to stay.

If Lahm embodied integrity and restraint, Thomas Müller was the player who brought anarchy and humour to the dressing room and together the two men created the perfect balance between discipline and fun that made the Bayern dressing room so special.

## CALM AND COMMOTION
### Ingolstadt, 7 May 2016

It's an hour and a half before kick-off and a win will mean their fourth consecutive league trophy. It's just four days since they were beaten by Atlético de Madrid in the Champions League semi-final and the team's still feeling the effects. They had given pretty much the best performance of the Guardiola era and it hadn't worked. There's nothing to reproach themselves for although Oblak saving Müller's penalty was probably a turning point.

We're in the 'Classic Oldtimer Hotel', famous for its collection of classic cars and motorbikes, amongst them quite a few Ferraris. The team talk's about to start but the room's still in total darkness. I can just about make out the computer generated image of a large red four on the whiteboard. They're about to do battle for their fourth consecutive Bundesliga title and only ninety minutes lie between them and glory. None of the team have arrived yet and there are just a couple of assistants at the back, talking on their phones.

Pep's down at the front, going over and over the message he wants to convey today. It'll be short and sweet. This is not a day for grand speeches but the Champions League disaster still hurts and if his men can get a win tonight, it would be fantastic. He has to find a way to get them motivated again. He considers different ideas whilst the lights flicker behind the number four on the whiteboard. Then Lahm enters the room. Silently, he slips into the seat beside the coach,

'Hi Pep.'

'Hi, Pipo.'

They lapse into silence. For two minutes, captain and coach gaze at the screen without saying a word. The silence fills the darkened room. They look as if they're hypnotised by the number four in front of them and both are probably thinking about everything they've gone through to get here. The scene sums up the relationship between them. They don't need words to communicate.

Suddenly the peace is shattered. Thomas Müller charges

into the room, shouting at the top of his voice and cracking jokes. He throws himself down on the other side of Pep and within minutes the three men are doubled up with laughter. This is Pep's Bayern – a perfect blend of Lahm's quiet intelligence and Müller's exuberant, irrepressible noise.

Guardiola found himself the object of an outpouring of affection during his final days at Säbener Strasse and at the many farewell dinners organised in his honour. His players were clearly going to miss him and time and again I heard him say, 'This is the best thing about being a coach. Winning the affection and respect of your players.'

At the end of July 2016 Pep returned to Munich in his new guise as City coach and was overwhelmed by the warmth of his welcome. Every last player was there to greet him and for Pep, it was one of the best moments of his whole career. Douglas Costa told me what the coach had meant to him. 'Under Pep I learned what playing good football really means. With him I improved my game every single day and only the best coach in the world could have achieved what Pep did here.' Xabi Alonso, Javi Martínez, Lahm, Neuer, Robben, Kimmich, Ribéry, Boateng, Alaba, Rafinha, Badstuber . . . all of them said similar things that night. But these guys were all team regulars and I wondered what other, less high profile players would have to say.

Claudio Pizarro started just nine games in two seasons, managing a total of 1,233 minutes' playing time. These are his thoughts on Pep: 'Pep has this special vision of football he learned from Cruyff but none of us had any idea what he was talking about when he first arrived. Tactically, he's way ahead of anyone else. By at least five years.'

Daniel Van Buyten appeared in the starting line-up sixteen times, which meant that he was on the bench for twenty-seven matches. He was just as effusive about the Catalan's impact: 'I've worked under great coaches, like Van Gaal, Hitzfeld and Heynckes, but Guardiola's far and away the best. I was thirty-six when he took over but I learned so much from him. He's definitely the best coach I've ever had.'

Jan Kirchhoff was in the squad on thirty-five different occasions but only played for 259 minutes in two years and never started a game. The longest playing time he enjoyed was thirty minutes of a Cup match against a fourth division side. He told *The Guardian*, 'Pep is the best coach in the world, without a doubt . . . If you want the honest truth, I'd say that he'll win the league and change this country's football forever. For sure. Wait and see, we're going to be watching a totally new kind of game.'

The coach has come a long way but to do so he's had to change, to come out of his shell and open himself up emotionally to his players. In my view, the attitude of his players in Munich was also crucial to this metamorphosis. They were open-minded, willing to learn from him and generous enough to make the changes he demanded. Unusual traits in the conservative world of football. Instead of shunning or defying him, these elite footballers welcomed him with almost childlike enthusiasm. All of which begs the question: can he do it again at City?

So far the signs are good and when Pep phoned one of his new signing targets he was greeted with a delighted, 'I can't believe you've got in touch, boss. I was almost giving up hope!' But what about when the novelty wears off? Will he manage to sustain his players' interest and enthusiasm over the next few years, through all the setbacks and difficulties that are bound to come his way? Are the City players prepared to pay the price of working for such a demanding and relentless manager? Certainly, the feedback at the end of his first few months has been positive. Fabian Delph already rates his new coach, 'I've learned more from Pep in three weeks than I have in my whole career.'

Pep has embarked on his latest project with the openness and enthusiasm that endeared him so much to his players in Munich. He's come out of his shell. Let's hope that's where he stays.

# BACKSTAGE 6

## LIQUID BAYERN
### Bremen, 17 October 2015

Bayern have reached just the maturity in their play that their coach has been aiming for. Right now they employ two principal routes of attack, plus a third alternative:

- Route A: Build up play 'outside'. The interior 'zones' are where the support play comes from and they also allow the players to impose a 'pause' while the play is constructed.
- Route B: Build up play 'inside'. The players use interior passing until the opposition midfield is reached then the ball's transferred 'outside' in search of the killer final ball into the box.
- Route C: Hitting long (usually diagonal) balls to the opposite side of the pitch, seeking to drag the opposition lines this way and that.

Bayern's great virtue is their capacity to alternate between all three of these tactics throughout a game depending on how the players and the coach read the oppositions' tactics. The team's completely mastered this strategy which unites different styles in one. Guardiola's more eclectic than ever. Even more of a chameleon.

His fundamental beliefs remain unaltered but he's added an endless number of options creating what could be described as 'Liquid Bayern', a fluid team which uses a variety of shapes plus a rich diversity of tactics. This is the point at which theory and action meet. Pep's meshed his ideas with the realities of German football (lethal counter attacking), his players skills' and talents as well as his own ability to teach and support them. He's had to adapt, interpret and re-assess.

The coach has become the conductor who knows the tune by heart, who knows that no orchestra sounds better than one where all the instrumentalists can express the full depth of their talent. It's meant using each man's obvious talents to their fullest extent and then digging deeper to draw out the skills and abilities as yet unrevealed. It's truly been the work of a 'maestro': by getting the maximum from his men and then asking for more he's been able to harness their skills to build a better, more harmonious group.

A team's style comes from the players themselves and the coach's job is to extract, exploit and unify these different styles for the good of the whole team. Right now, at Bayern, every one of Pep's players is not just in the position which best fits his characteristics but which brings the most value to the team. Every man understands and accepts that there are personal sacrifices to be made for the sake of the group. The team's game is plain, simple, unembellished football which seeks to achieve the objective via one of the possible three routes.

When they go down 'Route A' the centre halves, the pivote midfielder and the keeper are charged with sending the ball into the outside channels so that the full backs can advance the play. Each time the move is interrupted or hits a barrier the ball must be laid back to an 'inside' player who is there to support. His role is to keep the ball moving, to make combination passes and, hopefully, shuffle opponents about. The ball will stay 'inside' only for as long as is necessary until it goes back to the players on the wings. These little 'base camps' in midfield will support and try to drag opponents around using 'triangles' (Guardiola's favourite geometric shape) of passing options. The player driving play up the wing knows that his inside teammates are there to support, offer a pass and give the ball back as soon as he's in the best place to receive it. Not unlike a kid bouncing a ball off a wall trying to get a better angle each time. Progress continues down either of the wings until eventually the ball ends up in the penalty box.

(When there's a big switch of play from wing to wing, or interior to wing high up the pitch, it's usually the bugle-call for a big charge of midfielders into the box.)

The job of the full backs and wingers is to direct the tempo, form and verticality of the move. The 'interior' players (pivote, centre halves, inside forwards and the number 10) are there to support the wide men and take the right tactical decisions to help them advance into better space.

When the final 'charge' comes it is generally one of the wingers (or failing that, a full back), whose job it is to get high and wide into the box to provide the vital assist.

The centre forward, the '10', the other winger and one of the midfielders are the 'cavalry' who also move into the box whilst at least three players, the pivote midfielder, an inside forward and the full back from the other side of the pitch, MUST stay around the edge of the box looking for a possible 'second ball' rebound off the cross.

Route B ends with the same movements in and around the box but it starts differently. By this time, Pep's third year at Bayern, the majority of opponents no longer press his team high up the field. Bitter experience has taught them that no matter how intensely they press them, the technical dexterity and calm intelligence of Guardiola's players mean that they almost always get past them.

Obviously, mistakes happen from time to time. At Hoffenheim for example, when Alaba gifts the ball to Volland. But this is a rarity and even sides who usually play a pressing game, like Leverkusen or Dortmund, alter their strategy when they come to the Allianz Arena.

Bayern are now so dominant that they're almost always in control of the ball and the game whilst they're opponents desperately try to choke them of creative space. Their domestic rivals defend so deeply that Bayern rarely get the chance to counter-attack. You can't counter-attack when you're almost always attacking.

If the opposition manage to close the outside channels then Bayern opt for 'Route B'. It's 'inside', more linear and with fewer elements involved in construction than the first attacking route. The ball is moved from central defender to pivote midfielder to either of the strikers – usually Müller or Lewandowski.

The idea is low, vertical, fast passes to either i) re-organise the team's shape or ii) initiate the attack. In the first case, (i), the ball can be played back from the attackers to the organising midfielders or central defenders so that they can 'see the game' and judge if the distribution of teammates and opponents allows them to revert to Route A. Although attacking 'wide' is the principal route, the ball won't be sent there till the pivote or centre halves judge that the team's reorganised. If that's the best option then the ball will be sent, directly or indirectly, to the winger in search of that moment when he 'sounds the bugle' and the cavalry charge into the box.

Pep has clearly learned the lessons of his second season at Bayern and has made fundamental changes to the way Bayern advance. On one hand, using the 3-4-3 formation has fine-tuned ideas like the third man run, finding space to create 'free' men, playing forward with support from inside midfielders and passing triangles.

On the other hand, the plague of injuries he's suffered has obliged Pep to play with four and even five strikers, something which has taught this coach of 'a thousand midfielders' that it IS feasible to play with all those forwards and not unbalance the team.

It now gives him the confidence to reinforce his use of two traditionally 'open' wingers, pegged to the line and high up the pitch, with a number 9 striker who plays with all the traditional threat of that position, but who can also double up as a 'false 9' (Lewandowski). It also allows him to deploy a hard working no.10 player who confuses the opposition defence and midfield with his ability to 'arrive' in the right place rather than to 'stay' in one place (Müller).

Guardiola has learned all of this in his second season and is now applying it in his third. These ideas have also led to the creation of the perfect 'ecosystem' for Müller who now becomes the 'free' man in the attacking third with no responsibility for the construction of the game apart from receiving the ball with his back to goal, controlling it and putting it wide to either wing. It's Müller who effectively sounds the bugle so his teammates can start their charge into the box.

The team's effectively divided into two linked halves. The back division, formed by the keeper, two centre halves and the pivote midfielder situate themselves between midway up their own half and the centre circle and have a view of the whole pitch. It's these players who take the strategic decisions: whether to push the ball through Route A (wide) or Route B (through the interior) or whether to go for long diagonal passes over the opposition midfield to the wide men or strikers. Essentially, the team's brain lives in and around the centre circle.

The forward half of the team (two wingers, the striker and the no.10) move constantly in the first phase of the game, making sure that opposition players are distracted and disorganised. As soon as the 'trumpet sounds', however, they then burst into the penalty area to attack. These players must judge when they have exhausted and confused their rivals enough. That's when they strike.

Between the two halves of the team is the 'cartilage', made up of the full backs and inside forwards, who keep the team fluid and linked. Flexible footballers whose principal role is to support both halves of the team, to generate advantage and superiority and to close up possible defensive gaps. They are the engine oil which keeps the moving parts fluid.

Within this new simple 'ecosystem' each player can apply his own particular talents for the benefit of the team. Boateng and Alonso can take decisions, whether that's to support their teammates or provide precise long passes. Alaba and Bernat can sprint into spaces or run with the ball to drive an attack forward whilst Javi Martínez plays with restraint and discipline, saving his strength and pace for aggressive interventions to cut off the opposition in order to contain a counter-attack.

Lahm and Rafinha are the lubricating components who help facilitate whatever task is needed during a phase of play. Vidal bursts into space over and over again. Thiago's always on the ball or looking for it so he can take it where it'll most disorientate the opponent.

Costa and Coman are splayed wide on the lines, running and dribbling; Lewandowski knows he can attack the penalty box at the right time because the crosses will definitely arrive. Müller? He's loving his role as the explorer of space – his team's playing style has evolved into something simple but effective. He's fortified by the knowledge that his only task is to link to the wings and then look for space in which to be his anarchic best.

Smart, fluid, simple, liquid. It's taken two and a half years of hard work, observation and correction, learning and adaptation but Bayern's playing style is, finally, completely defined.

In the end Pep hasn't had to 'impose' a style on his men. It's evolved naturally from within the players themselves. His great gift has been his ability to draw out and unify their skills and find the right partnerships whilst neutralising any incompatibilities. He's done this whilst maintaining the 'fundamentals' of his game and has combined it all to create glorious football which works and gets results.

# 7

# FACING ADVERSITY

*Every time I make a mistake,*
*I seem to discover a new truth*
*Maurice Maeterlinck*

GUARDIOLA IS STILL a young man with much to learn. A surprising statement to some I'm sure, but true nonetheless. He's a hugely successful coach, possesses a genius for strategic and tactical planning and has more than his fair share of charisma. All this after just seven years coaching at football's elite level. He had an extraordinary start, winning six trophies with Barcelona in his first year. Most of his peers were well into their careers before really establishing themselves. I'm thinking here of great coaches such as Chapman, Pozzo, Hogan, Raynor, Rappan, Weisz, Erbstein, Guttmann, Rocco, Pesser, Sebes, Herrera, Busby, Maslov, Happel, Schön, Michels, Lobanovsky, Beskov, Menotti, Bilardo, Santana, Ferguson . . . (The obvious exceptions are Sacchi, Cruyff and Mourinho.)

Just thirty-eight years of age when he took over at Barcelona, Guardiola has continued to add to the triumphs of that first year, accumulating silverware and greater knowledge along the way. But after only seven years in the job, he still has a long way to go and a great deal more to learn. 'Learning' is just about his favourite word and it's certainly the concept he talks about most. He genuinely sees his own understanding as relatively limited and believes that there's still a world of knowledge and ideas to acquire.

In an earlier chapter I called Pep's time at Barça his 'teenage years'. He had yet to leave his 'easy' life, yet to abandon the comforts of home. (His job at Barcelona would have been rather less 'easy' had Pep not achieved such excellent results.) When the time came to make his way in the world, Pep chose Bayern Munich as the next stage of his adventure. We watched him grow and mature into 'adulthood' in Germany until it was time to move on once more.

## NECESSITY: THE MOTHER OF INVENTION
### Munich, 12 December 2015

Facing adversity is not an altogether negative experience. In Bayern's case, their difficulties have allowed the players to demonstrate their flexibility as they adapt to and perfect new playing systems. They have to master different playing positions and this in turn opens up whole new opportunities for the team. Domènec Torrent explains: 'The setbacks have forced us to think – and act – on the hoof and we've actually come up with some brilliant solutions. We've this problem with injuries at the moment but, in trying to find a way round it, we've found ourselves a new full back: Kimmich. Thanks to the experiments we've tried [to cope with all the missing players] he's proved what a great player he is, either as a full back or in midfield. Sometimes improvised solutions don't come off well but, now and again, they not only solve your current problems but create whole new opportunities for change and progress.'

Throughout his time in Munich Guardiola was heavily and constantly criticised although he also enjoyed widespread admiration for the work he was doing, particularly amongst his fellow coaches in Germany.

At the start of 2015 Manuel Neuer explained one of the things he most admired in his coach, 'Pep knows all the Bundesliga clubs much better than most Germans.' Fulsome praise indeed after only eighteen months working in the Bundesliga. Neuer intended to compliment his boss but his words proved a double-edged sword and were interpreted in many quarters as, 'this upstart foreigner thinks

Sitting on a ball, Pep watches Thiago and Müller practising free kicks. The training session finished a while ago but a few players have stayed back for some extra practice. They play Juventus in a few days and are keen to practise shooting. As always Guardiola will be the last one to leave the training pitch. *Loles Vives*

Guardiola talks the author through his game plan for Bayern's game against Juventus. It will be a sensational Champions League match, full of drama, emotion and superb football. *Isaac Lluch*

Thursday, 19 May 2016: Guardiola's last training session at Bayern. It's raining, as it was on his first day here and Pep decides to clear away the balls himself. This is his *adiós* to Säbener Strasse. *Loles Vives*

Bayern have just beaten Juventus in the Champions League after an agonising extra time. Estiarte, Guardiola, Planchart and Torrent show their delight as they go up in the coach's private lift in the Allianz Arena. This is where Pep has shared many of his most private thoughts over the last three years. *Martí Perarnau*

When the players returned from holiday in July 2015, they were met with the season's objective painted on the dressing room walls: the conquest of their fourth consecutive Bundesliga trophy. *Martí Perarnau*

All the walls at Säbener Strasse were adorned with motifs relating to the main objective of 2015-2016: to win the league for a fourth time, making Bayern the first champions to achieve this in the history of German football. 'Jeder Für's Team' (Every Man for the Team) was the dressing room's motto that season. *Martí Perarnau*

Guardiola wrote this good luck message for his successor at Säbener Strasse: 'The very best of luck Carlo, with all good wishes!' Ancelotti was delighted when he read it. *Martí Perarnau*

Pep is doused in beer by David Alaba as Bayern celebrate their 2016 Bundesliga title. *Getty Images*

Pep receives his Manchester City training kit from Director of Football, Txiki Begiristain, 3 July 2016, shortly after his unveiling to the fans. During this first appearance as City's new manager, he made his priorities clear: 'The first objective is to play well. After that we need to win the next game and then the next and then the one after that . . .' *Getty Images*

Pep, draped in a City scarf, is pictured at the club's training complex after his first press conference. *Getty Images*

Coming back to Munich: on 21 July 2016 Pep was back training his men in Säbener Strasse, although this time it was with Manchester City, not Bayern. He was given a warm, affectionate welcome by his former players (pictured, Xabi Alonso and Thiago with Domènec Torrent and Carles Planchart) and the fans. *Martí Perarnau*

Pep focused on the fundamental parts of his game from his first training session at Manchester City: bringing out the ball, sticking to positions, looking for free men . . . The midfielders (Fernandinho and Fernando pictured) are a key part of his playing style. *Getty Images*

Nolito is one of the five new players Guardiola brought to City in summer 2016. Wingers are essential to Pep's game. *Getty Images*

Guardiola has expanded the technical team who will help him achieve his objectives at Manchester City. Pictured, Pep with Domènec Torrent, assistant coach; Mikel Arteta, co-assistant coach; and Lorenzo Buenaventura, fitness coach. *Getty Images*

he knows more about us than we do ourselves'. It's interesting that during three sublime years in which he smashed every record going and won trophy after trophy, Guardiola was never once voted 'best coach' by the German press.

Throughout the Munich years the experiences that provided the best and most compelling lessons were the setbacks and difficulties he encountered. The greatest of these was probably the epidemic of injuries his squad suffered, most of which resulted from knocks and breaks rather than muscular problems.

Injury problems took their toll in all three seasons but let's look at 2015/16 in more detail. That year Bayern's squad suffered a total of nineteen muscular injuries of varying degrees, very much in line with the eighteen muscular injuries experienced on average by any elite squad during a season*. In fact, if we look at the stats for the whole of Europe it becomes clear that Bayern's muscular injury record is actually pretty good. The figures for season 2015/16 are as follows: Borussia Dortmund, fifteen; Chelsea, seventeen; Arsenal, twenty-five; Real Madrid, twenty-seven; Barcelona, thirty; Manchester United, thirty-one; and Juventus and Manchester City, thirty-three [*source: Efias.com*].

All this does great credit to the work of fitness coach Lorenzo Buenaventura, but what then do I mean by 'epidemic of injuries'? In part, I'm referring to the high number of twists, tears and breaks resulting from bangs, kicks and tackles on the pitch, most of them requiring a much longer recuperation process than muscular injuries. In 2015/16 the squad experienced an alarming twenty-seven injuries of this nature (50% more than muscular injuries).

The second contributory factor was Bayern's long established policy relating to recuperation. The policy, although state-of-the-art when it was first introduced at the club, had, in my opinion, long outlived its usefulness. We'll examine this in detail in the next chapter.

* *The figure comes from a UEFA study carried out by Professors Jan Ekstrand, Markus Waldén and Martin Hägglund*

# MEDICAL MATTERS

More important than the decisions we make
is the moment we choose to make them
*Henry Miller*

Doctor Hans-Wilhelm Müller-Wohlfahrt had been Bayern's doctor for nearly four decades, starting back in the 70s when Hoeness, Rummenigge and Beckenbauer were still playing. He had overseen the club's medical services since then and, after more than thirty years, his authority was unquestioned. Organisations can be slow to change, particularly in a place like Bavaria where people are, on the one hand, exceptionally open, friendly and liberal-minded and, on the other, deeply conservative and fiercely protective of tradition. In all his years at Bayern, the doctor had never once interfered in any other part of the running of the club but neither had he permitted anyone to meddle in the affairs of the medical unit.

This situation was radically different to the one Guardiola had been used to at Barcelona where the club's medical services (considered the most advanced and progressive in Europe) are a model of innovation and modernity. The aim of the medical team is to ensure that the recuperation process is fast, effective and safe and they use state-of-the-art technology and methods (all of which are stringently checked against current legislation) to ensure that the coach has as many men as possible available at all times. Barça's training ground now has an integrated sports clinic which boasts the most cutting-edge technology of any club in Europe. The medical staff also work side by side with the coach and are an intrinsic part of the squad's daily life.

Doctor Müller-Wohlfahrt's methodology, though highly respected, consisted, at times, of injecting players with Actovegin (a highly filtered extract obtained from calf's blood), an approach that was new and unfamiliar to Pep. The doctor, moreover, had never felt the need to base himself at the training ground or travel with the team to away league or Cup games although he did accompany them on

Champions League outings. If any of the players required medical attention, they were expected to attend the doctor's private clinic in Munich, even if they were overnighting in a hotel on the eve of a game. The doctor's treatment plans also tended to result in relatively slow recuperation times and, whilst this was his considered, professional approach, it also presented enormous challenges to Guardiola, as coach of a team of elite players coping with intense physical stress every day of their working lives.

I should say at this point that, personally, Guardiola and Müller-Wohlfahrt remained on good terms throughout their working relationship but it was, however, clear from the start that, professionally, the two men didn't see eye to eye.

In August 2013, Bayern were in the midst of their preparations for their match against Borussia Dortmund in the Super Cup when the doctor informed Pep that neither Neuer nor Ribéry (two of his key players) would be playing. Accepting the doctor's prognosis, Pep duly went ahead without them and lost his first official game in Germany. On the day, Neuer's absence in particular proved a serious blow. Thirty-six hours later, however, both men were back at training, fully fit. Nobody could quite believe it: two essential team members had been declared unfit to play but had recovered sufficiently to attend a full training session more or less the next day.

In my view, what happened next was a serious error of judgement on Pep's part. He was dealing with someone whose understanding of the demands of elite sport was diametrically opposed to his own but was reluctant to challenge long established practices so early in his tenure. He believed that over time he would be able to persuade the doctor of the wisdom of his point of view and that, for the sake of the team, they would work together to find an acceptable solution. He hoped that Müller-Wohlfahrt would be open to the idea of becoming more involved with the daily life of the team. This was a serious miscalculation and his unwillingness to take a more proactive approach meant that he had to tolerate the situation for much longer than necessary. Any football club will always be a melting pot of conflicting ideas and attitudes and the resulting debates and discussions often act as the impetus for innovation and development. Internal tensions can be the motor that drives the club's growth. However, in this case, the fault line ran too deep. Two of the club's key decision makers had fundamental disagreements about how to manage the health and well-being of the team's players and the situation was always going to be unworkable.

Pep grew increasingly dissatisfied with the medical services as the season wore on and the medical team continued to supply troubling diagnoses (the details are confidential) and frustratingly slow treatment plans. At the end of the season he informed the board of directors that he would require a permanent medical presence at the club from then on. At no time did he suggest that Müller-Wohlfahrt's services should be dispensed with and his proposal was that the doctor select and appoint a colleague who would be based at the club and therefore able to attend the players at all times. After a protracted delay the doctor's son, Doctor Killian Müller-Wohlfahrt, was appointed in January 2015.

In the spring of that year Bayern was hit with its first significant run of injuries. Some were muscular but most were traumatic injuries (fractures and sprains etc) which would take much longer to heal. Unfortunately, the club's medics provided inaccurate prognoses regarding recuperation times. For example, initially Pep was told that Franck Ribéry would be out for three or four days. In the end the player took more than eight months to return to full fitness.

Tensions were running high and Pep wasn't the only one feeling the pressure. Karl-Heinz Rummenigge was also deeply unhappy with the medical unit but chose the worst possible moment (after Bayern's Champions League defeat by Oporto) to vent his frustration, bursting into the dressing room and accusing the medical staff of having failed in their duty to the players. His outburst wasn't targeted specifically at Doctor Müller-Wohlfahrt and he made it clear that he held the whole medical team (doctors and physios alike) responsible. The dressing down lasted barely ten seconds because Guardiola intervened immediately, calming the situation down and instructing his players to get on with their showers. The next day a local newspaper broke the story of the doctor's resignation. Müller-Wohlfahrt had given a statement to the paper, which had a long history of publishing exclusives about Bayern's medical affairs, instead of speaking to the club directly.

It was terrible news for Guardiola, leaving him without his chief medical officer at the most crucial stage of the season, when the squad was struggling with a catastrophic level of injuries. He had even been forced to play some games with only twelve outfield players available! The other inevitable consequence was the storm of criticism that rained down on the coach who was blamed for the departure of a man who had been a club legend for over thirty years and this was further aggravated when the coach faced the press alone at the subsequent press conference. Apparently none of the directors were available that day . . .

## HELENIO HERRERA SACKED OUR DOCTOR
### Milan, July 1960

Coach Helenio Herrera joined Inter Milan in 1960, going on to win the European Cup in 1964 and 1965 with the Italian club.

On his arrival the Argentinian found that the club's medical services were run by an off-site doctor who treated the players at his own clinic in the city rather than at the training ground. His policy was also to issue medical instructions by telephone to the club masseur who was then charged with passing these along to the coach. In his memoirs Herrera describes his response to the situation, which bears remarkable similarities with Pep's.

'It's quite true that when I first arrived I asked the president to make certain changes to club personnel and, unfortunately and quite unintentionally, created a feeling of intense resentment about my actions. At no time did I ask the president to sack any member of staff who was fulfilling his duties professionally and effectively and people that think I was merely throwing my weight about are completely mistaken. Essentially, I carried all the responsibility for the team. If a player keeps getting injured, who takes the blame? Not the masseur or the doctor but Helenio Herrera and his excessive training methods. That's why I wanted the most competent people working with me and I certainly didn't request a new doctor on some kind of whim. But we all know that in Italy and Spain nepotism plays such a big part in staff appointments that any attempt on my part to get rid of a doctor or a masseur or a player was immediately interpreted as malicious and petty. It's really much simpler than that, although not everyone saw it that way. If I get rid of someone it's because he's not right for the way I do things. I'm not in any way questioning his professional abilities and accept that he might do perfectly well elsewhere. He just doesn't fit with my ideas.

'So, we get to day fifteen and I still haven't seen hide nor hair of the club doctor. It's obviously all about "long distance" medical care for this guy. Eventually he does appear and turns out to be a lovely chap, full of the joys. I know I'm going to have to wipe the smile off his face pretty quickly and, although I don't enjoy doing it, I basically tell him that he's about to have an extended holiday . . .

'His successor, Doctor Quarenghi is young and very smart. He comes to every single training session now.'

It's perhaps unfair to compare the two situations. Helenio Herrera was fifty years old at the time and an experienced coach who had managed ten different teams. Guardiola was much younger when he took over in Munich (forty-two) and his only coaching experience was at Barcelona. I do believe however that Herrera's was the better course of action. He made it clear from the start that he couldn't work with someone whose methods differed so greatly from his own. There was no question of him having doubts about the professional ability of the charming doctor, it was just that 'he's not right for the way I do things'. In contrast, Guardiola stuck with the status quo, hoping things would sort themselves out over time and, as we've seen, this proved to be a disastrous misstep.

By the time Pep moved to Manchester with his staff at the end of May 2016, his attitude had changed. He was clear that all decision makers at City had to be in agreement about certain key aspects of club life and insisted on taking charge of the future direction of the medical services immediately. One of his first acts was to appoint a much respected nutritionist to his medical team. Bayern had taught him a hard but salutary lesson.


## PEP'S PERSONALITY

A man's character is his destiny.
*Heráclito*


What appears to be a virtue can also become a defect, depending on what you do with it. Guardiola is an empathetic person. He's interested in people, willing to compromise and adapt where necessary and always happy to help someone out if he can. His natural empathy means that he's quick to identify with others' feelings. This determination to connect with people was evident from the start at Bayern: he chose to speak in German at his presentation ceremony, was happy to attend his first Oktoberfest (Munich's famous beer festival) clad in the traditional Bavarian *lederhosen*, agreed to the club's 'open door' policy at training sessions, tolerated the existing policy regarding medical care and understood that at Bayern the coach of the first team has no responsibility for the club's youth categories. He went along with it all because he felt it was in the best interests of the club to do so. And Guardiola always puts the interests of the club before his own.

His determination to accede to the many idiosyncratic aspects of life at Bayern – a club, don't forget, with its own very particular identity; 'Mia San Mia', the club slogan, effectively means 'We are who we are' – didn't always work in his favour. For Pep it was essential that, as coach of the German champions, he should make an effort to speak their language and therefore always addressed the press in German. Although an able linguist, he was less proficient in German than other foreign languages and made frequent grammar and pronunciation mistakes. From time to time communications director, Markus Hörwick, would pass on a request from a journalist that he switch to English (eventually Sky Deutschland insisted on doing post-match interviews in Spanish). Guardiola was determined to stick to his guns however, believing that switching to another language would reflect badly on the club. The coach of Bayern should always speak German, he believed, or at the very least, make a serious effort to do so. This policy backfired on him and his conferences were never as clear and as detailed as they would have been in English, not to mention Spanish or Catalan. Almost all the German journalists I spoke to thought that he'd got this badly wrong. They didn't care what language he spoke as long as they could understand what he said. It was really only Pep himself who was bothered about speaking the language of the club and country.

His natural empathy and willingness to prioritise the needs of the club got him into hot water in other ways and, ironically, had he been a little more selfish in his actions and decisions, life at Bayern might have been much, much easier. Take his policy regarding players for example. During his first year in charge Pep fought tooth and nail to keep Toni Kroos. The player had been in constant dispute with club directors and was unhappy with his salary as well as their refusal to accept his status as a vital part of the squad. Pep was desperate to hold on to the player, whom he saw as one of the linchpins of his team, the man who imposed order on their game once Lahm had set things in motion. The coach spent months trying to find a compromise between the two sides but in the end had to concede defeat as Kroos was transferred to Real Madrid. He could have given the club an ultimatum of course, 'Either Kroos stays or you're going to have problems with me too,' but threats and blandishments are not Pep's style and after two determined attempts to change the board's mind, he threw in the towel. The player was going to be a big loss to him but, for Pep, it was better to respect the club's wishes. Was he right? I think not. This is professional football, a world of elite sportsmen and serious competition and nobody thanks you for making the wrong decisions, no matter the reason. Sure enough when, a few months after Kroos' departure Javi Martínez broke his knee, thereby leaving the team without a key midfielder, no-one was prepared to stand up and publicly accept that getting rid of Kroos now looked like a disastrous decision. Instead, all eyes turned to Pep, eager to see how he was going to solve this latest problem.

Guardiola is a man who tends to interiorise things. When presented with a problem, he often assumes sole responsibility and may be unwilling to discuss it openly. At times he'll allow things to fester until he can no longer cope with the pressure and explodes. It doesn't have to be a particularly important issue but for a perfectionist like Pep, even the tiniest details can assume disproportionate significance. It's like watching a pressure cooker heating up, ready to burst. And there's constant provocation in his daily working life: a cheeky question from the press; a slight from an opponent; a player with a poor attitude; a bad decision from the board of directors . . . Pep deals with it all with calm dignity, swallowing his anger and saying nothing. But he's stored it all away and the pressure's building. Then one day he'll overreact and fly into a rage over some relatively minor detail.

Pep's also very emotional. His tears after winning his last Cup Final with Bayern were not untypical of the man but when I talked to fans afterwards they expressed how surprised they'd been. 'We thought Pep was like a machine, completely cold-hearted. Who knew he was so emotional? It's great to see he's got a heart . . .'

## I JUST WANT PEOPLE TO LIKE ME
Manresa, 23 June 2015

Pep's holidays end with a visit to Manresa, near his home town of Santpedor. He's been invited to the fiftieth anniversary celebrations of 'Ampans', a charity which works with youngsters with mental disabilities. He's visibly moved by the children's stories and begins to open up. 'If you really want to know what I want from life, from my job, I want to be liked. It's not easy though because I have to leave players out [of the line-up] and then they assume that I don't like them. They don't realise that I've made my decision based on tactical considerations or because of what's going on in my head at the time. They think I don't like them and I hate that because I never think our victories are down to me. Sure, I help the process along, but that's all. I don't consider myself better than anyone else and know I've had the good fortune to work for a great club with superb players. In my heart of hearts it's not really trophies that motivate me, it's the chance to create good relationships with my players. I like people. And I want them to like me.'

Why had Pep been so determined to hide his emotions, only 'letting go' on his last day? For two reasons: he's naturally introverted and he believed that he needed to protect himself. I'm not talking here about shyness but about an introverted person who's only comfortable and willing to open up when surrounded by trusted confidants. On those occasions he's expressive and chatty, happy to argue his position and always up for a laugh. I've taken numerous photos of him in the elevator in the Allianz Arena fooling around and having a joke, just as up for a bit of banter as his most extrovert players (David Alaba and Thomas Müller).

His natural introversion means the image he projects is that of a cold, aloof, nerveless competitor which perhaps explains people's confusion when he finally opened up in Munich, talking about the mutual affection between him and his players and describing the passion and commitment they showed every day at training.

'Love', 'affection', 'passion'. Strange words indeed to find on the lips of a man famed for his cold-hearted detachment. And it's precisely this discrepancy between the private and the public Pep that causes many people to distrust his heartfelt, if rare, public expressions of emotion. He's seen as someone incapable of becoming emotionally involved until it all gets too much on the last day and the floodgates open. Only then are people reassured that, yes, Pep is a caring guy who inspires not just affection but genuine passion in his players.

Guardiola's very trusting and over the years he's paid a hard price for his accepting nature. He's open and friendly and reluctant to find fault in others. Which is why he's found himself feeling let down and betrayed so often in the past. This is a man who would rather lose the argument than betray a friend, yet time and again he's put his trust in people who have proved unable or unwilling to show him the loyalty he deserves. He's too soft, too trusting.

Basically, Guardiola's one of life's good guys swimming against the tide in the tough, harshly competitive world of professional football. And this takes me on to one of his other faults: his propensity to take the weight of the world on his shoulders. Not satisfied with assuming responsibility for his own cock-ups, he seems to believe that he must also assume the faults and failings of his players, the club and, on occasion, even complete strangers.

And it cuts both ways. Without these flaws, Pep wouldn't be Pep. Without his passion, his unfailing dedication to his club and his players, and his constant striving for perfection, he wouldn't be the brilliant, innovative, trophy winning coach he is today. But that doesn't mean it's easy for him or for those around him. With Pep, nothing is done by halves. Everything has to be as close to perfect as humanly possible. Depending on the situation, this can be a blessing or a curse.

So, once again, I'd like to ask the obvious question. What has Pep learned from his Munich years? Should he make an effort to allow the fans and media in Manchester see his softer side? Well, having watched young fan Braydon Bent get the thrill of his life when he opened the door of a taxi and saw Pep Guardiola waiting for him, I'd say that, yes, he's just about ready to open up and let the world see the 'real' Pep. Warmer, more outgoing and as committed as ever.

# BACKSTAGE 7

## RESTORING THE PYRAMID
### Munich, 24 October 2015

It's been an historic day. Bayern have beaten FC Köln, bringing their total to a colossal thousand Bundesliga wins. The 'modern' German league was established in 1963 with Bayern qualifying for premier division football in 1965. They've spent fifty years amongst the elite of the nation's clubs and now, after 1,714 matches, the stats are impressive: 1,000 victories, 385 draws and 329 defeats.

Pep's radiant. The Bundesliga has issued a graphic showing the Bayern coaches with the best win ratios: Guardiola's way in front with an average of 84%. His predecessors trail him by a distance: Magath, 64%; Hitzfeld and Heynckes, 63%; Lattek, 62%. Then he gets more news from Spain. Today has been his 300th victory as a coach since he started at Barcelona B in 2007.

'That stat definitely includes Barça B?' is his only question. He really treasures the memories of his days with the Barça youngsters whom he led to victory in the Catalan third division.

But this has been a momentous occasion for another reason. Today Pep's restored the 'pyramid' and lined his men up in a 2-3-5 formation, a throwback to the football of the past, widely used in the years from the end of the nineteenth century until the 1950s. He's reached into the archives, dusted down an ancient idea and put it into practice.

The initial inspiration came from a conversation he'd had with Juanma Lillo. They were discussing the best way to overcome unambitious teams who 'park the bus'.

'You could go for an hourglass shape,' Lillo suggested.

Pep has never been afraid to resuscitate old ideas. We saw that at Barça when he used Messi as a 'false No.9' against Real Madrid in 2009. We've already seen the process he went through to implement that idea but today's change is different. It's not centred on one particular player. It affects his entire playing model and the whole organisation of the team.

Pep hadn't known the entire history of the 'pyramid' but Lillo was happy to explain.

When organised football was still in its infancy and concepts like tactics and strategy barely even considered, teams played exclusively offensive football, always moving in the direction of the opposition goal. If you go into any playground nowadays you'll see much the same phenomenon: the only objective in any player's mind is to get forward and score. Hungarian historian Arpad Csánadi informs us that as football became more organised, the initial 1-1-8 was replaced by other formations: English teams used a 2-1-7 in a very direct style of game whilst their Scottish counterparts preferred a more controlled 2-2-6 for their passing game. The idea for the 2-3-5 formation initially arose far from the football pitch in the august setting of Cambridge University where academics met to discuss football strategy.

From 1880, the pyramid became established as the universal playing model thanks to the success of Blackburn Rovers, amongst others. In some countries this formation was used exclusively until as late as the 1950s despite the success of systems like Herbert Chapman's WM (3-2-2-3), which was also used by Árpád Weisz in Italy. At the time there were also a number of interesting developments in terms of defensive football (Bold, Béton, Verrou, Il Método, Vianema), which arose out of the need to find successful strategies for weaker teams and flourished in the '60s with Italy's catenaccio.

The most important thing about Guardiola's decision to recuperate the old system was the thinking process behind it. The end result was exactly the same as the nineteenth century: his players on the pitch in a 2-3-5, but his reasons for using it were entirely different.

The idea didn't come from any kind of detailed knowledge of the system but was an intuitive response to three things: his need to dominate; his need to rotate his team; and his preference for using lots of strikers. Let's have a look at each of these:

## 1. Match Domination.

The analysis of FC Köln was definitive: they were going to 'park the bus' and hand control of the game over to Bayern.

Domènec Torrent was adamant: 'They're definitely going to shut themselves up in their own half Pep. They're becoming more and more defensive all the time.' And he was right. Köln start out with a 5-4-1 hoping to repel Bayern's incursions with a solid defensive wall. So Pep went for five strikers, only one 'true' midfielder and three full backs. It's the first time he's used this system. He used parts of it at Barça as well as at Bayern but today he's going all the way. During his first year at Munich he used a 2-3-2-3 against Manchester United, with Robben and Ribéry asked to sprint up and down the length of the pitch like wing backs. In his second season he also resorted to five strikers on numerous occasions although they tended to include inside forwards positioned near the midfield (Xabi Alonso).

He used 'forwards' to compensate for the lack of midfielders in matches which profiled as relatively easy. It meant the team could accommodate five strikers relatively easily without getting unbalanced by being divided into two units of players.

In March 2015 he faced Shakhtar Donetsk in the Champions League quarter-finals with five strikers. Robben and Ribéry were used as inside forwards charged with looking for that decisive dribble through their opponents' inside lines. It worked like a dream and Bayern won the game 7-0.

Today he's gone for a pure 2-3-5. Neuer takes a position about fifteen metres beyond the edge of his penalty box and he's as vigilant as ever, constantly scanning the play, ready to get involved if needed. Today he won't be required. At all.

Boateng and Rafinha, the two central defenders, are in front of their keeper, in the centre circle, but in Köln's half of the pitch. Arturo Vidal's the only organising midfielder (pivote) playing. Philipp Lahm is on his right and David Alaba to his left.

This line of three will have two main functions: to distribute the ball amongst their strikers while at the same time acting as a barrier against counter-attacks.

From right to left Coman, Robben, Lewandowski, Müller and Costa play in a line on the edge of the rival penalty box. Pep's gone for five strikers to match their rival's five defenders. The Bayern strikers position themselves in the spaces between the defenders and they're moving constantly. Only the two wingers on the outside stick to their positions, the others are dodging here and there, seeking gaps, receiving the ball from 'midfield' such as it is, trying to make the killer burst in to the danger zone or else recycling possession swiftly so they can start the attack all over again. And the guys on the wing are also in constant motion, wearing down their markers with their changes in pace and direction. One minute Coman's here then suddenly it's Robben. Now Coman occupies the space Costa's just left whilst teammates Müller and Lewandowski trick and tease the visitors in a whirl of movement. And if at any stage Bayern get bogged down, Alaba sprints up and takes up his place as the sixth striker. Köln struggle to even make it past the half-way line and Pep's team spends more than 70% of the match in the opposition half.

Pep's strategy's a triumph (4-0) and to mark this most auspicious of days the evening ends with free beer all round. For everyone in the stadium.

## 2. The need to rotate his players

There's a vital Cup game in Wolfsburg coming up and the coach wants to keep his key midfielders, Xabi Alonso and Thiago Alcántara, fresh. They'll need to be on top form physically and mentally. Xabi's role is a crucial one – he'll be responsible for distributing possession to his teammates and Thiago's expert dribbling and passing will also be key. Both roles require peak fitness which means that the two players are often missing from the starting XI before any big matches.

This leaves Pep with one guaranteed midfielder for the Köln game: Arturo Vidal (Rode's injured and Javi Martínez isn't yet match fit). Vidal will be supported by Lahm and Alaba and together, the three of them will line up in front of their central defenders. Given the opponent they're facing, Pep reckons it's a risk he can afford to take.

3. His preference for lots of strikers.

'It's weird, I know. I've spent my whole life saying that it's all about the midfielders and here I am, using five strikers.' Pep's words just a year ago when Lahm and Thiago were out of commission. Back then the coach tried out a number of different systems with five strikers, always using two of them as inside forwards. One match, the return leg against Oporto in the Champions League, was crucial in reinforcing his faith in using five attackers. Bayern had been hammered in the away game (3-1) meaning that Pep was forced to go for all-out attack at home. There was nothing for it but to use five strikers (although two of them were really re-deployed full backs). That night Bayern's forwards, Lahm, Müller, Lewandowski, Bernat and Götze, lined up in the spaces between the Portuguese defenders. Behind them, Thiago and Xabi were kept busy distributing the ball from one side to another. It was another stellar performance and Bayern won 6-1 (5-0 by the fortieth minute).

Their success that day convinces Pep that he can confidently re-use his five striker strategy, thereby defying the conventional wisdom that fewer, not more, strikers are needed for effective attack. By now his men have got this tactic down to a fine art and are able to attack with five strikers without losing any of their cohesiveness and unity.

This system gives Bayern an added benefit: the players passing the ball have more options to choose from. Pep expands on this during the post-match dinner, 'Passes from the midfield or further back are more likely to be safe and efficient if they're aimed outside, towards the wingers but we're more likely to do some damage if they go inside (although they're more likely to be intercepted). But five strikers give us so many more men to pass to. The other players can choose to pass to the outside (less risk) or to the inside (more risk but more threat to the other team). It just gives us so many different options.'

Guardiola's men have fully realised the objectives he laid down way back in the early days of his tenure. All of them know his tactical 'stockpile' inside out and they execute their tasks with practised ease. They've assimilated everything he's taught them and, more importantly, have found new, undiscovered resources and talents within themselves. These are their triumphs: their willingness to learn, their determination to succeed and their ability to master every new stratagem and tactic. Sky TV pundit Roland Evers gets it spot-on when, mid-commentary, he calls Lahm a '*Verteidigende Mittefeldflügelstürmer*', which translates as 'defender-midfielder-winger-striker'.

Today's been Pep's shining hour. He's asked his players to implement a complex, high-risk strategy and it's been a resounding success. He's reinstated a system, long ago abandoned for other safer, more pragmatic strategies, and has fine-tuned it, adding his own crucial tweaks and adjustments. Pep's pyramid in action looks nothing like the chaos we see in football footage from the 1930s. It's a model of razor sharp tactical planning and ruthless organisation. He's prepared a brutally offensive game whilst protecting his weak points and ensuring group cohesion. This pyramid isn't rigid and unyielding, its very success depends on the dynamic flow of each of its component parts.

Don't view this as a nostalgic return to the Cambridge of the nineteenth century when the football 'pyramid' first appeared. The strategic thinking behind today's game plus the world class performance on the pitch, make it anything but. It's a state-of-the-art, outstanding example of twenty-first century innovation. In one of those strange twists of fate football often brings us, today in the Allianz Arena we've looked on in wonder as the theories of the great football minds of Victorian England have converged with the strategic brilliance of Pep Guardiola. And all because of a pyramid . . .

# 8

# NURTURING TALENT

To achieve excellence you need to train
but to surpass it you need to change
*Xesco Espar*

FOR PEP EDUCATION is an obsession. He finds lessons in everything he reads, sees and experiences – the good but, more especially, the bad. People tend to assume that elite coaches are the experts in all things football but you'll find coaches at all levels within the game with just as much understanding and knowledge. What sets top coaches apart is their ability to work under intense pressure, manage world class footballers and hold their own against other first rate competitors.

Guardiola started his coaching career in the third division, something conveniently forgotten by those who say he'd cope less well in a club with fewer resources. He learned the ropes with Barça B, leading what was essentially a group of kids to victory in the league and it's an experience he'll never forget. Pep understands that his own knowledge is not necessarily superior to that of a third division coach and he therefore drives himself to continue his own education. Remember how he summed up his time in Munich? 'I came here to learn more than to teach. I knew I had to adapt to Germany and I've learned a huge amount. It's been a fucking brilliant experience.'

Pep genuinely believes that this process is vital to his career progression. And there are many areas he'd like to improve: his knowledge of the game, his communication skills, his ability to analyse well under pressure and to plan for every contingency. As Reginald Revans said, 'In order to survive we must continue to learn at the speed of change.'

Several years ago Pep explained to me how he sees this process, 'You learn by watching and listening. Observation and reflection.' A football coach has to watch and analyse games; apply the teachings of his mentors in new contexts; debate and discuss the ideas of his assistants and peers; and experiment with new moves and tactics as well as talking these through with his players. He must also spend time focusing on his opponents' games, examining their tactics and identifying their mistakes. He'll spend hours and hours reading analyses and reports and talking tactics with other experts whether in his own or a different field. It's an ongoing process and he must be ready to challenge everything he knows in order to augment his knowledge and use the lessons of the past to grow. As Ángel Cappa says, 'The future of football lies in the past.'

Krishnamurti talked of the importance of maintaining an open mind, 'You cannot learn if your thinking is stuck in the conclusions and assumptions of the past.' And Belgium doctor Maurice Piéron says of football coaching, 'Any coach who fails to take the time to observe is the lesser for it. The coach should spend more than 80% of any training session or match observing what's happening.'

Volleyball coach Julio Velasco shares his own experiences, 'You know, I've learned so much more working with less able players than I have with the more gifted guys. With the weaker players I had to make much more effort to find the key to helping them improve.'

Coaches learn from the men who form them, implementing their ideas first as players and later as coaches. The knowledge passes down through the generations, from master to apprentice, and it's often possible to trace the influences back to the source. Think of Jimmy Hogan – Josef Blum – Karl Humenberger – Rinus Michels – Johan Cruyff – Pep Guardiola. Or, Herbert Chapman – Vittorio Pozzo – Karl Rappan – Helenio Herrera – Fabio Capello – José Mourinho.

Philosopher José Antonio Marina writes that our 'ability to learn' (as well as biological mutation and natural selection) has been a crucial part of human evolution. He calls this the third evolutionary power, 'Not only do we have the capacity to learn more than other animals but we are also able to decide exactly what it is we learn.' Perhaps we could call this process, 'selective learning'. Marina's ideas are directly applicable to the evolution of football, 'The function of intelligence (and therefore the function of the brain) is not to understand or feel, it's to direct the action. We don't think in order to understand. We think in order to do. "Talent" might therefore be described as intelligence in action at its sharpest and most efficient.'

Paco Seirul.lo continues this theme, 'A coach has a good idea so he decides to try it out. It might take a while to perfect it but, when it does eventually start to work well, his opponents notice and then they have to come up with their own ideas in response . . . It's basically the same process as evolution. It's how all the different species have evolved. At the start you have a certain type of insect which is a source of food for birds. Hundreds or thousands of years pass and this same insect has developed a poison which kills the birds that eat it. To survive the birds must evolve, either by not eating the insect or by developing an antidote to the poison. That's evolution in a nutshell and if you genuinely want to understand the evolution of football, I'd recommend reading *On the Origin of Species*. It's exactly the same process. Let's say one day you decide to play with one less defender, leaving three defenders with two men in front of them in a 3-2-3-2. That's going to impact on the players. The way they interact will change. And what's likely to happen next? Well, usually your players will make mistakes and they start to lose the ball. And that's actually the great advantage we have in football. The impact of the change is immediately obvious, in this case, we lose the ball! The players haven't communicated well enough and now our opponents can take advantage and take the ball of us. Every time you introduce a new or different element, everyone around it is affected, for good or for bad. That dichotomy always exists. And there's bound to be a passage of time between the change and all its effects becoming clear but it's a very short period of time, as we've seen. We make the change and almost immediately we lose the ball.'

Guardiola's obsession with education has nothing to do with intellectualism. It's not about acquiring knowledge for the sake of it, it's about developing his understanding so that he can manage better, direct the action better. It's a very pragmatic obsession. It may seem strange that Guardiola spends so much time and effort creating his 'masterpiece' (he only considers it to be complete once he's imparted everything he knows) and then moves on to the next one, without pausing to savour the fruits of his labour. We call him a maverick because he's an obsessive, nonconformist perfectionist but perhaps it's just a matter of survival. He's realised that spending time glorying in his successes would be self-indulgent and dangerous. He's someone who's understood that to cease to grow is to die. 'Growth consists of learning and changing so that you continuously create a new and better version of yourself,' writes Imanol Ibarrondo. We should all be in constant movement, never allowing ourselves to become stagnant. Growth and progress should never stop.

When Guardiola said that he was moving to England to continue his education, he really meant that he was going to continue to educate others. Any teacher learns through educating others and for Guardiola, the process is the same.

Psychologists Ron Gallimore and Roland Tharp studied the learning process through their work with John Wooden, the legendary California University basketball coach (he won ten NCAA titles between 1964 and 1975). They recorded their findings in a book, *You Haven't Taught until They have Learned*, which captures the essence of the purpose of training: it's not about the 'teaching' that happens, it's the 'learning' that's important. I'd define 'learning' here as the absorption of the coach's ideas or the process by which the player develops his talents, including those yet undiscovered, under the coach's guidance.

When, halfway through his final season at Bayern, Guardiola said that he had already achieved what he had set out to do, people were horrified. 'What's he talking about? He's off his head. We still haven't won the Champions League!' From Pep's point of view however, he'd done his job. His players had learned what he'd set out to teach them. Obviously, there was still a lot to do, still trophies to fight for but the fundamental objectives of his mission in Germany had been realised.

This is undoubtedly an unusual point of view and it's therefore understandable that fans and media alike sometimes struggle to understand Pep. But Nick Faldo tells us that 'only the best want to improve themselves. That's what makes them the best.'

It's not enough to continue to learn and grow, you must also change. Never give in to complacency and always demand more of yourself. Reinvent yourself, change what you do or apply an old skill in a new context.

And practice makes perfect. Marina tells us that when Tchaikovski composed his Violin Concerto in 1878 Leopold Auer refused to perform it because he considered it 'impossible to play' but nowadays any reasonably talented music student can manage it with ease. It's all about practice.

Initially the Bayern players couldn't produce more than ten consecutive passes in a rondo without one of the players in the centre intercepting it, but three years later there are numerous clips showing lightning fast rondos where they reach fifty, sixty or more. How did that change? They practised, were corrected and they mastered the skill.

Professor Santiago Coca explains the purpose of training in these words, 'so that we play this game to the best of our ability and the players can express their talents'. Marina says that talent 'isn't like a scarce and highly coveted gemstone . . . That's an outmoded view and is the antithesis of any kind of creative vision of an intelligence which is capable of creating and developing what we are able to do, our inner resources and our talents.'

Talent isn't a gift. It's the process of channelling our resources in the best manner. And how do we do that? Through practice and training. We are all born with a certain genetic make-up but, as Marina says, 'not all our genetic attributes will be fully expressed. Everything in our immediate environment impacts this process and education is one of the elements in our environment. In fact, education is the element that generates the talent.' In football terms, training is the education the players receive and through it they activate and express the genetic elements that allow them to excel at football.

Arrigo Sacchi has said something similar, 'The coach's objective is to construct a footballer through training and playing. To win you need intelligence and hard work and I've always said that this is a team sport, not one played by eleven individuals. But each person matters, as do his particular characteristics and talents. All footballers have to love the sport. They have to be honest, hard workers. And they need talent although that isn't the main criteria. Our job is to develop each player so that eventually the team moves like a single unit.'

Julio Velasco poses this question, 'Perhaps we coaches prioritise talent because we don't want to have to work too hard?'

We talk of a coach 'training' his men but this is misleading. The coach teaches and guides his players but he can't 'do' the training for them. In this sense training involves the player expressing all his abilities: physical, technical, tactical, intellectual, emotional, competitive. A good coach facilitates this process and nurtures his players' talents. 'In terms of epigenetics, our genetic inheritance constitutes the origin of a process of growth which involves continuous adjustments and balances,' says Marina.

And for Pep, experimentation is a vital part of the learning process, 'If you want to learn you have to experiment. It's not enough just to do what other people tell you to do. The only way to correct a defect is to first have suffered its consequences.'

There's no more instructive experience than defeat. Stefan Zweig wrote in *Fouché*, 'Nothing weakens any artist, any general, any statesman more than constantly getting his own way. It's only in failure that the artist recognises his real relationship with his work, only in defeat that the general sees his own mistakes and only in his fall from grace that the statesman comes to fully understand the political system. Long term wealth makes you soft and sustained applause blunts your edge. Only by braking do we bring a new tension and creative elasticity to the spinning wheel. Only by suffering do we develop a deeper, broader understanding of the realities of life.' And, I'd like to add, living in need is stimulating to the senses.

Guardiola has experienced relatively few defeats in his career as a coach: scarcely 10% of his games have ended in failure, a better percentage than any other coach in history. He's rated No.1 in the

Elo rating system with 2,151 points, ahead of the late Hans Pesser (an Austrian player and coach) who has 2,143 points.

However, because being defeated is a relatively rare occurrence for him, he tends to remember the details of the matches he's lost. Not the unimportant ones, such as the five games he lost in the Bundesliga once Bayern had secured the title (out of a total 102 matches played in Germany, Pep lost only nine). On the other hand, his defeat against Real Madrid in the Champions League will be forever etched on his mind because he blames himself for failing to stick to his own ideas and Bayern's Champions League game against Atlético has also stayed with him, although on that occasion bad luck was to blame rather than human error.

We say that losing can be a valuable lesson but I'm not so sure. Often, we're so busy making excuses that we make no effort to understand what's happened and the reasons for it. It's also tempting to simply ignore anything that feels too painful. This is something Guardiola works particularly hard to do well: to analyse his defeats so that he can learn from them. After a brutal defeat against Wolfsburg in early 2015, in part caused by the failure of the new tactics Pep had just introduced, he wrote 'the bible' up on his office whiteboard. This would be his tactical guide for all future planning and from that day to this he always, always refers to it before putting the final seal of approval on his match day plans.

## THE ANSWER'S IN 'THE BIBLE'
### Munich, 2 February 2015

The game's been a disaster and a dejected Bayern troop out of the Volkswagen Arena after an agonising 4-1 defeat. Guardiola's new tactics haven't worked. His team were unrecognisable out there today. Fractured, weak and totally disorganised. He set out with the best of intentions but it's been a fiasco. He wanted to give them an added advantage, another weapon in their armoury, another variant in an already tactically complex game. His men had understood his proposition and had practised long and hard all week. His idea was to move straight to attack mode once they got the ball, without waiting for the classic Bayern reorganisation. But today it's all gone to hell and after the game Pep tells his assistants that they won't be using the tactic again. He goes over the game in detail, analysing every move and mistake and the process leads to a more inspired idea: he's going to write 'the bible'.

He's got a new office in the training ground. It had been difficult to concentrate in the original one which sits between the massage therapy room and the canteen. His new office is more isolated, tucked away at the end of the second floor corridor and he's had the walls painted with a special wipe-off finish. It's like having gigantic whiteboards all around him and he records everything there instead of on the little yellow slips that used to be scattered all over his desk. And that's where he writes 'the bible', three short, simple sentences written in red:
- Two against four in attack
- An extra man in midfield
- An extra man in defence

Pep insists on analysing his victories with the same critical eye, which is why he's often taciturn and silent after a win. He might look like a man who has no idea how to celebrate whereas in fact he's just trying to find the lessons, anything he needs to do better. Kaspárov sheds some light on this, 'When things go badly we naturally want to do better next time but we should always be looking for ways to improve, even when things are going well. Not doing so just leads to stagnation.' And Guardiola agrees, 'It's when you win that you have to be most vigilant.'

The final word goes to the great Benjamin Britten. 'Learning is like rowing against the current. If you stop rowing, you'll start going backwards.' Learning is the motor of all evolution.

## CULTIVATING TALENT THROUGH GOOD HABITS

> I want my coach to correct me
> when I do things badly.
> *Stephen Curry*

Spaniard Jesús Candelas is a futsal coach who argues that the search for improvement must be ongoing, 'Even when we're at the top of our game we should still be asking "where can I improve?"'

And the answer should be: 'Everything, always.' There should be no barriers to development and growth. But how do we achieve this? By cultivating talent. We've already seen that talent is a process rather than a natural gift so it makes sense that it's something that can be cultivated through constant practice. José Antonio Marina strikes a note of caution here, 'Not all kinds of practice bring improvement. It has to be "directed practice", in other words, a well-planned, very specific training session which provides what I call, "profound learning". It's not about just repeating a particular action, it's about having clear objectives and doing it to the right standard. Malcolm Gladwell's suggestion that 10,000 hours' practice is enough to become an expert in something has been widely discredited for one good reason: practice must be effective and well-directed in order to yield the desired results. There's absolutely no point in doing 10,000 hours of the wrong thing.'

Marina continues, 'Of course, anybody can claim that anyone can achieve anything as long as they have the right training but it's undoubtedly true that no-one becomes "a great talent" without doing a lot of work. Moreover, once you get to a certain ability level, it's only "directed practice" that makes the difference.' Experiments carried out by the Berlin Academy of Music proved that the one thing that distinguished the virtuoso students from their peers was the amount of work and practice each did. Remember Julio Velasco's words: 'A coach should approach his work like a craftsman, not like a shop steward. That's where the real joy is. We are the artisans of the training and formation of sportsmen.'

We've already seen the huge strides made by Guardiola's players at Bayern (notably Boateng, Kimmich, Neuer, Lahm and Costa), but it's important to recognise the investment made by the coaching team and the players: 835 training sessions, 161 official games, 37 friendlies, 530 team talks and about 2,000 one-to-one sessions watching and analysing videos. This is equivalent to more than 1,500 hours of playing time and practice as well as another 1,500 office-based hours. In other words Pep's players invested around 3,000 hours in this process of 'profound learning'.

## ONE LAST TIME
### Munich, 19 January 2016

It's Tuesday and Pep spends a large part of today's training session having his men practise his new ideas about how to press and rob the ball then move straight into position for the attack. It's been pretty gruelling and the second time this week they've focused on this move. They've done two and a half hours already and the coach's still shouting, 'Das Letzte!' ('One last time!')

The players all know that it's anything but. Medhi Benatia trots back on to the training pitch. He's just come back from the treatment room and he's chuckling, 'We all know damn well that when he yells "Das Letzte!" he doesn't really mean it. We learned long ago that it only stops when he says, "Lads, I promise, it really is the last time."'

Pep's not yet reached that stage and he goes on and on demanding more as the clock ticks and the shadows lengthen over Säbener Strasse. They're almost on their

> knees, completely shattered when at last he says the magic
> words, 'Lads, I promise . . .'
>     Benatia gives me a wink, 'Now it's over.'

American philosopher William James said that life was nothing more than the sum total of our habits and researchers at Duke University estimate that more than 40% of what we do every day doesn't involve spontaneous actions; we're just repeating habits.

José Antonio Marina explains the importance of habit, 'We have a limited capacity to undertake new activities in a focused and concentrated manner. Think back to learning to drive or if you've ever tackled a new language. These things require intense concentration and can be exhausting. But there's a stage at which it starts to become automatic. The actions become habits and you can perform them without thinking. It's habits that help us develop our perceptive and moral sense and our intellectual and motor skills. Education is basically the acquisition of habits.' Marina's words echo those of Greek philosopher Aristotle, 'We are what we repeatedly do. Excellence, then, is not a single act but a habit.'

Coach Fran Beltrán wrote, 'You know you're playing good football when you don't have to think about it anymore and that's why players have to train, to build habits.' This is true of all sports. If Usain Bolt started his races pondering the fine points of running, he'd never win. If Stephen Curry stopped to think about how to aim at a basketball net, he'd always miss and if Leo Messi deliberated every time he took a shot, he'd never score. All of these men do their thinking (usually under intense pressure) in training (their 'directed practice') not when they're competing. The habits they acquire at training are a vital part of understanding the dynamic nature of intelligence and the success of the action carried out. Emma Stone has said that she only knows one way to sing well live, 'A lot of practice. You have to learn the song inside and out. It's only when you know it really well that you can afford to improvise.'

But how do we reconcile this idea of constant repetition with the complexities of football? Paco Seirul.lo has the answer, 'We repeat specific elements of our game but always vary our approach. Because if I keep doing the same thing over and over again, you're eventually going to notice and catch me out. So we have to simulate situations where automatic repetition doesn't work. If our game is too repetitive then we'll never win because everything we do will be so predictable. We have to watch and develop the way our players interact. It's not about using a different vocabulary. It's about working with different concepts.' The interaction between players is a fundamental part of football and the synergy this creates can make a crucial difference to the team's success. It's a consideration for any coach as he plans his ideal line-up. He may choose not to go for his best players, but rather those who work best together. Getting the right mix might be down to the coach's instincts and vision, or the players might indicate what they'd prefer or it might emerge naturally over time.

'Profound learning' only occurs when everyone is committed to continual progression and the 'student' is guided and corrected along the way. As Marina says, 'The pupil must know immediately if he's performing well or not. Practising without knowing how you're doing is like playing bowls with the scoreboard covered up. The evaluation must happen soon after the act itself.'

In March 2016 in Dortmund, many onlookers were surprised to see Guardiola speaking to Kimmich about a mistake whilst he was still on the pitch. At the time it seemed a strange thing to do but, in retrospect, was it really so unusual? Think about the chess players who meet up after a game to carry out a painstaking and often painful analysis. Even the US army has discovered the importance of post-operation analysis. West Point Academy's Colonel Thomas Kolditz confirms as much: 'Doing this has literally completely transformed the way the army works.'

# SORT IT OUT NOW
## Dortmund, 5 March 2016

Pep believes in sorting things out on the spot. It's always been an obsession for him but this season he's taking it to an extreme. Of late, he's been very sure of himself, very certain in his convictions and has not allowed even the slightest infraction of the dressing room rules. He's also more rigorous than ever in terms of how he corrects his players' mistakes.

His men have really messed up the last few minutes of their 0-0 draw against Borussia Dortmund (although it's no big deal because the league title's almost in the bag), so, after hugging Tuchel goodbye, Pep heads straight for Medhi Benatia, who's still out on the pitch, having come on for Xabi Alonso in the last minute.

'Medhi, did you give Kimmich his instructions?'

'Sure Pep, I told him but there was a lot of noise.'

The coach runs over to Kimmich.

'Did you hear Benatia's instructions?'

'Sorry Pep, I didn't.'

'Fuck! You were meant to move into centre midfield!'

'I'm really sorry. I just didn't hear him.'

'I wanted you to move in front of the defensive line and maintain that position but instead you moved away from that organising position and we lost control. I need you to listen when people pass on my instructions.'

'I'm so sorry. I had no idea . . .'

Then it's all over and Pep gives Kimmich a hug. The young player's like a son to him.

'You were brilliant out there today, Josh. Really, really good. I told you you could do it!'

'Thanks Pep. It was a hard game but I did okay in the end.'

'What do you mean "okay"? You fucking aced it. You were bloody sensational Josh. Sensational! I'm so proud of you.'

So can the application of 'directed practice' ever go wrong in football? Not really, as long as the coach provides immediate correction and demands the sustained, intense work that allows his players to develop the right habits. Good habits allow talent to shine.


## THE IMPORTANCE OF RECALL

One's memory is the only paradise
we can never lose
*Jean Paul*

Talent isn't a gift, it's a process. The coach cultivates his players' talents through training, practice and immediate correction. This process then creates habits. His players don't need to think about what they're doing, they just do it, interacting with each other so that synergy is created.

But how does a coach ensure that his men retain his teachings? Well, memory is the basis of human intelligence and talent arises from the most efficient use of memory. So a coach must focus on helping his players remember what they learn. Nobody was surprised when Pep dedicated most of his early training sessions in Manchester to showing his players how he likes play to start: bringing the ball out from the back, constructing the play in a particular direction as well as pressing and regaining possession. As we'll see, he had some very good reasons for doing so.

Pep was driving back from a week's holiday in Switzerland in June 2015 and was chatting to me with his phone on hands free. 'I've been thinking about the football calendar – the way we have to play a game every three days. It just doesn't give us enough time to prepare all the tactical variants I want to use. The lads have mastered defending with either three or four at the back – they can switch rapidly between the two but there's a lot more still to do. There are so many little details left to cover and there's no way on earth we can keep training the way we do. I've thought about it long and hard over the holidays and have already talked it through with Dome [Torrent] and Loren [Buenaventura]. I've decided, from next season on, to start moving into small groups to work on all the little details.

'So, we'll start, say, at 10 am with the midfielders and defenders and work on the relevant tactics and moves with them. Even if it's just half an hour, it'll be worth it. Then, an hour later, we'll do the same with the attacking midfielders and the strikers. So they're not spending longer in training but what we do is better targeted and more efficient.' Pep implemented his plan and followed this routine at least once a week from then on. But he was left dissatisfied. There just wasn't time to cover everything he wanted to in training.

In February 2016, just after the announcement of his departure, the two of us were taking a stroll in Munich when he said, 'In football we just don't have enough time to train. That's why we have to focus on tactics. There's no way we can afford to spend two weeks of our pre-season working on fitness and speed. That's really the only time of the year that we can give them in-depth training: learning, implementing, understanding and correcting the tactical game we're going to play.

'Concepts, concepts and more concepts. They need to learn it all right at the start and then we'll spend the whole year developing it.'

This is the main reason that he expanded his technical team at Manchester. He now has Domènec Torrent, Brian Kidd, Carles Planchart, Mikel Arteta and Rodolfo Borrell working with him as well as Lorenzo Buenaventura and his fitness team and Xabi Mancisidor, goalkeeping coach. This will allow Pep to work with small groups on different tactical aspects of the game whilst his assistants focus on other parts of the training plan. His objective is to increase the number of hours dedicated to improving tactical expertise.

In fact he used his very first training session at City (5 July 2016) to run through some tactical ideas with the players which he'll work on again during the season. His idea is to provide total immersion in the tactical fundamentals of his game which he can then follow up throughout the season leading short, specific sessions in small groups so that the players 'remember' the concepts they've learned. This process will be further enriched by the experimentation that will also happen throughout the competition.

According to Ortega and Gasset, 'To be truly imaginative you need to have a good memory.' And Björn Borg also recognises the importance of memory, 'The secret of staying cool under great pressure is preparation and practice so that your muscular memory functions all by itself.'

In his book, *Endgame*, Frank Brady explains how Bobby Fischer prepared in the run-up to beating Borís Spassky in the World Chess Championships. As well as spending many hours training, Fischer made one book his constant companion for six months: *Weltgeschichte des Schachs* (*The History of World Chess, Volume 27*), which described in detail 355 of Spassky's games with a diagram for every five moves. Fischer made copious notes, marking Spassky's missteps with a red question mark and his clever moves with an exclamation mark. And then he memorised them all. 355 games and 14,000 individual moves. For the next few months Fischer enlisted the assistance of friends to help him practice. He would ask his friend to pick any game from the book, tell him the location and the name of Spassky's opponent and then he would recite every movement. Perfectly.

Memory supports the creative process and when they play, footballers are in a constant process of recalling what they have learned and absorbing and filing away what is happening in the moment. Steven Rose describes memory this way, 'The act of remembering creates another memory so that the next time we bring it to mind, we're not actually remembering the initial event, but the memory created the last time we thought about it.'

# LONG BALLS DOWN THE OUTSIDE
## Munich, 5 October 2015

Thomas Tuchel's Borussia Dortmund come to the Allianz Arena today so far unbeaten this season (eleven wins in fourteen games). Bayern are also unbeaten and this crucial league match promises to be an epic clash. Pep's worked throughout the week around the basic idea of a 3-4-3 which can, thanks to Müller's versatility, switch to a 3-3-1-3 or a 3-3-4 in attack, a 4-4-2 without the ball and a 4-5-1 if they have to defend in the penalty area.

They then find out that Tuchel's put half of his men into completely new positions. In the Bayern dressing room nobody's getting too worked up about it however. Captain Lahm nips over to Pep's office and knocks on the door:

'Have you seen their line-up Pep? We'll need to play using width and sending the ball long.'

'Spot on Philipp. Use the wings, and pass it long from the back.'

'Are you going to talk to the lads?'

'I'll have a quick word. Will you tell Jérôme [Boateng], Xabi [Alonso] and Thiago to come and see me.'

Within minutes the three players and their captain are standing in Pep's office. This won't take long so nobody sits down. Pep talks them through what's going to happen.

'They're using loads of midfielders to fill the centre of the park so remember what we've worked on. We have to avoid playing through the middle. Xabi and Thiago, send the ball wide. Jérôme, lots of long balls from you. If we do pass inside make them low, vertical and hard so that they can't steal the ball from us. Just remember the things we've worked on and you'll be okay.'

Bayern go ahead early on thanks to a long ball from

Boateng to Müller (the defender sprints over to high five his coach) and then, in the break the coach reminds his men what they've learned during the week, using some video clips prepared by Carles Planchart.

'We're moving forward down the outside, avoiding the inside as much as possible. We only look for Lewy, Müller or Götze on the inside if Jérôme can give us hard, low passes. If not, we go for long passes and play over the top of their pressure.'

Bayern win 5-1 (Boateng provides another assist with a fifty metre pass) and afterwards Tuchel declares, 'Bayern surprised us with their long balls.'

The Bayern players explain what happened. Xabi Alonso: 'Pep has shown us a whole range of tactical approaches and we can change our game at the drop of a hat, whenever we need to.' Jérôme Boateng: 'During a game all it takes is a signal from Pep and we all understand the tactical change he wants. He just gives us a sign and we all know exactly what to do next.'

How do we define 'intelligence' in a player? A smart player will have a good memory, he'll have absorbed the hundreds of instructions he's received during training and he'll retain them so that his brain can activate the process of synaptic transmission when the time's right.

Of course it doesn't always work and there were many days in Munich when the combination of habitual practice and good recall just wasn't enough. On those occasions they had to rip up the plans, re-organise and rely on a bit of improvisation.

## A LITTLE PIECE OF PAPER
### Munich, 12 December 2015

'We're sunk, Dome. We're going nowhere like this.'

'Yes, we've definitely stalled. We need to make some changes.'

'We could put Lahm on the wing but if we push Philipp forward, we'll have to change everything behind him.'

'It's definitely radical. We'd have to make loads of other changes.'

'Let's do it.'

Bayern's first half performance against FC Ingolstadt has been disappointing. Pep's men have lost their ordered, controlled football and their defenders are struggling to cope with the visitors' aggressive pressing.

This is the second time in a row they've faced an opponent who hasn't opted to sit back but has gone for targeted attacks on Bayern's midfielders and defenders, thereby preventing them from building their game by playing out via their keeper. Vidal initially plays in the pivot position but due to the lack of order in Bayern's play that decision lasts barely twenty minutes. Kimmich takes over in organising midfield and Vidal plays left midfield. Javi Martínez plays to Kimmich's right. Bayern might have scored in the first half, a lob by Lewandowski that Ingolstadt's defence manage to clear, but Neuer's saved them twice from going a goal behind.

During the break the coaching team discuss how their team can regain control. They decide to bring Thiago on for Vidal but Ingolstadt have made some changes and moved into phase two of their plan: they've tightened up at the back and their formidable defensive line is neutralising all of Coman's excellent runs on the right wing.

'If we push Lahm up on the wing, we'll need to make eight changes of position and switch to a completely different playing formation.'

Domènec Torrent's got it right. Pep's suggestion means

driving a horse and cart through the team's current formation but the coach is determined: 'We're trapped Dome. We need a massive shake-up. It's got to be this way. Let's do this now.'

It's going to be better to sketch out the new positions on a piece of paper than use his usual sign language. There's just no way all eight players will be able to work out what he wants from a few hand signals. In the fifty-eighth minute Pep grabs his chance during a throw-in. He hands Lahm the piece of paper with his instructions. He wants the team to move to a 4-2-4 and he wants the following eight changes:

- Lahm moves up to the right wing
- Coman goes to the left wing
- Rafinha swaps side to become right back
- Badstuber moves into the left back position
- Javi Martínez moves back to left-sided centre back
- Thiago abandons his left attacking midfield role and plays alongside Kimmich as a 'double pivot'
- Lewandowski moves from the left and into position as a centre forward
- Müller changes from the No.10 role and plays as joint centre forward with Lewandowski.

Lahm quickly reads the instructions and takes just over a minute to pass them on. He runs over to Coman and talks him through the changes to be made then does the same with Javi, who passes the paper on to Thiago, Rafinha and Badstuber. There's a convenient corner kick to defend and Lahm uses the time to communicate the changes to Bayern's strikers.

Pep's changes do the trick: Bayern's players are now in exactly the right positions to start to pressurise and disorientate Ingolstadt's defence.

Without necessarily hitting the heights, the home side's play becomes more fluid, more coherent. Having two wingers and two central strikers hugely increases the passing options for the Bayern midfield and Boateng with his long passes.

And that's how the opening goal comes. Lewandowski breaks from his marker, Boateng puts the ball into space in front of him. The Polish striker dances around the advancing keeper and scores his fifteenth goal in sixteen league games. This was Boateng's third goal-assist pass, a stat that underlines his ever increasing importance to the team. He's been an excellent central defender but he's now become a fundamental part of the entire construction of Bayern's game.

Minutes later Coman, Müller and Lewandowski show just how well they manage space when their expert play leaves Lahm clear to score the second goal of the afternoon. He slams it away with his left leg and will joke with the press later that this was the instruction Pep had given him, 'Pep's note said that he wanted me to score with my left foot.'

If memory and habitual practice are a vital part of football then today's experience (and a little piece of paper) has been the exception which proves the rule.


## LANGUAGE AS A WEAPON OF CONFUSION

*The limits of my language are the limits of my mind*
*Ludwig Wittgenstein*


We've already seen the crucial role memory plays in any footballer's development. Now for another key part of the process: the way in which the coach passes on his knowledge. Football coaches tend to spend a limited number of years at a club before moving on and must decide whether their impact lasts only for the duration of their contract or whether the knowledge they pass on becomes a long-term legacy. Whatever their intention, every coach must confront, on a daily basis, one of the greatest challenges any manager can face: how to communicate effectively with his players.

Communication is enormously difficult and language, at times, only adds to the confusion. I'm not just thinking here about multi-lingual teams like Bayern. Words can be confusing, whether spoken in your mother tongue or not. And there's another aggravating factor. In football, communication usually takes place at moments of stress. An instruction given in the heat of competition, at a moment of tension or disappointment or when the player is exhausted is easily misinterpreted. It's no-one's fault. Human communication is imperfect because we ourselves are imperfect. We talk about 'the universal language of football' and there's no doubt that, on one level, football does transcend cultural and language barriers. At a deeper level however, I'd argue that the language of football has become universally confusing.

Richard Sennett, the Centennial Professor of Sociology at the London School of Economics and University Professor of the Humanities at New York University, says, 'What we can say with words is perhaps more limited than what we can do with things. It's possible that the craftsman's work [and football is the work of a craftsman] establishes a field of manual dexterity and knowledge that transcends our capacity to explain it: even the most accomplished of writers would balk at the idea of describing how to tie a slip knot, for example.'

There are lots of good anecdotes about messages and instructions being 'lost in translation' in sport. Take Jeff Van Gundy, the Houston Rockets' coach, who said of his Chinese pivot, Yao Ming, 'He only understands half of what I say . . . Just like any other foreign or American player.' And another basketball coach, Kresimir Cosic, might well have considered a player understanding even 50% pretty good going. The Croat famously said of Stojan Vrankovic, 'I told him he'd earn a place if he put his arse into training and his head into the game. Seems like he got it the wrong way round.'

It's not easy for any coach to transmit his knowledge through words and images. Guardiola doesn't like using computer simulated training programmes because no virtual football pitch can convey the exact movements he wants his players to use or the dynamics of a real game of football. And his tactical plans cover such a complex range of combinations and permutations that words alone could never accurately convey them.

Which is why he makes so much use of video footage, 'I use videos to demonstrate my ideas. Without them, training would be exhausting.' All of us can relate to what he's saying, I'm sure. Putting up a shelf wouldn't be the same without the helpful little diagrams in the instructions manual and even then, it can be an excruciating process. And as for tying a slip knot . . . a teach-yourself video or a live demonstration would definitely be required.

Seirul.lo recognises the difficulty of communicating effectively, 'When the coach says, "I want you to press," what does it really mean? It could mean that everyone heads straight for the ball so the players closest to it will obviously get there before the guys who are further away. Or you could take it to mean that you wait until the guy with the ball goes wide and then only the players closest to him start to press. Or it could mean that you have to wait till the ball crosses the half-way line and moves into an area where there are fewer rival players. That's when you press because it'll be easier to rob the ball. And so on and so forth. These are all perfectly clear, sensible interpretations and yet they also confuse the issue enormously. As a rule everything in football is clear yet confusing. Why do I say that? Because we all know that the same results will not always follow the same actions. Nobody ever manages to define it with any precision.

'That's why there's so much confusion between coaches and their players. Every country tries to address this issue as part of their training programmes for coaches but what one country thinks of as breaking free of a marking scheme, for example, might be totally different from the way they define it in another country. It's not just about language. It's to do with differences in the way concepts are understood and defined. Each nation's game is rooted in the particular traditions of that country. Probably because we play it with our feet. If we used our hands it would never have put down the kind of roots it has.

'Everyone in basketball uses the same terminology because the lexicon was established by the NBA. It's a different story in football where we don't even use the same numbers for positions on the field. In basketball everybody's clear about what a No.1 is and the only variants are in what that player should do: score from a distance, pass, dribble etc . . . Everything else is taken as read: this guy's a No.1 and that guy's a No.2. There are universal names for every position because the NBA oversaw this process. But the origins of football are quite different. Football started out being played on the street and people used their own terminology to describe what happened. As its popularity increased so too did the terminology that was used. If you consider that there are some countries who still have no official coaching academies, it makes sense that people are still using different terminology to describe the same concept.'

There's no way of establishing precisely what percentage of Guardiola's instructions during training sessions are understood by his players. What is clear however is that when he first arrived at Bayern, the players grasped very little of what he meant and by the time he left they were absorbing almost everything. Clearly, the ability to absorb and comprehend new information and knowledge varies from player to player. The obvious way to ensure effective communication is to keep repeating what you say, try to improve how you communicate and back up your explanations with detailed correction on the pitch, using the process of 'trial and error' over and over again until the message goes in. But there's a problem here. Doing it this way demands a great deal of time, the one resource which is in desperately short supply in modern football. Guardiola believes that the way he communicates has a primary role in the progress and transformation of his players and has therefore invested time and effort in improving his own communication skills and finding the best resources to aid this process. In truth however verbal/written language and audiovisual tools have enormous limitations. There's another way to communicate effectively.

## FOOTBALL AS A METALANGUAGE

A pass connects, a ball thumped long isolates.
There are coaches who teach what's both basic and difficult:
How the players can connect with each other.
*Diego Latorre*

Another good way to ensure the effective transfer of knowledge from coach to player is the use of a 'metalanguage': their own language containing all the relevant vocabulary they'll need to describe the particular concepts and playing models they use. Or in other words, the use of football as a language in its own right.

Previously, I've written about the 'Barça language'. I was trying to define the work of La Masia (youth football) where Barça's young players were developed and I realised that the teaching methods and playing models they used there actually constitute a language. Coaches, trainers and players all use a distinct vocabulary to refer to the football they practise: codes used in both written and spoken form, special terminology and a distinctive numbering system.

'The interactions between players consist of passing, trajectory, the use of space, advantage,' observed Paco Seirul.lo. 'There are ways to observe the game which allow you to see if an idea is being fully implemented or not. But clearly, in order to observe correctly you must first understand the elements that make up the playing model. It's impossible if you only look at the move, and ignore the passes which create it. Every pass is a message. There are players who give neutral passes, "Here you are. Make what you can out of that." But other players are saying, "Here you are, do your best." Or "Here, have a bit of fun." These are passes with intention, they express something and there's only one player who has achieved true mastery of this kind of pass: Andres Iniesta. Iniesta passes the ball like a father teaching his little son tennis for the first time. He sends every ball with exactly the right force and to precisely the right place because he wants his child to hit the ball easily and have a good time. This is exactly what Iniesta does only he's playing at the top level of the sport with other elite footballers. With Andres the message is, "Here, do your best and have some fun," whereas for most players it's, "Here, make what you can out of this." With his passes Iniesta tells his teammate how to continue the conversation, that is, the game.'

Seirul.lo believes that football is indeed a language, a 'metalanguage' in which a pass is a means of communication, the playing model is the grammar we need to master and the codes, numbers and terminology, the alphabet.

Barcelona developed their own language in the 1990s inspired by the work of Johan Cruyff, a football genius, and the hard, patient work of dozens of coaches who themselves became fluent in the 'Barça language'.

Guardiola is a native speaker and made sure that his players at Barcelona mastered the language to a level of absolute fluency. Now at City, as he faces the enormous challenge of trying to win the Premier League he must make a crucial decision. Should he communicate with the players in the traditional way or should he attempt to go one step further and lay the foundations of a new 'City language'? Such an undertaking would require a great deal of time, resources and a huge amount of collective energy and dedication. It would also ensure that the legacy he leaves involves much more than cherished silverware and fond memories.

Pep's conscious that this is an opportunity. Manchester City is the ideal place to create a unique 'football language' and the club offers all the necessary resources: an academy, youth teams, a large team of 'teachers', the backing of the institution itself . . . All he needs to do is unite all these elements and work on them with care and patience.

Pep's sophisticated football ideology was created in Holland, developed in Barcelona and enhanced in Germany. Hopefully England will mark a new milestone in its progression. Our protagonist possesses the charisma, energy and passion required to create a new language. But does he want to try? Will he even have time to establish a complete, comprehensible language that will last for generations? Does he have the vision and conviction to do it? Does he have the support he'll need to see it through? Or, to paraphrase James Kerr, is he prepared to 'sow the seeds of the trees he'll never see grow?'

## SHARING KNOWLEDGE

If I've learned anything it's because I've always had my eyes open
*Alessandro del Piero*

Now for the choice any coach makes when he leaves a club: does he leave all his knowledge behind him or not?

The great Roman architect, Marco Vitruvio wrote, 'The different arts consist of two things: craftsmanship and theory. The craftsmanship belongs [only] to the people who have practised and mastered it; the theory is then shared with all educated people.'

In football terms, Guardiola is a craftsman. But he also shares and communicates theory. Pep left Barcelona in 2012 after having established an ambitious project to document everything relating to their positional play. And to this day he continues to collaborate with the Catalan club. He's preferred to keep this work quiet and will probably not be happy that I'm sharing this, but I think Barça's supporters will be delighted to know that Guardiola continues to contribute ideas, information and documentation.

Equally, when he left Bayern, Pep left all the documentation relating to the exercises and playing models he developed in Munich since arriving there in 2013, including detailed notes about specific tactics. I think Bayern fans might also be interested in this information. He left all of this in the custody of Hermann Gerland, his assistant coach, who's been a permanent fixture at Bayern since the 1990s.

I've no idea precisely how Barcelona and Bayern will use this documentation in the future but both clubs can be sure that they have in their possession a cultural/tactical guide of the highest order. What's clear is that Guardiola doesn't fear sharing his knowledge with others. Just consider his close friendship with rival, Thomas Tuchel. Pep had no hesitation in sharing the details of his playing model with him and he's done exactly the same with the many coaches (from all levels of football) who visited him at Säbener Strasse: Sampaoli, Zidane, Dorival Júnior, Sanvicente, Gattuso, Fran Beltrán, Patricia González . . . More than fifty of his peers came to Munich to seek his guidance and opinions.

Pep's wife, Cristina Serra, told me, 'I think Pep shares too much in your book. Too much tactical information. He's very open about these things in his press conferences too. Other coaches don't do that. Some of them share absolutely nothing, they obfuscate and refuse to give away the tiniest detail about their tactics. Any coach who reads your book will get a complete rundown of Pep's tactics . . .'

Her comments define Guardiola's character to perfection. He feels that he should share his ideology, without worrying that others will steal his ideas, copy them and exploit his weaknesses. He instinctively knows that his own development is partly dependent on the pressure he's put under by his rivals.

And the greater his opponent, the better for everyone, most of all for football: 'Great coaches like Mourinho made me better,' he told the Manchester press on his first day. But should coaches care about the development and growth of the sport or is it better to focus solely on winning? Each person must decide for himself, depending on his/her personal ideology but in Guardiola's case the answer's obvious.

For Pep there's also an element of 'giving something back'. As a rookie coach, and as a player with an interest in coaching, Pep benefited from the guidance and counsel of illustrious men like Bielsa, Menotti, Cruyff, Lillo, Julio Velasco, Sacchi, Mazzone. He now believes that, having reached the top, he too should lend a hand to others and is always happy, as far as his hectic schedule allows, to speak to any young coach who's interested in his methodology. He also makes it a priority to support and guide players who have the potential to move into coaching. Men like Xavi, Busquets, Milito, Mascherano and Iniesta in Barcelona and Xabi Alonso, Badstuber, Schweinsteiger, Javi Martínez, Rafinha and Neuer at Bayern. The goalkeeper in particular is a superb reader of the game who soaks up knowledge and information. Pep invested a great deal of time talking tactics in Munich, particularly with Neuer and Xabi Alonso. 'I'm delighted if I help a player on the way to becoming a coach in the future. Johan and others did it for me and it's right and proper that I do it now with my players.'

Sociologist Richard Sennett points out that Robert K. Merton 'tried to explain this process of the transfer of knowledge in science through his famous "on the shoulders of giants" idea. The phrase referred to two concepts: the fact that the work of great scientists establishes the terms of reference for those who follow them; and that knowledge is, by its very nature, cumulative. It expands over time as human beings climb on to the shoulders of giants, just like acrobats in a circus creating a human tower.'

And this is exactly the reason for the efforts of coaches like Juanma Lillo to document, 'intellectualise' and describe in detail the theory behind positional play (and develop it into the game of 'disposition'). It's also why Guardiola refuses to treat his own knowledge and ideas as if they were military secrets. Perhaps I need to be absolutely clear on this point. On a day to day level, (strategic and tactical planning, line-ups etc) Guardiola insists on a 'closed door' approach. The tactics his team practise during the week are the tools he'll use for competitive matches in the coming days. When the coach does share he carefully limits his explanations to his theories regarding his playing model and a general description of his methodologies, in other words, his football philosophy.

I'd just like to finish by saying that football is a combination of ideas which travel the world on the backs of those coaches who create them. Perhaps that's for a future book . . .

# BACKSTAGE 8

## MÜLLER, A SURPRISING ICON
### Gelsenkirchen, 21 November 2015

Domènec Torrent's absolutely clear, 'Müller epitomises the way the team has changed under Pep's tutelage. They've all absorbed everything he's taught and Thomas is the symbol of that process.'

If there's one player who, three years ago, was light years away from Guardiola's ideas and attitudes, it's Thomas Müller. Not because he wasn't interested in what the coach had to say but because of the kind of man he is. With almost any other player it was possible to identify characteristics or patterns of behaviour that made them, potentially, the perfect symbols of the transformative power of Guardiola's training and methodology. But not Müller.

The talented and super-efficient Neuer might be a likely candidate, or Lahm, with his natural intelligence and superb skill. Or perhaps you'd consider midfielders Xabi and Thiago more emblematic of Pep's playing style, one for his talent at distributing the ball, the other for his sheer creativity. Rafinha and Badstuber's resolve and determination might be what stands out for you or Coman and Rode's humility. And let's not forget Alaba's versatility, Martínez's aggression in defence or indeed the enormous progress made by Boateng. And what about those three expert dribblers, Robben, Costa and Ribéry, each one a key part of Guardiola's game along with Lewandowski, whose ability to adapt to rapid and radical change has defied all expectations. Any one of them might be said typify the characteristics of a 'Guardiola-type' player. But Müller? No way.

Thomas Müller is the antithesis of the kind of player Pep was looking for when he arrived at Bayern. He's not particularly technically talented, quite the contrary. He's lost more balls than any other Bayern player over the last two and a half years. He doesn't dribble particularly well and he's never been the fastest guy on the park. His headers are unexceptional and he could use some work on his shooting skills (with either foot), he loves to press his rivals but often does so with his head turned towards his own teammates, thereby losing sight of his real objective. Pep tried to convert him to an attacking midfielder but quickly had to admit defeat. Müller just didn't 'get it'.

And yet . . .

This is a prodigiously talented footballer. And not just because of his extraordinary knack for scoring goals, almost always from a strange angle or using an unusual part of his body. In fact, so distinctive is his style that a new word has entered the football lexicon in Germany where they now talk of the ball being 'Müllered' as it hits the back of the net.

It's not just his colossal scoring record though. The player is also admired for his boundless energy, his unstinting commitment to the team, his contagious optimism and his insatiable need to keep winning, no matter the circumstances. But it's more than even this. Müller possesses one special quality. He's *Die Raumdeuter* ('the Space Interpreter'), the man who appears in the right place at exactly the right moment. The nickname was coined by a group of fans on Football Manager during the World Cup who believed that this was the player's greatest talent: his ability to see and move into spaces nobody else has noticed at just the right time.

Before Guardiola arrived at Bayern Müller was already an established figure in the first team, having come through Hermann Gerland's youth system, been promoted by Louis Van Gaal and used as a most unorthodox striker by Jupp Heynckes. Pep also saw him as a valued team member and he played in 151 of his 161 games in charge. In other words, over the three-year period, Müller missed just ten games.

That's not to say however that the two men gelled from the start. In fact it took two long years before Pep was completely satisfied with the player's output. Time and again he asked his maverick striker to take on other functions within the team: as an inside forward, a winger or centre forward. But Müller continued to struggle with the demands of Pep's positional play despite the many flashes of genius he sporadically produced. Remember him as a false No.9 in Manchester in October 2013 or in Rome a year later thundering down the left in attack? As Lahm, Neuer, Boateng and Robben revelled in the new playing model, it looked at times as if Müller was drowning – until the solution presented itself in Pep's third season when he hit upon the idea of creating a special 'ecosystem' for his wayward striker. The effect was dazzling and the player's obvious delight in his new role was clear for all to see. Müller himself was happy to credit Guardiola publicly with the transformation, praising his coach as the force behind the hard work, adaptation and unity of the whole team.

Müller's ideal position was as second striker behind Lewandowski but his success was due less to his position than to how he interacted with the players around him. When the team was able to field two pure wingers like Costa and Coman, be open on the wing and able to send balls right into the penalty box, Müller's job became so much easier. Boateng and Xabi would pass him the ball which he would then send out to one of his teammates on the wing, running into the penalty box with Lewandowski, with whom he formed the most efficient of partnerships. Pep said of this moment of the game: 'It's not that I quite like my wingers to play open and very wide. It's absolutely essential to my game. What I like more is wingers playing on their natural side rather than off their wrong foot and coming in – although I've often used them that way. But just look at Gento, one of the greatest wingers in history [Paco Gento, the Real Madrid winger who won six European Cups between 1956 and 1966]. Gento played on his natural wing and he pushed and ran – chasing the ball to the line and then crossing. The reason that I like wingers who go outside and cross off their better foot is that when Costa or Coman hit the line and cross it allows Lewy and Müller to charge on to a ball which is curving out into their path.'

In order to create this powerful four-man attack (Lewandowski and Müller plus two wingers) it meant the team needed to have either one pure defender or a pure midfielder but that was something Pep now found easy to balance.

What mattered most was finding the best way to exploit Müller's special talent for finding space. In thr autumn

Müller was in top form and Guardiola was enjoying the tricks he would regularly perform during games. For example during the free kicks where he usually took charge of the set-up, sometimes pretending to fall over while running to kick the ball (like he did in the 2014 World Cup) or faking confusion with a teammate by bumping into him. But his fooling around didn't stop there. Whenever he was taking the kick-off, he'd keep his foot on the ball even after the referee blew the whistle, causing opponents to sprint across the halfway line before the ball had moved. That was the moment that Müller the showman would protest to the referee, demand that the offenders be sent back to their half at which point he'd instantly start the game and catch the other team confused, vexed and off balance. It would crack Pep up with laughter and Müller would do it repeatedly.

There was another factor helping Müller to adapt to the new playing model: the leadership responsibilities he had begun to show. Over the last two year the dressing room had had two unquestioned leaders: Lahm, the kind of quiet, reserved leader who directs and supports the emotional life of the team through his behaviour rather than with words; and Schweinsteiger, a more expressive, forceful character, whose body language always conveys exactly what he's thinking. Now things had changed because Schweinsteiger and Toni Kroos had gone and, although Xabi and Thiago had the right qualities to fill the role, both felt that the official team leaders should be German. It's a code that the two men take very seriously. But Thomas Müller was the perfect candidate. Lahm continued in his role of the calm, unperturbable captain, discreetly guiding his teammates without having to say too much and Müller became his volcanic sidekick. He was the one who laughed and joked, geed everyone up and shouted and yelled when necessary. He was the one who nagged them and kept them all in line.

On 9 November Bayern play a friendly in Ratisbona against Paulaner Team, an amateur side created especially for this competition and composed of players from around the world who have applied to take part. It's organised by one of Bayern's sponsors and Neuer and Müller, who are about to go off on international duty, play for just fifteen minutes. Pep uses the game to give some playing time to Badstuber, Kirchhoff and a few of the younger players. He also wants to try Philipp Lahm (aka Pipo) as a false No.9. This is a huge compliment from the coach who has already asked his captain to play in three of the defensive positions, three of the midfield positions and on the right wing. The only thing left to try (other than putting on the keeper's gloves) is the centre forward's position so today's his big chance. And it works: he gets one goal and shoots at goal eight times. It's entirely possible that Lahm's never enjoyed his football as much as he has today in this new position. Müller looks on in glee and files it away in his repertoire of jokes for later use.

Domènec Torrent's said that Müller's become the player who's most emblematic of Pep's time at Bayern and I'm interested in hearing what Pep has to say. 'Müller definitely symbolises the game we want and he interprets it brilliantly. It's one of the things that's given me most satisfaction:

making him a better player than he was before and, let's face it, he was already a superb player!'

'I'm more impressed with him every day,' says Torrent.

'I was always a fan,' agrees Pep.

'Pep, remember what happened when we were down to ten men [Badstuber had been sent off in the fifty-second minute], and immediately had to face a corner. Benatia wasn't on yet and Thomas had to take charge of our whole defensive organisation. He signalled to the other guys and everyone immediately knew what to do.'

Perhaps Bastian Schweinsteiger's departure has forced Müller to take on a greater leadership role?

'I hadn't thought about it before,' muses Pep, 'but it might well be the reason. Basti's got a strong personality and once he left perhaps Müller felt that the time was right for him to step up. There's certainly no doubt that he's become one of the leaders of the team. And he does it very, very well. Look at the way he celebrates a goal. He always, always, thanks whoever's provided the assist and goes over to hug him. He never celebrates alone. He always runs back to his teammates and looks for the guy who gave the assist. He's smart too and knows it's a good idea to let someone else take a penalty now and then. And look at tonight, when he scored the third goal to make it 3-0, instead of celebrating by himself, he immediately took his glove off so that he could shake Robben's hand and thank him for giving the assist. Dome, I'd like to use that image in one of our team talks. It's the perfect image of what it means to be a true leader in this game: someone who conducts himself with humility and who's always prepared to acknowledge the work of his teammates.'

The moment Pep's referring to is especially significant because Robben's been behaving increasingly selfishly on the pitch recently, to the extent that at times he's prevented teammates scoring easy goals. His conduct has caused intense friction with Lewandowski and Müller's gesture tonight seems intended to convey two things: 'thanks for the assist . . . and that's what this team's all about, passing well and helping each other out.'

# 9

# IF I MUST LOSE, I WANT TO CHOOSE HOW

*Don't die like an octopus.*
*Die like a shark.*
*Maori Proverb*

GUARDIOLA TENDS NOT to revel in his victories. I'm not talking here about post-match celebrations, when he's more than happy to join in the fun. But there will always be a point, sometime later, when he begins to reflect more seriously on the day's events and starts to dissect the game, examining every detail with forensic attention, much like a pathologist performing an autopsy. Usually, he'll find more than one mistake that could have been avoided. Perhaps the idea of 'triumph as an imposter', as Bielsa puts it, is so deeply ingrained in Guardiola's psyche that it's impossible for him not to end up brooding over missed opportunities or avoidable errors in the wake of every triumph.

He's more magnanimous in defeat however (with his men, never with himself) and, as I've already mentioned, has only suffered forty-five defeats in eight seasons. Some of these losses resulted from his own miscalculations, others were due to his players' mistakes or bad luck and a few were entirely unimportant. Pep has experienced two particularly crushing defeats, both at the same stage of the Champions League competition: the 2012 semi-final when Barça were eliminated by Di Matteo's Chelsea and the 2016 game when Bayern lost to Simeone's Atlético. On both occasions, Pep's men had performed brilliantly, producing lots of chances: Barcelona had forty-six shots at Petr Cech's goal and Bayern produced fifty-three against Oblak. In both matches, Pep paid the price for his front-foot, attacking football. A misstep from one of his own men led to a lethal counter-attack and, ultimately, defeat and elimination from the competition. In both cases his players failed to convert a crucial penalty.

These experiences have caused Guardiola to look for a way to perfect how his playing model protects against setbacks and counter-attacks and we'll no doubt see the results of his work in City's game. He's clear however that match domination and an attacking style are, and will always be, fundamental to his game: 'This is something we have to work to preserve. What's the point of creating a playing model that people love and then changing it? We have to respect the people who love the football we play. If we get knocked out of the Champions League in the last sixteen we'll just have to deal with it but we'll never, ever change the way we play. It doesn't matter whether we're up against Juventus or Barcelona. Other teams may beat us but it will never be because they've dominated possession. That ball's mine and you'll only get it off me if you counter-attack. You have to live and die for your own game. We can't change and we shouldn't change. They can call me reckless as much as they want. I'll be back next year. I am what I am and my job is to convince my players that we're moving in the right direction. At the end of the day it's not about winning or losing but about sticking to your own path.'

Let's take the four weeks between Bayern's defeat of Benfica on 5 April 2016 (1-0, Vidal) on the away leg of the Champions League quarter-final and 3 May when they were knocked out on away goals by Atlético. Between those dates, Bayern suffered their last defeat under Pep (1-0 against Atlético in Madrid), just their nineteenth loss in 161 matches and only the fourth of the season.


## A SACCHI TEAM

Defence is about attacking your opponents' attack.
*Arrigo Sacchi*


Munich, 4 April 2016
'They're pure Sacchi. I'm completely serious. Benfica play like one of Sacchi's teams. They're a machine with the best defensive organisation

in Europe at the minute and they're not even a defensive team. Quite the contrary! They base their defensive line really high up the pitch and press constantly, closing down all the space so that there's not even a hair's breadth between the two back lines. They've got super-fast strikers and all those youngsters, Renato . . . People here in Germany don't tend to watch games from the Portuguese league and it doesn't get much coverage in England or Spain either. So nobody really appreciates just how good Benfica are. But I'm telling you they're the image of one of Sacchi's teams.'

Pep's hardly left his desk for twelve days. He's been analysing Bayern's rivals in the upcoming Champions League quarter-finals and has only left his office to go and see Johan Cruyff's family in Barcelona. The Dutchman's death on 24 March was a devastating blow for the Catalan who has lost a football father figure as well as his greatest mentor.

He's spent the twelve days dissecting ten of Benfica's games: their home and away matches against Sporting Lisbon, Atlético de Madrid, Zénit, Sporting Braga and FC Porto. He's watching the games in full panorama – all the pitch in vision all the time, so that he can seek out tiny details. Carles Planchart's done some extensive analysis too and has given Pep his conclusions but, as always before a big game, the coach wants to do his own detailed evaluation which he'll then compare to the work of Planchart and the rest of the technical team. Pep's already paying a price for his twelve days of intensive, desk-bound planning and has stiffness and pain in several areas of his back. One of the club physios has had a go at releasing some of the tension but it hasn't worked. His back's still in a mess (especially the lumbar area, the upper back and the psoas muscle) and he's having difficulty walking.

'I haven't moved out of this seat for twelve days and I've done no exercise. No wonder I'm in this state.'

He's studied Benfica inside and out and now feels like he understands their brand of football perfectly. He's also changed his routine so that he can devote himself to planning how to convince his men of the danger Benfica represent and, for the first time in three years, doesn't attend training. His men managed to scrape a win against Eintracht Frankfurt (1-0) yesterday in the kind of low-key, unexceptional game that often follows an international break. Having said that, Ribéry's bicycle kick goal was extraordinary and Lahm, Alonso and Bernat were on better form than ever. Bayern's attacking players, normally so reliable, had been slow and lacklustre however.

So, on Sunday 3 April Domènec Torrent takes training whilst Pep prepares a series of videos focusing on the structure of Benfica's game. At midday he breaks another tradition and calls his men to the meeting room on the floor above the dressing room. He then spends forty-five minutes giving them an exhaustive breakdown of Benfica's 4-4-2: their high defensive line positioned almost at the centre circle; their fabulous marking and the way they back each other up; how tight the two back lines are (it's almost impossible to get a clean pass through them); the way they force their rivals into offside mistakes; and the quality of their aerial ability. It's a meticulous analysis of the Portuguese side, possibly the most detailed breakdown Pep's offered his men during his three years in Munich and, as they leave the ground that afternoon, no-one is in any doubt that they're about to go up against a gifted, dangerous rival.

Monday's training session starts thirty-five minutes late because the coach is still working on the way he wants Bayern to disarm Benfica. On this occasion there won't be three pre-match chats. He wants to do four and it's becoming increasingly obvious just how serious a threat Pep considers the Portuguese side. He can only see one way to beat them and explains his strategy to his squad, 'We can't play a direct game, looking for Lewy and Müller because we'll end up offside. Lewy and Müller, you're going to have to sacrifice yourselves. You need to dart about, pulling defenders with you but never looking to receive the ball. The ball's got to move from the inside out to the wings but I want you to do something different from usual. I don't want the winger trying to break away and dribble the ball forward. They'll gobble us up if we do it that way. No, the winger who gets the ball must send it back to someone on the inside and that guy has to beat his marker and send it out wide again. Hopefully, by doing that we'll confuse them and they'll end up out of position. It's going to be complicated lads but that's what I want you to do: inside-outside-inside-dribble-outside until we get to the point we can put it away.'

It's easier said than done as we'll see on Tuesday evening in the Allianz Arena, particularly with Bayern's strikers looking sluggish and slow. Only Ribéry's on top form.

Back on pitch two, Säbener Strasse, everyone's hard at work in a closed door session and the team practises the model Pep's proposed. Thiago, Lahm, Xabi, Alaba and Vidal look like they've understood perfectly but their finishing's poor.

'Dad, how did you miss that?' shouts Arturo Vidal's son, Alonso.

'I just can't get a single fucking goal,' moans the Chilean midfielder

He's not the only one. The strikers look so lethargic that Pep's getting jumpy, 'Fucking hell lads. We've not managed to fucking score yet! Nobody's leaving till we get a goal.'

'Tomorrow Pep. Tomorrow we'll be slamming them away,' Müller reassures him.

At the press conference Manuel Neuer and Douglas Costa show off their in-depth knowledge about Benfica and Guardiola too is quite happy to talk tactics and run through the playing model the Portuguese are likely to use. As he always does when he's in this mood, Pep shares much of what he knows about their rival's game and it's obvious how much work he's put into his pre-match analysis. I'm not certain that this is the wisest approach. Sometimes it's better to play your cards close to your chest.

One of the German journalists calls Benfica a defensive team and Pep sets him right, 'Just how many of their games have you seen?'

'Very few actually.'

'No. Not "very few". None. You've clearly never seen them play because if you had you wouldn't say that they're a defensive side. Benfica is a team with great defensive organisation but they play attacking, offensive football.'

Much like Arrigo Sacchi's legendary Milan, a side who played defensive football without being a defensive team. Sacchi's Milan were superbly organised defensively because their star players were all attackers. And Sacchi used them to produce a game that consistently tricked their opponents into believing they were a defensive side whilst, in reality, they were quite the opposite.


## A MAJOR HEADACHE

*It's about competing well even when you're not on form.*
*Lorenzo Buenaventura*


### Munich, 5 April 2016

Today Pep's line-up has just one variable: which of his top midfielders will be on the bench. He's had this 'problem' for a while now: there's only ever room in the team for two midfielders. This time it's Xabi Alonso who won't be playing although the coach hums and haws about his decision right up until the last possible moment. During the warm-up Alonso's passion for the game is obvious as, whilst the other substitutes play a mini-rondo, he watches a couple of minutes of the historic Bayern games being shown on the stadium's giant screen. He's transfixed.

Elsewhere Müller's practising headers with Lahm as usual but he's off form. He only manages to put away two of the full back's eight crosses. It's a better performance than he managed in the warm-up before the Juventus game (zero out of eight attempts) but he's looking glassy eyed and distracted.

The game starts with an impressive goal from Bayern. The Benfica players are kept busy chasing the ball from one side of the pitch to the other and then Douglas Costa sends a long diagonal pass to Ribéry, who gives it to Lewandowski, who then passes to Bernat whose cross is then headed home by Vidal who has just arrived on the run. His son applauds furiously from the stands.

'The players already in the penalty box don't score against this kind of team,' says Pep later during dinner. 'It's the guys who arrive just at the right moment and work their magic.'

The game plays out exactly as Guardiola has predicted. Benfica play in a tight, ruthlessly effective 4-4-2 formation. As Bayern try to drag then around the team shuffles across as one – stubbornly organised. As instructed, the Bayern players don't look for Lewandowski and Müller, but for Ribéry and Costa, so that Thiago or Vidal can make their carefully timed sprints forward ready to receive the ball. The home side spend the first twenty minutes sending long passes back and forward and it's clearly disrupting the visitors' game but then things start to go wrong. Pep's men seem to get tangled up in the spider's web woven by coach Rui Vitoria, Bayern's game deteriorates and, above all, they begin to lose their rhythm.

The Bayern players troop off at half-time, disappointed with their game so far. Manel Estiarte's chatting to Valentí Guardiola, Pep's dad who's in town for a visit.

'We're not playing well,' says Valentí.

'And our tempo's down,' agrees Estiarte.

Pep runs through the strategy again in the dressing room and the team go out with his instructions ringing in their ears: get the ball out to the wing, pass it back inside and send it back out again. But now Benfica are using a lot more long high balls, knowing that Mitroglou's height gives him an advantage over Kimmich. Guardiola takes Kimmich off and sends on Javi Martínez, who'll say later: 'My skull's aching after all the balls I had to head away.'

Javi's playing his hundredth game with Bayern and now that he's come on, Benfica lose their height advantage. Later however the stats will show that Benfica won 56% of the aerial clashes. The Portuguese team only have two chances in the whole ninety minutes but they're both excellent shots. Javi Martínez blocks the first with his stomach and Neuer saves the second one with his arm. Bayern miss five great chances as, one after the other Müller, Vidal, Ribéry and Lewandowski (twice) fail to put the ball away . . . Müller fails to keep his promise to Pep and the strikers are still looking decidedly shaky. Only Ribéry impresses. Over dinner, Guardiola addresses this issue. 'These things happen. You never get consistent performances out of a striker. They're not like midfielders, they tend to go through peaks and troughs. The droughts don't last forever but it's a bit worrying that three of them are on a low at the same time.'

Lewandowski's particularly off form. At the eighty-eight minute mark he finds himself in a one v one with Ederson, the Benfica keeper. He dribbles round him, beats him and then decides to pass to Lahm instead of taking the shot himself. It should have been a sitter but instead he messes up the pass and Lahm has no chance of getting to the ball and scoring. A second goal would have given Bayern a strong advantage in the tie and it would also have been Lahm's first Champions League goal.

Pep knows he's got a problem, 'Lewy looked knackered out there today. He needs a rest. Müller too. I think I'll only play one of them at Stuttgart on Saturday. The other one can rest and then play in Lisbon. We'll use four in the midfield and only one attacker for the Benfica game. Hopefully that way we'll attack better than we did today.'

Whoever's on the bench at Stuttgart will definitely play in Lisbon.

The 1-0 result leaves Bayern's fans pretty disappointed although perhaps this was to be expected. Most people were pretty unconvinced by Guardiola's warnings about the Portuguese team. He knew from the start that they'd be difficult to beat.

'I told you. Benfica are a strong team. People seem to think that if a team's not from Spain or Germany or England, then it's bound to be rubbish. If people took a bit more notice of the Portuguese league, they'd realise that they've got some damn good teams.'

Guardiola spends a few minutes immediately after the final whistle talking to Douglas Costa at the side of the pitch. The player's performance has dipped so much that the coach suggests that he needs to give some serious thought to how to correct his mistakes. He tells him he'll need to focus on his weak areas and improve the quality of his football, he's made a few serious mistakes today in his pressing and man marking. Pep needs him back on the scintillating form he showed earlier in the season. The two men talk it through and then exchange a hug.

Pep's actually the person who's least disappointed with Bayern's performance today:

'I told you how Benfica play, didn't I? We played well but we messed up our chances. We're struggling up front and can thank our lucky stars that Franck's on top form. Let's see if a bit of rest does the trick for our strikers.'

Tonight Bayern have matched Real Madrid's 2013/14 record of eleven consecutive Champions League wins. Bayern have just won their eleventh consecutive European game and Guardiola has completed his 150th game in charge of the German side. He's won 114 games, drawn eighteen and lost eighteen. He quotes these figures to his dad, telling him delightedly, '76% were victories, dad. Better than with Barça.' (He achieved 72.4% at Barça.)

Valentí's beaming too. He's proud of his son but he also expects a lot from him. Pep learned his ferocious work ethic from his dad and has always considered himself a coach of limited talent who must work harder than everyone else to compensate for those limitations. Valentí, who worked as a builder, has always drilled into his son the importance of hard work and it's a value that Pep's carried forward into his own career. Tonight's no different and his mind's still on work, going over everything that needs to be done over the next few days. 'The game today has given us so much more information about Benfica. We don't need to depend on videos now we've seen the real thing at first hand and my players understand much more now than they did yesterday. We must use that knowledge to improve our game when we next meet them. They've lost Jonas for the return leg and I intend to make a few changes of my own.'

Pep's keen to know if Benfica's magnificent defensive organisation is the result of Rui Vitoria's recent work or whether Jorge Jesus masterminded their game. Miguel Pereira, a much respected Portuguese journalist tells us, 'I think it's a mix of both. When he was in charge of Vitória Guimarães, Rui Vitoria was famous for his strong defence. Back then he used a 4-4-1-1 with a lot of young players and his current Benfica side is very like the Vitória Guimarães team that beat Jorge Jesus' Benfica in the Cup. They were superb in defence that day. And Jesus also worked hard to improve his defence in his last few years at the club. He started out at Benfica with a very offensive style of game and his defence was often neglected and exposed as a result. The latter years changed that quite a bit and he had a fixed rota of defenders who made the back four strong but who also knew how to support the midfield in pressing and closing. I know that Lindeloff, Semedo, Ederson and Renato have made their first XI debuts this season but they were actually training with Jesus last season and it was his idea to turn Almeida into a full back and use Samaris and Pizzi to strengthen the whole defensive block. So you could probably say that the Benfica of today is the result of a superb legacy which has been developed and improved by a coach who's managed to get the best from a young squad.'

Pep's fascinated. He's not learned anything that he can use to beat Benfica on the return leg but it's helped him to understand the Portuguese team's progression.

'I really admire what Jorge Jesus has achieved. He's done a great job. And Rui Vitoria also helped the team develop. They're both fucking brilliant coaches. Between them, they've managed to create another Sacchi-style team.'

A week later Lewandowski's sitting on the bench in the Stadium of Light and Müller's playing, just as the coach has planned. Bayern eliminate the Portuguese champions and qualify for their fifth consecutive Champions League semi-final (two with Jupp Heynckes and three with Pep Guardiola). It's their sixth semi-final in seven years since they got to the final in 2010 under Louis Van Gaal and they've almost matched Real Madrid (six consecutive semi-finals) and Barcelona (seven in nine years).

# KEEPING THEM FRESH

Baseball is 90% mental, 10% physical
*Yogi Berra*

## Munich, April 2016

Between 2 April (Bayern's victory against Eintracht Frankfurt) and 5 May (when they beat Atlético), Guardiola tries to give his three strikers a break by limiting their playing time. He alternates their matches with some time on the bench: Lewandowski plays 700 minutes out of a possible 900, Müller 669 and Costa 528. Of the three the only one who regains some freshness is Lewandowski. Thomas Müller's still struggling and his performance continues to deteriorate right up to the Euros when he hits an all-time low.

There are a number of factors which can affect a player's form: cognitive or physical exhaustion, a dip in self-confidence, the playing model, what's happening at home, personal problems, his understanding of and 'fit' within the playing style . . . There are so many factors in operation at once that it's impossible to say how much each impacts on the player when he's at the height of his form and when he hits a low. Which is why Lorenzo Buenaventura restructures training from now on in an attempt to reduce the fatigue some of the squad have been suffering.

The assistant coach has planned the next few weeks down to the last second. The games come at them thick and fast with almost no time to catch breath in between. Bayern play eleven games in the thirty-five days between 2 April and 7 May. Their period of rest and recuperation in between games varies between sixty-two and ninety-eight hours.

Given that it takes a minimum of seventy-two hours to recover even basic levels of physiological recuperation, in at least half of their games, the players don't have enough time to recover their energy. Buenaventura therefore limits training to the absolute essentials, prioritising recuperation and adding a few short training exercises to maintain power and muscle tone. Just competing keeps the players match fit. Rest, recuperation, good food and short bursts of muscle-building work will do the rest.

And it's not just the technical staff who're looking for equilibrium. The team itself switches up and down the gears depending on the importance of each fixture. They kill themselves during Champions League games but, almost unconsciously, pace themselves for the league matches. Guardiola supports by choosing his line-ups with extra care and in the way he plans and prepares for the games. He wants to maintain the group's competitive drive so he rotates the players constantly. With the exception of Sven Ulreich, assistant goalkeeper, the whole squad is used at some point or other. Key players like Ribéry, Thiago, Vidal, Javi Martínez and Kimmich alternate between the pitch and the bench. They need the rest time. The two players he takes greatest care with are Philipp Lahm and Xabi Alonso, the club's veterans. From January on, the technical team make sure they're rested as much as possible and Lahm ends up playing only five games while Xabi has four. Since March neither of them has played more than three games in a row. The policy works and both men are in top form for the Champions League matches.

In contrast, David Alaba has managed nineteen consecutive games since January. And he's played every minute of them all. He's a monster physically but the central defenders' injuries (Boateng, Benatia and Badstuber) have forced Pep to use him as a central defender or a full back. His coaches are well aware that Alaba needs a break: he's the player they've had to call on most to play in positions he's not used to.

## ALABA IN CENTRAL DEFENCE
### Munich, 7 November 2015

The young Austrian's sitting in one of the black chairs in Pep's office. The room's fairly spartan and the coach's name's not even on the door. All there is is a print of the Bayern Munich club badge. There's a small white sofa, a white table for Pep's laptop, his chair, a couple of black chairs and a red fluffy rug. There's also the whiteboard which he uses to plan for matches, moving the coloured magnets around to represent his players' movements.

Alaba's sitting opposite Pep who's doing the talking but ten seconds in something unexpected happens: the player realises that he's still wearing his baseball cap (he always wears it, turned round back to front) and snatches it off, apologising to the coach for coming into his office so informally dressed.

'David's a lovely boy,' Pep says a few hours later over dinner with Cristina. 'I was telling him what I wanted him to do in the match and the minute he realised that it was a serious chat he took off his hat. He felt like he was being disrespectful and was so apologetic. I'm fascinated by that. It just shows how sensitive and well-mannered he is. I thought I couldn't get any fonder of him than I was already.'

Pep's called Alaba in because he wants to ask a favour: he wants him to play in central defence again.

'I put him there at the start of the season because Javi Martínez and Badstuber were out and Benatia was about to have that bad injury. At the time I promised him that when all my central defenders were back, I'd return him to full back. That's where he's at his strongest, where he performs best because he can run all day. I've kept my promise up till now but now I need him back there again. That's why I asked him to come and see me, to ask him to do me this favour again and to tell him that he won't be able to go up and attack much because I need him protecting our back. He's a great kid who understood exactly what I was asking and agreed immediately. David's the perfect player. He's multi-talented. And, it seems, he's got good manners as well.'

The training session on the eve of the Werder Bremen game fits Buenaventura's model exactly: warm-up, a few rondos, positional play practice drills, five on five plus three 'wild card' players who switch side to play with whichever team has the ball, simulating the 'superiority' of numbers which Guardiola always aims for in matches. It's all light work. There's no physical or mental pressure. Just forty-five minutes. Yesterday they worked on the power-building exercises.

'We're doing everything with as little pressure as possible. We're in the sprint to the final now. The final lap before the finishing line,' says Buenaventura.

Saturday 16 April is Guardiola's 400th match in the top division (295 victories). His men help him celebrate by beating Schalke 3-0.

## THE LAST DEFEAT

Where there is strength you sometimes find weakness
*David Llada*

### Madrid, 27 April 2016

In the pre-match team talk Guardiola reminds his men of the strong points of Atlético's game: their pressing high up the pitch at the start of the match (the first fifteen minutes), their compact lines of defence, their ability to stay connected in groups of players if they're forced to shuffle across, their fabulous record of scoring at set plays and how dangerous they can be on the counter-attack. The coach also tells his men to expect a dry pitch where the grass will have been left to grow as high as possible. It's aimed at slowing down Bayern's passing.

Just as Pep did for the Benfica game, he's prepared four tactical talks before the clash with Atlético. He needs four sessions to cover everything he wants to share about their rival. During one of them he breaks his own rules and shows his men an entire video of a section of the Champions League quarter-final match between Atlético and

Barcelona in 2014, which ended in victory for the Madrid side (1-0). Guardiola shows them the first fifteen minutes and tells them to expect a similar level of pressing. In the 2014 game Atlético hit the post three times in the first twenty minutes and Barça were absolutely swamped.

'Lads, you need to expect more of the same from them, so keep your heads. Just bring the ball out as cleanly as you can and win your one v ones. Those first twenty minutes are crucial and if we can get through them without conceding a goal we'll have the psychological advantage for the rest of the game.'

But his men do the opposite: they're sluggish and slow from the start, losing all the 50/50 balls (Atlético win 75% of the twenty-nine one v one clashes in the first ten minutes) and almost immediately conceding what will be the only goal of the match. Guardiola stands cursing on the edge of the pitch, his fists clenched. Everything that he drummed into his men is playing out in front of him.

His players all accept responsibility for the disaster later at the post-match dinner. The manager had given them due warning and they'd started badly, in the wrong state of mind to face such an aggressive opponent. Some positives have come out of today's game and Xabi, Thiago, Lahm, Javi and Costa are all keen to point these out: their defensive management of corners and free kicks; the team's strong response to conceding the early goal and their refusal to let it throw them off; their total domination of the second half and the many chances they created (seven of which were very, very close). There's more optimism than despondency amongst the players, more calm acceptance than bitter regret but they do all recognise that they failed to follow the coach's instructions and that doesn't feel good.

The press and supporters round on Pep, slamming his tactical decisions and holding him solely responsible for the defeat. The general argument is that putting Müller on the bench was a fatal error because 'this is a player who should play in all the big matches'. I disagree and think that Guardiola did the right thing by leaving him out of the starting XI. For me, his big mistake was bringing him on for Thiago in the seventieth minute.

After their first ten minutes of woefully lacklustre football, Bayern find their feet and begin to have more time on the ball because of Atleti's defensive formation. The Madrid side play deep in order to break, but this lets Pep's team dominate the ball and push higher and higher up towards the rival goal. There are as many 50/50 challenges as earlier in the game, but Bayern are now winning many more of them. As the game turns, the Germans begin to dominate completely and start to look dangerous: they shoot at goal nineteen times, keeping Oblak under constant pressure, hit the crossbar (Alaba) and fail to convert at least seven excellent chances.

By midway through the second half it looks like an equaliser is inevitable. Atlético aren't managing to close down all the inside channels (one of their specialities) and Bayern are controlling the game and creating more and more chances.

Guardiola decides to bring Müller on for Thiago, believing that the German is more likely to produce a goal (despite the fact that he's been so off-form lately) and that Thiago's absence at this stage won't impact his team too much. Sadly, he's quite wrong and the change actually ends up slowing down the Bayern attack.

Four minutes later Ribéry loses the ball and Fernando Torres ends a superb counter-attack with a shot off the post. Bayern's onslaught, which just minutes ago seemed unstoppable, collapses. They've played brilliantly for forty minutes but, although they produce a few more chances, the rest of their match is a shambles. Guardiola sees that his men are losing control and sends on Benatia. For me, Thiago's departure has weakened Bayern's midfield and damaged the whole construction of their game. After Müller comes on. In other words, the exact opposite of what Pep's detractors are saying.

Guardiola definitely makes a mistake with regard to Müller but not because he leaves him on the bench. His great error is in playing him at all. This argument will apply equally to the return leg and the Cup Final as well as later, at the Euros, with Löw in charge.

To claim, as many Germans do, that Müller is essential for all important games is just as arbitrary and ill-judged as saying he should never play at all. When he's fighting fit and on form he's a sensational player, but just like any other footballer, if he's below par his presence in the team can do more harm than good. And that's exactly what happened between April and July 2016 when he suffered a serious dip in his performance. This is nothing new in football or any other sport. All athletes have highs and lows. Müller has undoubtedly been the symbol of Bayern's glorious, attacking, dominant game for most of Guardiola's third year in charge, it's just that he's lost his edge when it matters most . . .

## LOOKING FOR A GAP

*I fight my hardest battles with myself every day*
*Napoleón Bonaparte*

### Madrid, 28 April 2016

It's 1:30 in the morning and Pep sits down with his brother Pere and a couple of friends to discuss today's game and how to approach the return leg. The players have already gone to their rooms, all of them pretty hacked off with today's result as well as the way they'd gifted Atlético the match in the first fifteen minutes. They're happy enough with the way they played in the second half when they created seven good chances. No-one else has managed to play so well against the Madrid side. Simeone's defensive line is like a solid, unbreachable brick wall and although Bayern's previous opponents, Benfica and Juventus played well defensively, today, in the first quarter of an hour, the Spaniards repelled the German offensive with consummate ease.

Pep's prognosis is as follows: 'There's no way I can say what's going to happen on the return leg. We can't tell the lads that, because we had seven good chances today, in the next game we'll have fourteen and get three goals at home. I don't know how it'll go. None of us do. Every game starts from zero and this is such a complex game that you can never say for sure what's going to happen. That's the magic of football I suppose. It's why we're all so passionate about it. Maybe they'll get another goal and we'll have to score three. Or we might get five. Who knows? All we know is that we need to work really hard to ensure our lads are as well organised and disciplined as possible.'

Now that the official part of the evening (the team dinner) is over Pep can relax with his brother and his friends and spend a couple of hours talking football in the comfort of the Eurostars Madrid Tower Hotel. Every few minutes they're interrupted by fans looking for selfies with Pep and then Jorge Mendes, a well-known Portuguese football agent, also makes an appearance to pass on his good wishes for the second leg. Mendes is currently in negotiations with Karl-Heinz Rummenigge over the potential signing of Benfica player Renato Sanches and it's strange to see him here, in the small hours of the morning, after a crucial Champions League game, chatting casually with Bayern's coach who's trying to work out his strategy for their next game.

During the conversation with his three confidants, Pep repeatedly says, 'I need to see the game again.' He's told Carles Planchart not to bother analysing today's game. He'll do it himself and will prepare the videos he'll show his players next week. He wants Planchart to concentrate on Saturday's match against Borussia Mönchengladbach. It's going to be a big day because if Bayern win they'll have sewn up their fourth league title in a row.

'I definitely need to see the game again.'

He keeps saying it despite the fact that he already has every detail etched on his brain. Every move, every mistake, those first minutes of chaos, Bayern's initial failure to win the 50/50 challenges and the good stuff too: the extended period of Bayern domination, Vidal's brilliant runs from deep which meant he repeatedly arrived in the box just at the right time, Douglas Costa on sparkling form . . .

### THE OVERTURE
Madrid, 27 April 2016

Pep scratches his head. 'The main thing is that we start the moves intelligently. Bringing the ball out from the back well is vital to our attack.'

His brother Pere interrupts, 'But is that really true, Pep? Is it so important to bring out the ball like that?'

'Of course! It's absolutely vital. It's just not the same if the winger gets the ball from the centre half compared to from an inside forward. If he gets possession from the centre back it gives the other team time to organise their defence. But if the play's been worked forwards until it's the attacking midfielder who delivers the ball it's far harder to defend – especially if the midfielders have drawn the defenders to them. It's one of the fundamental parts of our game, bringing out the ball cleanly. That's why we messed up at the start, because we brought it out badly.'

It's very late, already the small hours of the morning but my thoughts inevitably turn to music and chess. I remember conductor Christian Thielemann's rhetorical question regarding Beethoven's fifth symphony, 'Can you have a good symphony without a good overture? Of course not.'

I recall Garry Kaspárov's words too, 'Your opening moves are much more than the trivial mobilisation of your troops. They establish what kind of battle it's going to be and is your first and best opportunity to take the game in the direction you want it to go, where you'll be best placed to beat your opponent. The start of your game is the most difficult, the most subtle phase of all.'

We end the chat with some thoughts from Juanma Lillo. 'There are two kinds of coaches,' says Pep. 'Those who begin their attack from their own penalty box and those who begin it when their rivals take their goal kick. Only if you play out, building out from the back with clean, accurate ,intelligent passing can you install yourself in the opponents' half.'

So if he recalls every moment of the game so vividly, why then is Pep so desperate to see it again?

'Because I have to come up with a different way of attacking Atlético. I'll have to watch it several times more, not to understand what happened, but to work out what's likely to happen on Tuesday and what we must do to beat them.'

He won't be making immediate decisions about how Bayern will play, nor about which of his players he'll use but he does have a rough idea about the kind of line-up he wants.

'One thing's for sure. I won't make the mistake I made two years ago against Real Madrid. Win or lose, I want to play our game, not someone else's idea of what our game should be. I know I want Lewandowski as centre forward with Müller behind him plus two guys on the wings. But there's a lot more to work out and I'll make those decisions after I've watched the game again.'

There are a few options and scenarios: 'One option is to take a new approach to the first fifteen minutes of the game. They'll be pressing us high up the pitch and I might ask my defenders to send lots of long balls to Lewandowski for our midfield to follow up and look to win layoffs or the second ball. It's not how I like to construct our game but it is a good way to neutralise their pressing and I think our supporters would like that approach. It would help us get fully switched-on and involved in the game from the start and short circuit Atlético's initial charge. But I'll need to come up with a few alternatives: if they put out a 4-4-2, with Torres and Griezmann at the front that's totally different from a 4-1-4-1 with Carrasco up front. Dome [Torrent] and I will have to design an emergency plan for the last half an hour in case we have to produce a heroic comeback. It feels like we'll have to play lots of mini-games within this one game and we'll have to be totally prepared for them all.'

Guardiola's also thinking about something he mentioned after the Benfica match: 'It doesn't matter how much analysis you do and how much information you give the players, there's nothing like playing an opponent to teach you exactly how they play. We've done that now and my men know exactly what kind of team Atlético is, what they do well and where their weaknesses are. It's also true of course that Simeone and his team know us a little better now and I'm quite sure he'll be analysing our domination of the second half and thinking up ways of handling it better. If we manage to pinpoint exactly what went on today, we'll be in a good position to come up with the right solutions.

'Basically we need to bring the ball out from the back using a three against two approach and I'll maybe put Vidal in with Boateng and Javi. I know it sounds odd but Arturo is a guy who starts his run as a defender but arrives in the penalty box like a forward.

'The other thing we need to do is stop them getting away with the ball, stop them counter-attacking. There's no way we can stop them counter-attacking completely but we have to do everything we can to stop them.

'The third key is in the right channel: we need to move the ball really rapidly, our winger needs to tie down their full back, Lahm must do the same to their inside midfielder and I want Costa to pick up the ball behind where Lahm's position is and make his diagonal right to left run so that he can shoot on goal, cross or send the ball back out wide if he's closed down. This tactic could be decisive and I'll need to study it in depth. I might follow David Trueba's suggestion.'

'What does Trueba say?'

'He says that when he has to finish a novel he shuts himself in a monastery and works on it till it's done. That's what I'm going to do on Sunday. I'll leave the recuperation session to Dome and shut myself away somewhere. Maybe a hotel or a church,' he jokes with a wink. 'Or maybe I'll just stay at home for the day and watch today's game over and over until I see how we can do some damage. This stage is the most intense part of what I do. At the end of the day it's the players who have to play the game. All I can do is instruct and organise them, give them the right tactics to get them to the final.'

Guardiola mentally runs through a range of different possibilities: play a 4-3-3 so that the attacking midfielders try and exploit the channel between their centre halves and full backs; use a diamond midfield four; use five strikers with Costa and Müller as inside forwards ('but not for the whole ninety minutes'); and he keeps coming up with different strategies depending on the line-up he's considering. He needs to find a gap in Atlético's defence and organise his players so that they can use that gap to bring the whole wall tumbling down. He says again how unpredictable football can be.

'We can prepare and plan all we like but then Müller appears, knocks the ball in off his backside and suddenly you're in the final. Football's a science, for sure, but it's an inexact science.'

Eventually it's time for bed and Pep gives his little brother a hug. Pere tells him, 'Go with what you believe Pep. Whatever feels right to you.'

Guardiola shares his final thoughts as he goes up in the lift to his room on the twenty-fourth floor just before 4:00 am. He obviously feels deeply about this: 'I really want us to have a good game on Tuesday. I want the whole of Germany seeing these players producing the kind of brilliant, inventive football I know they're capable of.'


## BEFORE THE BATTLE

I may make a mistake but at least I'll still be me.
*Antígona*


### Munich, 2 May 2016

Arturo Vidal throws himself full length at the ball and ends up sprawled on the grass, having banged his side against one of the metal bars around the pitch. He yells in pain and stays down. Then, when he tries to get up, he feels dizzy and sick. The medical team check him out and it looks like he's got some rib damage. It's just thirty hours before the Atlético match and Vidal hobbles into the dressing room and tells the coach, 'Don't worry, Pep. I won't let you down. I'll play, broken rib or not.' In the event a painkiller will get him through the match.

On Sunday afternoon, after lunch with David Trueba and some other friends, Pep shuts himself away at home and watches the whole away match from start to finish. He's looking for a chink in Atlético's armour, he needs to find the weakness he can exploit on match day in the Allianz Arena. It's vital to come up with a new kind of attack which will allow his men to shake Atlético up and destabilise their defensive wall. It's bad news that Atlético's captain has made such an unexpected and speedy recovery (just ten days) from his hamstring injury. Simeone's defensive wall's going to be stronger than ever.

Around eight o'clock on Sunday evening Pep thinks he's found their weak spot. It's in the small channel between the central defender and the left back. Koke normally covers this area but Philipp Lahm will be able to drag him far enough away to allow Thomas Müller to charge through. It's a small opportunity and he has to exploit it fully.

Guardiola spends the whole of Monday morning in his office at the training ground working on the tactics for the game and the videos he's going to show his men. The Bayern players have often commented on how much they value Pep's analysis. He always gives them detailed information that proves invaluable when they play. Today, Pep's analysis is as accurate as ever. He's gone over all the errors they made in Madrid, basically losing all the individual battles because of a lack of competitive tension and then identified Atlético's weaknesses, paying particular attention to 'Koke's channel'. Bayern will have to draw Koke away from that zone. Lahm will provide the diversion whilst Müller pushes through the space.

Out on Number One pitch, which is completely closed from viewing today, the team run through three movements. The first one will be used during the first ten minutes of the game and consists of sending long balls to Lewandowski. Expecting an aggressive, all-out attack from Simeone's men, which is what happened in Madrid and also what Juventus used successfully in the Allianz Arena, Guardiola wants to go with long balls from his defenders to his centre forward so that he can bring the ball down and pass it to the midfielders. Neuer and Boateng will be sending the long passes and even if Lewandowski doesn't manage to control it, at least the action will be well away from the German goal. We saw a bit of a dress rehearsal for this strategy last Saturday in the Mönchengladbach game but it's no longer an experiment. Pep's made up his mind: Bayern will deal with Atlético's pressing by using long balls to Lewandowski.

Bayern's coaching team reckon that after a short-lived all-out attack, Atlético will move to phase two of their plan: solid defending from the midfield back. This will be the moment for Bayern to revert to their more traditional game of bringing the ball out from the back. The team practises bringing the ball out non-stop for about twenty minutes. Pep has only one question mark over his line-up: should he use Benatia or Boateng?

'Boateng brings the ball out brilliantly but he hasn't played for three months and I don't know if he's fit enough for such a tough game. Benatia anticipates well . . . I just don't know. I can't decide which one to go for.'

During training Benatia complains of some muscle pain. It doesn't look too serious but it resolves Pep's doubts for him: he'll have a chat with Boateng on Tuesday. He'll look him in the eyes and if he sees complete self-confidence, he'll put him in the starting eleven. Just a few months ago Boateng had had to play in a lot of pain. He wasn't injured but had taken a bad knock to one of his legs and was clearly suffering. He came through the match with flying colours though, and that kind of resilience makes him a good bet for the Atlético game.

### BOATENG'S RESILIENCE
#### Munich, 7 November 2015

They finish lunch at the Dolce Hotel and get to the stadium at 2:30. Pep asks Boateng to come to his office. The player hasn't attended training the last couple of days because of a muscle problem after taking a bad knock during the Arsenal game. Pep's decided to put him in the starting team anyway.

'Jérôme, I've two reasons for asking you to play today: firstly, I need you to ensure we bring the ball out well and secondly, and most importantly of all, I want you out there despite the fact that you're in so much pain. I want you to show me you can do it. Over the last two years you've done well but whenever you've had the slightest discomfort you've opted out. By the time spring comes, we'll be facing some really big games and maybe you'll have to play even if you're suffering after a knock. I need to know now that I can count on you. I want to know that you can cope with the pain and play your game as if everything's okay.'

Boateng plays beautifully for forty-five minutes, gritting his teeth and getting the job done without complaint. Pep's so pleased with him that at half-time he tells him he's earned a rest.

After working on bringing the ball out (Boateng, Alonso and Lahm will be the men responsible), the team move to the third tactic Pep wants them to use: breaking through the channel Lahm will try to forge between their central defence and left back. The coach wants to play a four-man diamond shaped midfield. A 3-4-3 when Bayern have the ball. To achieve it, Alonso will drop back to make a three with the central defenders. Vidal will move into the base of the four-man midfield – Müller at the forward tip, Lahm and Alaba on either side of the diamond. Up top Costa and Ribéry wide and Lewandowski at centre forward. Pep's trying to overcome the way Atlético always achieve numerical superiority on the wing. If Costa attacks he faces both Filipe Luis and Augusto Fernández. If Lahm joins in then Koke will be there for a three v two. Pep wants to make Costa and Lahm occupy the three Atleti men but then move the ball so quickly in the inside channel, via Alonso and Vidal, that Müller can burst through whatever space Koke has vacated to cover Filipe and Augusto. It's not a gaping weakness, but Bayern need to exploit it to the maximum – hence the 3-4-3 and diamond shaped midfield. There's one more instruction for Vidal, Alonso and Boateng: the passes down the right side must be firmer and quicker than on the left in order to exploit the slightest space Koke's movement leaves.


## DOWN AND OUT

I couldn't live without champagne.
In victory I deserve it; in defeat I need it
*Winston Churchill*


### Munich, 3 May 2016

Reluctantly, Pep lifts his grey sweater and shows Cristina the state of the white shirt underneath. It's torn to pieces. What's strange is that it's only the fabric that's in shreds, the buttons are still all in place, neatly fastened. It looks like a giant hand has grabbed his shirt and ripped it up.

'Just as well you were wearing a sweater on top,' says Cristina.

The condition of the shirt perfectly reflects Pep's state of mind. He's in bits. As are his players and all of Bayern's supporters. German has a wonderful word to describe great performances: *souverän* (supreme). And that's exactly what Bayern's game has been today: supreme, confident, superlative. It's just the result that hurts so much. The away goal rule means that Bayern won't be going to the final and they're devastated. Stupefied.

Xabi Alonso's in a state of complete shock. He's searching for a word to describe the enormity of what's just happened, some kind of explanation he can get his head round . . . But there's nothing. He's all cried out and feels completely drained. After the game he sobbed on the pitch like he's never done before. Xabi knows that today's game was perhaps his second last opportunity to make it to a Champions League final in the starting XI. He's already won the trophy twice: once with Liverpool and once with Real Madrid, but he wanted to emulate Clarence Seedorf's achievement of winning the trophy in three different leagues. It's taken him a while to pull himself together and get changed. He then drags himself through the corridors of the Allianz Arena, almost breaking down again when he meets his wife, his mum and his agent, Iñaki. They all hug and kiss him and it's nearly too much. Nobody knows what to say. There's nothing anyone can say. Xabi hugs his dad, Periko, who used to play for Real Sociedad and Barça. Periko's also trying to contain his emotions and his face is a rigid mask. They don't need words to express the pain at being eliminated. A look's all it takes. Jon, Xabi's eldest son, shatters the silence, 'Come on, Dad. Time to go home.'

Outside the lift, David Alaba's looking as lost as Xabi. One of his friends gives him a big hug, whispering words of comfort into his ear but David's not listening. He's stunned and can't believe it's ended this way. He's going over and over his own mistake – the one that allowed Atlético to score. There had been a number of players involved in the foul-up. The original misplaced Boateng pass, his reckless attempt to press the ball to correct his mistake, the slight step forward by Alonso, leaving Torres space he could use and then Alaba slamming on the brakes to try and play Griezmann offside, thereby losing any chance of winning the race with the French striker. And that final piece of bad luck: the involuntary slight deflection which sent the ball into Griezmann's path for him to tuck away. A series of tiny errors that have cost Bayern their place in the final. David Alaba knows it and feels the pain of everyone. Nothing can ease the agony. Reassuring words and comforting hugs just won't cut it and it's going to take days for him to get over this.

Thomas Müller's deep in thought. Completely silent. His silence sums up how awful they're all feeling. Müller's a chatterbox, always ready with a laugh and a joke, always with something to say, even at the most inappropriate of moments. His unpredictability extends way beyond the football pitch and in real life he often puts his foot in it by cracking a joke at just the wrong moment. No-one really minds though. It's just the way he is . . . But that's not how he is tonight. He's a pale shadow of himself, a lost soul wandering round inside the stadium, head down and silent, fully aware that he messed up today. His penalty miss reinvigorated an Atlético side which had been fading fast. But it's more than that. His playing was chaotic and erratic. None of his teammates would dream of criticising him for it but everyone knows that Müller's mistakes badly damaged the flow of their game today. The man who so often saves the day with a lightning fast sprint into just the right spot has let them down badly.

Guardiola's coping stoically. He's been through something very similar, four years ago when Roberto Di Matteo's Chelsea knocked Barcelona out at the same stage of the competition. Barcelona dominated that game too so the similarity is striking. Over the 180 minutes of the semi-final Bayern have had fifty-three shots on goal but, once again, a team who came to play tight, defensive football has managed to eliminate Guardiola's side.

The coach has nothing to reproach his players for. Their biggest mistake was the disastrous minutes at the start of the away game, 'If we can get through the first twenty minutes [of the away game] without conceding a goal, we'll be in the final,' he'd told them before the match in Madrid.

But that's not how it's turned out and Saul's goal during those dreadful fifteen minutes of the away game, plus Griezmann's effort tonight have meant the end of Guardiola's hopes of making it to the final. Atlético's formidable defensive organisation, despite failing to prevent Bayern's constant attacks on goal, combined with their explosive counter-attacking has made all the difference. It's the same kind of organisation that Helenio Herrera's Inter Milan produced although Herrera liked to use a sweeper. Just like Herrera's Inter (European Cup winners in 1964 and 1965), the Atlético full backs are happy running up and down the wing, their centre halves boss the penalty area and the team seems to possess a sixth sense about where gaps will arise and how to close them. The midfielders have made huge sacrifices all night, putting in double effort to ensure that there's no space, no time, no opportunities. The Madrid side has made full use of Torres' acceleration into open space as well as Griezmann's astonishing ability to control the ball no matter who's pressing him (much like the great Luis Suárez of that '60s Inter team). 'El Cholo' Simeone has turned Atlético into a superbly talented team and his crowning glory is the defensive organisation they've developed. Like Herrera before him, Simeone has made his defence the centre of his strategic plans and, like Herrera's Inter, it has transformed their game and turned them into a top class, winning team.

From the first second of the game Bayern set out to tear down the *rojiblanca* wall. It's pouring with rain but Bayern are fizzing with energy and everyone knows exactly what to do. They've had three meetings with the boss and two training sessions dedicated to today's game. They've heard Pep and know the tactics inside out. Pep has followed up on his conclusions after the away match in Madrid.

With the ball, Bayern's profile is a 3-4-3, diamond midfield. The defence is composed of Javi Martínez, Alonso and Boateng. The diamond has Vidal at its base, Müller up top, Costa and Alaba right and left. The front three has Lahm as the right winger, Ribéry on the left touchline and Lewandowski in a personal battle with the Atlético captain, Diego Godín.

Each winger has a different task. Lahm, on the right, stays open so that Costa can burst through the inside channel which Bayern hope will open up between Atlético's left back and left centre half. Pep's asked these two to play fast, daring, attacking football.

This is the gap Pep spotted and his men push through in wave after wave of attacks this evening. The left wing play their usual game. Ribéry wide but Alaba inside him looking for a passing game, looking to draw the Atlético defence out, move them about and to take a shot if space opens up. It's about running from the right, passing and moving down the left.

During the warm-up Müller practises heading at goal with the crosses Philipp Lahm sends him. He only scores one goal in eleven attempts. Another bad omen?

Pep's prepared for the epic battle ahead. Atlético win the toss and start with possession but within seconds Bayern have robbed the ball off them and they're away, playing the football of their lives.

Undoubtedly tonight Bayern produce the best game of the entire Guardiola era. It's not necessarily the most aesthetically pleasing football and the final result is devastating but, pound for pound, this is their best performance in three years. It's a mix of positional play and the direct, vertical game Pep's dreamed of since the day Xabi Alonso signed. He also has his wingers attack, the trademark the coach has wanted since the start whilst using his inside forwards to smash through the central channels. They maintain possession for 45% of the game and make 650 good, clean passes, treble the number their rivals manage. Atlético spend most of the game on the back foot, hunted back into their own area. Bayern are like a human steamroller, crushing their opponents' resistance with ruthless efficiency and breathtaking speed; it's not about blind haste, they move with calculated speed and the rain and the wet grass prove a huge boon. The ball's flying and every pass arrives at its destination a second faster than the away game. Madrid's defenders are struggling to stop them.

From the start Xabi Alonso, Boateng and Lahm spot Atlético's weak point. Alonso and Boateng drive more and more long, low, fast passes and watch as their rivals arrive late for almost every one. Lahm's noticed that the gap Pep told them about has just got wider and he slams his advantage home. He feints inside, drives outside and twists and turns his marker, all to increase the space Costa's got to push into.

Bayern push through to their opponents' area, driving Simeone's men back towards their goal and their superb goalkeeper. The Atlético players are locked so tight together, they're struggling to breathe. Already they're having to play for time, taking as long as possible when the ball goes dead, especially for goal kicks. They use these few seconds to help them survive but are immediately pushed back again by the Germans who look unstoppable.

Neuer is the only man who's not crowded into the *rojiblanca* half so it's inevitable that Bayern take an early lead. Xabi Alonso gets the credit with a shot from a free kick which deflects in off Atlético defender Giménez. Atlético are like a fish out of water, fading fast in the face of the home team's onslaught. Bayern are given a penalty which should put the last nail in Atlético's coffin and Thomas Müller steps us to take it. But Oblak, Atlético's star of the whole tie, saves it and gives life to his struggling team. (In his three seasons at Atlético, Oblak has only managed to save three out of a total of twenty-one penalties.)

'We need to go on defending the way we have been,' says Periko Alonso, Xabi's dad at half-time.

Bayern's attacking's been outstanding but their defensive work's been even better: Atlético have only managed two long range shots on goal in forty-five minutes and have presented no threat to Neuer. Cristina, Pep's wife, is walking up and down the corridors with Valentina, their youngest daughter. She's feeling the tension, 'We're so close, we're almost there. It's such a shame about that penalty! With a 2-0 lead we'd be almost over the finishing line but it looks like we just have to suffer for a bit longer. We're almost there . . .'

Cristina doesn't know how right she is. The Bavarians are noticeably less fired up as they go out for the second half. They think they've already got past the most difficult stage of the game and they know that their domination has been absolute so far.

Bayern amuse themselves passing the ball around in the first few minutes. Meanwhile Simeone's made an important change and winger Yannick Carrasco comes on. The Belgian has recovered from the injury that kept him out of the away match and El Cholo has asked him to look for a chance to counter-attack. Atlético are desperate for some breathing space.

Bayern's 'downtime' lasts barely four minutes and they quickly recover their pace and intensity. Xabi's sending the ball flying from one side of the park to the other and Vidal seems to be everywhere at once. Lahm organises the attack and the forwards push on.

Then, and we've seen it so many times in football, Atlético get lucky. Bayern push through their defences for a shot on goal. And miss. Their opponents follow this with their own attack on Neuer's goal and hit the jackpot. Griezmann thumps the ball into the back of the net, effectively buying them their passport to the European final.

Bayern are suddenly struggling. It's going to be impossible to turn the game around. They now need to score two more goals against a side that's only conceded five in the competition so far. Three goals is a tough ask. Only once this season has an opponent managed to get three past Simeone's men. Atlético, moreover, are like a team reborn. Griezmann's given them the shot in the arm they needed and Carrasco and Torres' runs are easing some of the pressure in their half.

Pep's men stick to the plan and continue to produce masterful football but they're still facing a solid defensive wall. It feels like Thiago, with his trademark defence-splitting pass might be the solution and possibly Coman, to add his anarchic runs from wide but Pep can't sacrifice Xabi, who's having the game of his life out there, or Vidal, who's also outstanding, or Lahm, also playing his best football of the last three years . . . Pep decides to bring Coman on for Costa (the Brazilian has never regained the scintillating form he was on between August and December). The Frenchman's dribbling isn't perfect but he'll have two fantastic chances to get Bayern's third goal in the dying minutes of the game. Neuer emulates Oblak by stopping Torres converting a penalty for Atlético's second goal.

Bayern's second goal comes in the seventy-fourth minute. Ribéry makes space, crosses for Vidal and he heads back across goal for Lewandowski to put the home side up. Bayern batter Atlético still more, the chances come and go, but Alaba's brilliant chance which deflects off a defender is saved by Oblak who twists in the opposite direction to which he was originally going in order to concede a corner.

The keeper's had a sensational night and his efforts, added to Atlético's excellent defensive organisation, are largely responsible for getting them through to their second Champions League final in three years. The 'Expected Goals' algorithm which calculates the number of goals in a game dependent on the number of shots and the quality of the team's normal shooting power, reflects all this. Normally, according to this theorem, Bayern would have scored 4.24 goals to Atlético's 1.4. But Bayern's finishing hasn't matched the number and quality of their chances.

So, for the third time in three years, Guardiola's team don't make it past the Champions League semi-final. They lost to Real Madrid because Pep failed to trust his own instincts and opted for the wrong tactics. Then, a combination of Messi's genius and Bayern's injury epidemic saw them go out to Barcelona, but tonight's been very different. They've played superbly and have still failed to get through. No wonder there's an all-encompassing sense of stunned disbelief in Munich tonight.

Nobody feels like eating in the players' restaurant. The food's left untouched. Lucas, the Spanish waiter offers them champagne, wine and beer but no-one wants to drink either. Not even to forget. Of the starting XI only Neuer and Javi Martínez stay in the Players' Lounge. Pep leaves early with his family after trying to force down a few mouthfuls of pasta.

'It's like Barça–Chelsea all over again. But this is worse . . .'

Domènec Torrent and Carles Planchart are in an even worse state than Pep. They're going over and over the match – the number of times their players did all the right things without reward, the dominance of the shots on goal, the missed penalty and how brilliantly Oblak performed.

They'll be here till 3.00 am trying to get their heads round what's just happened. Tonight Bayern launched wave after wave of deadly force again Atlético's blockade. But it's all been for nothing. Pep's team is out of the Champions League.


## NOBODY ALWAYS WINS, NOT EVEN PELÉ . . .

Glory is about joy. It's not about winning from time to time.
Glory is about loving to practise, about enjoying every day.
*Rafa Nadal*


### Munich, 4 May 2016

Perhaps Guardiola's too reckless, too willing to take risks in order to test his own ideas. He's certainly unusual in the modern game where there's an almost unhealthy obsession with titles and trophies. He is, nonetheless, absolutely determined to continue to take risks in his quest to develop and perfect his own playing model and ideas. We can expect an even more radical approach at City where his football will be as bold and innovative as ever (although he'll obviously need to spend a significant period knocking his new team into shape).

'We have to do this for the guys who've invested so much in the game, in this playing model. It's not about what people say about us, it's not about the column inches in the papers, no, it's for everyone who's worked so hard to produce this quality of football. There are so many coaches who've put themselves on the line down the years to ensure that these ideas survive. And I've a duty to pass what I know on to future generations. Guys like Xavi and Busquets will eventually take on the mantle at Barça and they'll pass their knowledge on just like Johan Cruyff did for me and as I tried to do for them. Mascherano is someone else who'll make a fantastic coach as will guys like Xabi Alonso, Manu Neuer, Javi . . . That's what it's all about.'

It's the day after Bayern's elimination from the Champions League and Pep's already deep in analysis. This is how he deals with any defeat: he accepts it and moves on, examining his own mistakes as well as what his opponents did well. He scrutinises the match from every angle, determined to learn from it, correct his mistakes and take his understanding of the game one step further.

'The main lesson I've learned from my time in Munich is how to lose. I always want to win but obviously that's impossible so at the very least I'm determined to choose how I lose. Sometimes a defeat can give you so much more than a victory and that's what's happened here. It wasn't like losing to Real Madrid [the 0-4 of 2014]. The game against Atlético was quite different. That's the important thing. If you have to lose some of the time, then at least you should choose the way you do it. Do you know what the great thing about this tie was? We played two outstanding games against a tough opponent like Atlético, a team that's enormously hard to beat. And we only managed that because of the courage and generosity of my players. We may not have made it to the final but we played the kind of football that's made the whole world sit up and take notice. That's not nothing. And it's all thanks to my players. They were tremendous. So brave.

'There are a lot of coaches around today who play a very reactive game . . . I mean them no disrespect but we're different. We're carrying on the work of Cruyff, of Juanma Lillo, of Pedernera, of the Brazil of the 1970s, of Menotti and Cappa, Ajax, the Marvellous Magyars . . . We're their natural heirs and of course we'll lose sometimes. But the sun will still rise the next day and we'll go on dreaming our dreams, doing our thing. In football, nobody wins all the time, my friend. Not even Maradona won every game. Not even Pelé.'

# BACKSTAGE 9

## 'CRACK!'
### Munich, 13 February 2016

It's a gentle, tranquil Saturday morning in Munich. Tomorrow Bayern face a rough, hostile derby against Augsburg but today's training session won't be too tough. The coach doesn't want any accidents. Boateng's out and so is Javi, still recovering from the arthroscopic surgery he's undergone for his torn meniscus. Benatia's out too. Bayern's defence is hanging by a thread.

A hush has fallen over the training ground at Säbener Strasse. There's almost nobody around except the players and technical staff and the only sound that breaks the silence is the distant pealing of the city's church bells. They ring out throughout the morning but it's a gentle, calming sound, almost imperceptible, like the sound of running water.

Pep's men are practising positional play and the steady *tac-tac-tac* of the ball blends with the sounds of the bells.

All's right with the world and the session's going well. Until suddenly the silence is shattered.

*Crack!*

It's the unmistakable sound of a bone snapping and everyone freezes. The moment seems to stretch . . . There's a sense of total shock, nobody can believe it. They watch in horrified silence as Holger Badstuber, the cornerstone of Bayern's defence, collapses, howling in pain. He's writhing in agony and in desperation. He's leaned badly on his ankle and it's broken. He holds on to his injured leg, lying on the grass, his screams continuing to puncture the calm tranquillity of the morning. Suddenly twenty-five teammates are around him. They're all devastated. A few of them are so upset they have to move away from the scene and one of them vomits. Lahm runs off to call the ambulance and Pep stands with his hands on his head. He, like most of his players, is fighting tears as he stands helplessly by whilst Badstuber screams. Doctor Braun, a constant presence these days now that the club has changed its policies regarding medical care, is on the spot in seconds. He straps up the break, gives Badstuber a shot and tries to reassure him.

*Crack!*

Like the branch of a tree snapping.

The minutes last forever. Two minutes of Badstuber's screams. Two minutes of nightmare proportions. The most talented defender in Bavaria and Bayern's great hope for the last five years has fallen victim to injury. Again. Since 2012 the player has had to go under the knife six times and any one of the injuries could have ended his career. Six times he's recovered and clawed his way back to the top. This is his seventh injury. But as the minutes pass and Badstuber's anguished screams continue everyone's thinking about the seemingly never ending nightmare the guy's been through.

They're still frozen to the spot, feeling totally numb when the ambulance arrives to take the German defender away. Domènec Torrent and Hermann Gerland are the first to react and they calmly call the end of the session and send everyone off to the showers. Tomorrow they've got the derby match and the team will need to recover from today's events and play their usual masterful game.

When the team bus arrives at Augsburg, everyone's feeling very differently. Badstuber's surgery's been a huge success. It's a clean break and there should be no problems getting back to full fitness. The player himself sends his team mates an upbeat Whatsapp message. He's keen to thank them for all their support. It's like the sun's come out again. Kathleen Krüger, the match delegate, has sorted out t-shirts with messages of support for Badstuber and the team and technical staff wear them ahead of the game. Pep insists on keeping his on throughout the whole match.

The efficient Ms Krüger has also planned another surprise. After dinner at 7.00 pm (Bayern always dine at 7.00 pm on the dot when they're staying away in a hotel together) the technical team and players are all invited to watch the Serie A match between the two Italian leaders, Juventus and Napoli. At 8.45, Pep, Torrent, Planchart, Estiarte and most of the team sit down in a private room in the hotel and watch their future European rival, who win in the last minute thanks to a goal from Zaza.

The next day Bayern produce their finest away game of the season. Domènec Torrent is delighted, 'That was our best game. Along with the Cup game in Wolfsburg in October [1-3].'

Badstuber's accident seems to have fired Bayern's players up. They show their rival no pity. As usual Pep is focused, not just on the immediate objective of the day (to beat Augsburg and get the three precious points they need to stay ahead of Borussia Dortmund), he's also thinking about his tactics for the upcoming Juventus game. He's tried out the line-up he wants in Turin and, although he's told no-one except his closest circle, as long as nothing else changes (and nothing does), these same men will be playing that day.

Four 'little guys' make up today's defence: Lahm (1.70), Kimmich (1.76), Alaba (1.80) and Bernat (1.72). Their short stature means they're at a disadvantage but this is more than offset by their skill at bringing the ball out. It's going to be a big risk facing last year's Champions League finalists with this particular defensive line but his men have made huge strides in the quality of their game and he reckons it's a risk he can afford to take.

The Bavarian derby is a celebration of Bayern's attacking prowess: thirty-six shots on goal, a Bundesliga record. Pep smiles. His men are on a roll. Just in time to go to Turin. With a 'little guys' defence'.

# 10

# ARTISTIC SOUL, RATIONAL MIND

*There are many ways of winning
and very few ways of enjoying yourself*
*Rodrigo Zacheo*

WHEN GUARDIOLA TALKS about his football 'fathers' he's referring to something that's a crucial part of football and our understanding of it. The history of this sport is, after all, the story of knowledge being passed down from master to apprentice, from coaches to their players who themselves will go on to pick up the baton. Jimmy Hogan was a huge influence in Josef Blum's career and he in turn inspired Karl Humenberger, who managed Rinus Michels for five years. Michels then went on to coach Johan Cruyff, who passed his ideas on to Pep Guardiola, who has now shared them with Xavi Hernández and Xabi Alonso . . . The evolution of football has only taken place thanks to the generosity of these men who have been willing to share their expertise either directly with their brightest players or in the form of the legacy they leave at the clubs who employ them. The fact that these men have been prepared to travel, pass on their knowledge and continually challenge the status quo has created the conditions for football innovation throughout history.

There are so many examples of this in football: Gusztáv Sebes starts out copying the work of Hogan and Hugo Meisl; Cruyff imitates Michels; Mourinho, Helenio Herrera; Guardiola, Cruyff . . . And in the end, the students' achievements exceed their mentors for the simple fact that they've been carried upon the shoulders of giants . . .

Therefore, in order to fully understand Guardiola, we must familiarise ourselves with the work of his mentors and in particular of course, his two greatest influences: Cruyff and Lillo. Cruyff: intuitive, spontaneous, creative, artistic, perceptive, uncomplicated. Lillo: rational, intellectual, reflective, profound, erudite, complex.

It shouldn't really surprise us that, given that his mentors possess such different personalities yet coincide so much in terms of their football ideology, their combined influence has inspired both the creative and the rational sides of Guardiola, a man with the soul of an artist and the ruthlessly efficient mind of a winner. The student is the reflection of his masters' teachings.

When Pep sits on a ball in the middle of the training camp, silent and brooding, he's usually reflecting on the upcoming game, how to manage it or exactly what advantages his chosen line-up will give him. This is rational, hard headed, calculating Pep. When we see him in the middle of a game, waving his arms about, shouting furiously and ordering changes of position, this is passionate Pep in full creative flow. Reflective and complex like Lillo; intuitive and instinctive, like Cruyff.

## IDEAS THIEVES

*Ideas are like fleas. They jump from one person to another*
*but they don't always bite*
*George Bernard Shaw*

Guardiola often describes himself as an 'ideas thief' who's not only learned from his mentors but who's constantly on the lookout for new inspiration. He listens and watches, ready to absorb any new information or experience which he may then adapt and use in his own game. He'll say, 'Ideas belong to everyone and I steal as many as I can.' That's how he came up with the idea of asking Messi to revitalise the false No.9 position and, down the years, there have been endless other nuggets he's picked up and then transplanted. Whether he's leafing through a book about rugby which inspires him to perfect the culture of his team or sees how Atlético defend a throw-in and then adds it to his plans for Manchester City . . . Pep never misses the opportunity to find and re-use ideas and inspirations.

He observes, reflects, 'steals' the idea, absorbs it and then applies it to new circumstances and contexts.

It's exactly the process that led to him playing Messi as a false No.9 and the restoration of the pyramid formation in Munich. Guardiola didn't invent these ideas but he was astute enough to draw from the past and identify potentially useful concepts that he could adapt to his current methods. He absorbed these concepts, extracted their essence and produced his own new version.

In Chapter Two I quoted Miquel del Pozo saying that Guardiola has never been interested in pausing to contemplate his masterpiece once it's complete and del Pozo tells us that this attitude reveals 'the genetic characteristics of an artistic and creative mind. The only thing that matters is the moment of creation and when it's complete, he loses interest.'

The philosopher, José Antonio Marina develops this theme further, 'Creativity is based in the wealth of all that has gone before but, afterwards, there's a fundamental decision to be made. Great artists have always agreed that an important part of their work consists of discarding much of what they've produced.'

Marina's words take me back to Munich and a conversation I had with film maker and writer David Trueba, who's a good friend of Guardiola's. We were chatting about Bob Dylan and the creative process he followed when he was composing. I've already referred to this in Chapter Three but Trueba had much more to say, 'This is how Bob Dylan wrote his songs: he'd get up early in the morning and fill pages and pages with verse. I mean, a lot of pages. Then he would go back and ruthlessly strip it down to the bare minimum. He might dump as much as 50% of what he'd written so that he'd be left with the pure essence of what he wanted to say. So basically his creative process consisted of producing a huge amount of work and then distilling it down to the fundamentals.' This is exactly the same thing Marina has described.

Trueba goes on, 'Pep goes through a similar process to Dylan's as he prepares for matches. He fills page upon page in order to be left with the essential verses at the end. And this isn't a new thing for him. Even back when he was at Barça B, he prepared for matches this way, filling pages and pages with his notes. You should ask him to show you his notebooks. It's all in there. Copious notes and several pages on every single game with all the details, the facts, the mistakes, the things that worked . . . It was like he wrote a treatise on each match and then distilled it down to the essentials.'

The creative process that Guardiola goes through consists 'stealing' ideas, absorbing them, extracting the essence, applying them in new ways (using them to innovate) and creating his own masterpiece. His methodology consists of obtaining and preparing detailed information, binning the majority of it and ending up with the core of the new idea.


## AN OBJECTIVE, DRIVEN ROMANTIC

Good football is the football you remember.
*Roberto Fontanarrosa*


There are two sides to Guardiola's character: the hard headed rationalist and the passionate artist. He has the sentimental soul of the artist as well as the warrior spirit of a fierce competitor who always wants to win, combining the radicalism of a typical *Cruyffista* with a kind of Teutonic eclecticism. This is a midfielder famous for his lightning fast passing who wants 'foot on the ball moments' from his players, an introvert who often bares his soul; a coach who believes that football is all about ideas but exhorts his men to 'run like bastards'; an insatiable winner who seeks to be the master of his defeats . . . Essentially, we're talking about two people here: Pep and Guardiola.

'Pep is a surprising mix of someone who's very results driven and a natural romantic, although he's not an aesthete,' says Xavi Valero, former goalkeeper of Welsh club Wrexham FC as well as several Spanish clubs and, since 2007, goalkeeping coach for a variety of clubs including Liverpool, Inter, Chelsea, Napoli and Real Madrid. 'The second time I met him I was really surprised by the things he said. He's absolutely not one of those *ars gratia artis* (art for art's sake) types. I'd expected him to be a bit pretentious, full of himself because that's how he's often portrayed . . . Instead I found a man of deep convictions, a coach who's capable of taking eleven footballers and a ball and transforming passion into reason and a "how" into a "what" and creating a thing of beauty . . . For me, that's Pep all over, a romantic rationalist.'

Xavi Valero sums Pep up perfectly but perhaps the man himself can offer an even better explanation of his character. Here's how Pep described his passion for football one day over lunch in Munich. 'People love to quantify football. It's all about numbers, numbers, numbers. And I always say to them, "How can winning one league title change your life? Or a Champions League trophy? We need to work to produce something that people can admire!" The work that we do has to come from within, from our very souls. Don't get me wrong, the numbers never lie and I live to win, you know that. You know that I always want to win. Always. And I've never said that people have to agree with me. If the things I say don't move you, if you don't feel even the tiniest shiver up your spine or the slightest emotion, then stick with what you're doing, follow your heart . . . But I for one will continue to work to help my players express the best that football can offer and, hopefully, inspire and move those who watch our game.'

If City fans really want to understand their new coach, they'll have to first understand both these sides of Pep. Sometimes they'll see him looking miserable after a victory. They should know that he's probably unhappy with some aspect of the team's game. Other times he may appear untroubled by a defeat because his men have followed the plan to the letter and been beaten by something beyond their control. The new coach might be overheard one day praising a player who's messed up. Don't worry, there's nothing wrong with Pep's eyesight, he just likes to ensure that none of his players feels like a spare wheel. You'll hear him insist that he wants good football: precise passing, a solid, organised defence and intelligent attacking. Then you'll see him celebrating a lethal counter-attack, or a lucky break or a set piece performed to perfection. People will call him a cynical hypocrite for demanding one thing and then celebrating another as though it's unreasonable to insist on your own ideas and then applaud a result that comes through other means.

Those who claim that he often contradicts himself will, I'm sure, find plenty of evidence of this. Many people will struggle to understand his decision making (his line-ups, the distribution of players on the pitch, his changes of system, his game plans . . .) and that's okay because it's complicated. He's a man who has no time for convention and cliché. As Ignacio Benedetti says, no-one can analyse what he doesn't know and understand . . . I promise you though, the best way to understand this man is not to get bogged down in the line-ups he chooses. It's his game plans that really matter.

Guardiola aspires to create a playing model which integrates the total football of Michels and Cruyff with the speed, energy and verticality of the Germans plus the poetry of the Brazilians and the pragmatism of the Italians. Of course he's not unique in this and many coaches before him have developed a similar model, inspired by the Argentine team River Plate, also known as 'La Maquina' (the machine), which sowed the seeds of integrated football back in the 1940s. River Plate was the precursor to many other great sides who either intentionally or spontaneously played football that, to varying degrees, came close to the idea of total football. I'm thinking of the teams led by Sebes, Maslov, Michels, Happel, Lobanovsky, Sacchi and Cruyff. This is the kind of football Guardiola has always aspired to and his experiences in Munich have only served to deepen his resolve. He's more determined than ever to follow this path not just because of his romantic soul and his warrior spirit but, more pragmatically, because in Germany he's proved it can work. Ultimately, Pep wants Manchester City to express themselves both pragmatically and freely although clearly he'll need a lot of time to realise this dream.

So is he more of a romantic or an achiever? Does he lead with his head or his heart?

It's fascinating to me that a football coach can so effectively combine his intellectual understanding of the game with intuition and 'feeling'. I've witnessed both these approaches in action on so many occasions but here's just one example.

## 'FEELING IT'
### Munich, 21 and 22 January 2015

It's the morning of Wednesday 21 January 2015 and Guardiola's arrived at the training ground early. He needs to change his plans for the day. He had intended to do another session similar to yesterday's but tells me he's 'just not feeling it'. This is a very Guardiola turn of phrase. He needs to 'feel' the exercise he's focusing on, he needs to be comfortable with it. He also needs to be in the right mood and feel okay physically. Like all of us, Pep has off days. Maybe he's had a bad night's sleep or is just worn out and a bit down. Or sometimes he's just feeling lazy. On those occasions he may not 'feel' the training exercise he's planned. It doesn't happen often, maybe three or four times since he's been at Bayern, three or four days when he's changed the training routine at the last minute because his head isn't in it or he doesn't feel physically up to it. Today's one of those rare occasions and he draws up new plans for training. Domènec Torrent and Lorenzo Buenaventura modify their own plans accordingly and postpone the original exercises until tomorrow.

It's Thursday 22 January and the players are working on their second session this week of practising returning to their positions after winning the ball. Buenaventura will lead them in explosive drills in which each player will perform twenty-four different movements involving resistance training, dribbling and sprints. Before they do that, Pep takes a session practising winning the ball back followed by immediate attack, rather than a return to positions. It only lasts thirty minutes today but he's absolutely clear about his instructions. Today he's 'feeling' it. His men practise three different kinds of attack once they've got the ball back.

The first variant consists of a diagonal ball from Alonso, aimed at curving into the path of Robben making a run from the outside into the opposition penalty area. The second is an identical diagonal pass but this time curving from the inside to the outside so that the winger can take possession in an 'open' wide position and then look to cross for a Lewandowski finish. The third type of attack is the most complex. It starts with a direct pass to Robben whose orders are to cut inside to the inside forward channel and to link with Lewandowski who moves towards him. When the winger gets his centre forward's pass he'll send the ball right across to the other wing where the receiver will be either Müller on the wing or Bernat arriving in the right hand side inside channel. The network of moves shows who plays in tight spaces, who plays near each other and who links via long passes. And the relationship between these three types of positional play will determine whether the football this team produces is highly fluid or more static. Those who play within tight spaces, those who link by positional association and those who create the play over wide distances – all are fundamental to the positional play Guardiola practises.

It's clear then that Guardiola's is a permanent struggle to marry the rational and the emotional, the complex and the simple, the reflective response with the spontaneous action, thought with feeling. His instinct tells him when he's got the balance right. Above all, he's got to 'feel it'.

# BACKSTAGE 10

## HEROISM
### Munich, 16 March 2016

Maria's sobbing. Her Uncle Pere's standing up on one of the seats in the stadium, also crying. Manel Estiarte, his own eyes welling up, stands massaging his right hand which he's just slammed against the wall. He thinks he might have broken a couple of fingers.

Tears, pain and looks of anguish . . . One might think that the three of them have just witnessed some dreadful accident but what they're actually feeling is pure euphoria. Against all the odds, Bayern have managed to equalise (with a Müller header) in the dying minutes of a tie that appeared lost. Earlier, Maria, Pep's eldest daughter, left her mother and siblings to come up here; Pere, Pep's brother, came over to get away from the Italian fans in the stands; and Estiarte, Pep's right hand man, then joined them. He needed to get away from the agitation and tension of the Bayern players watching the game, Javi Martínez, Tom Starke and Jérôme Boateng.

So Maria, Pere and Manel watch Bayern's heroic comeback from this tiny corner of the stand's main staircase, opposite door 105. It's a comeback that looked pretty improbable after a desperate first half.

'It'll be a miracle if we manage to pull this back,' says Pere at half-time. 'We definitely need a miracle. But if we do manage to pull it off, that'll be it, we'll be flying.'

To everyone's surprise, Juventus have hammered Bayern mercilessly. This is a game that should have been fairly predictable and everyone seems taken aback by what's happened, in the Italian camp just as much as the German.

Five days ago Pep was chatting to his son Màrius and Estiarte over dinner at the stadium after their 5-0 defeat of Werder Bremen (taking them that bit closer to the league title) and began talking them through his ideas about today's game, 'Manel, we know the Italians only too well. You and I are pretty much half Italian ourselves. Well, okay, you're 100% Italian. You know what they'll be after: a one-off chance that they can convert. They'll look for some incident: a corner, a foul, whatever. If they make it to the seventy-fifth minute mark and they're still alive, they'll put three forwards up against us and if we haven't managed to shut them down before then, we'll have a hellish last fifteen minutes. It's a bugger that we didn't do better in Turin [2-2]. They'll definitely look for that one-off chance and if that doesn't work then, being Italian, they'll want to play the "heroes" and then they'll really make us sweat.'

'Shut up Pep. I don't even want to think about it before Monday. Let's not talk about the game. Otherwise I'm going to be up all night.'

But Pep doesn't appear too concerned about his friend's insomnia. He's not going to be put off. 'We'll have to maintain our organisation and not lose our heads.'

'What do you mean by "not lose our heads"?' Màrius wants to know.

'What happened against Madrid. We have to stay in our positions and let the ball move.'

'And have you talked all this through with your players?' asks his son.

'No, it's too soon for that. I want to let them have a good night's sleep first.'

Guardiola and Estiarte believe they know exactly what

to expect from Juve because both of them have a special empathy for the Italian game. Pep's time in Brescia had a huge impact on him and Estiarte's lived in Pescara since he signed for their water polo club in 1984. Pep's already watched all of Juve's games this year and spent the entire bus journey to the Werder Bremen match going over the first half of yesterday's Sassuolo–Juventus clash.

'Without the ball they always defend with five men and then when they've got the ball they switch to a 3-4-3.'

The Werder Bremen game is straightforward and Bayern break yet more records: Lewandowski's now on twenty-four goals after twenty-six league games; the team makes 993 passes; Coman provides three goal assists, equalling Ribéry's record (October 2012); Lahm achieves 167 touches; Thiago scores two goals . . . Bayern have been a whirlwind today but even that doesn't stop Domènec Torrent worrying about the Juve game. He's so uptight he's having trouble sleeping and is up in the small hours every morning. This goes on for the next three days. He wakes up at four, five, six am, checks the time on his phone and starts to think about Juventus . . . Then, out of the blue, the night before the big game, he's sleeping like a baby.

It's never been Bayern's performance that worries him. It's more what the Italian giants are capable of. 'We're in good shape and the lads are all completely focused. They know what they're doing. Every single player understands the reason for every movement, for everything we do on the pitch. It's all really coming together now.'

Torrent, like Carles Planchart, is convinced they're going to beat Juve. 'There's no doubt in my mind. We're going to win. You can never take anything for granted in football but I really believe that our game and our current form make us the stronger side.'

By Saturday night Pep's just about decided on his line-up. The only choices are: Vidal or Thiago and Robben or Coman. Then, at Sunday morning training, Robben complains of some pain in his left adductor muscle after a six-a-side game. It doesn't look like a serious injury but everybody's pain threshold is different and what would be a mild irritation for the likes of Vidal or Javi is a big deal for a player like Robben. Even so, when it happens nobody has any idea that this is going to turn into something more serious and that Robben's not just going to miss the Juve game but the rest of the season as well.

Pep's been a bundle of energy this morning, leading the session with an almost ferocious intensity. 'There has to be a bit of competitive tension. Without that the team's dead. You have to maintain that level of aggression and there will always be people looking to wind you up, which is great, because it helps keep the tension high. We all need friends. But we need enemies too.'

Lewandowski stays back on his own for another twenty minutes at the end of the session to practise penalties. 'He's keen to start taking penalties. I'm really pleased that Lewy's always looking for ways to improve,' says Pep.

Monday comes and goes without any major developments. Robben definitely won't make it to the game but the club isn't making that public for the time being. What nobody knows yet is that Kimmich is suffering a bit with muscular problems. With guys like Ribéry and Coman available the team can do without Robben but Kimmich is irreplaceable. He's the backbone of the team, the guy who's led Bayern's defence single handed since February. The team revolves around him and without Kimmich, all their plans and ideas would fall to pieces but he won't countenance the thought of not playing and is anxious to allay any doubts the coach may have. 'Pep, I'll play no matter what. No amount of pain's going to stop me. You can count me in.'

As a precaution, the young German's training is restricted to a recuperation session with Holger Broich and the rest of the squad barely do an hour of proper training. They do the rondos with a bit more care than usual. Everybody's desperate to avoid unnecessary bumps and bangs. Then they move to tactical work: practising bringing the ball out, the full backs positioning themselves near Bayern's pivote midfielder and Costa in the inside forward position.

The snow starts in the early hours of Tuesday morning and goes on for the next twenty hours. Training's restricted to a few drills to build explosive power, the rondos, positional play and a few other tactical moves. The weather conditions mean they have to abandon their plans to practise the runs down the wings and crossing for the strikers to shoot at goal.

Before training starts Bayern find out that Marchisio and Chiellini will be out of Juve's line-up and midway through the morning they get the news that Dybala's also injured and won't be coming. Estiarte informs Pep but the coach doesn't see any reason to change his plans. 'Let's not kid ourselves. This doesn't change anything. We only got a draw in the away game and those three didn't play then either. So this changes nothing. In fact, missing those players will probably mean that they'll be working even harder for their one-off chance.'

Both teams' press conferences are exercises in diplomacy. Massimiliano Allegri calmly delivers the news about his team's injuries. 'We're missing three players but it's no big deal. It would need to be something much more serious than that to worry us. What is clear however is that tomorrow we're going to have to play a very defensive game.' Football legend Gigi Buffon adds his own comments. 'It's going to be a game worthy of a Champions League semi-final. Bayern have spent five years consolidating their position at the highest level and they're a fantastic side. Tomorrow we're just going to have to see which team has the most guts.'

Guardiola's similarly laid back. 'You can't sit worrying about the result for ninety minutes. Just the last fifteen! You know, I never really get too uptight during our games. I really enjoy them.'

As he speaks, Pep has no idea that tomorrow he'll be worrying about the result for a lot more than ninety minutes and he'll be feeling anything but pleasure. The best made plans . . .

The next day, during the pre-match talk the normally meticulous Guardiola makes an unusual slip. The team's followed the same ritual for three years now and, as usual, the players are called into one of the hotel's meeting rooms two and a half hours before the game. One after the other they troop in and sit down. Hermann Gerland checks that everyone's here, turns off the light and shuts the door. That's Pep's cue to start. This is his third and last talk (remember, he never goes into the dressing room before a game) and as usual he starts by giving them the line-up. He steps up to the whiteboard and begins. 'Right gentlemen, today's line-up is: Manu, Rafa, Kimmich, Benatia, David, Xabi, Arturo . . .' Somebody coughs politely at the back and Domènec Torrent jumps up and interrupts his boss, who's still moving his magnetic 'players' around the whiteboard.

'Sorry Pep, did you say Rafa?'

This is followed by a loud noise from the back of the room. Rafinha's on his feet and shouting in fake annoyance, 'Shut it Dome, you bastard.'

Everyone cracks up with laughter. Everyone, that is, except Pep who apologises for his mistake.

'Sorry, Rafa; sorry, Philipp.'

Rafinha's still enjoying the joke. 'Dome, you total bastard. If Pep hadn't noticed I'd have had my chance . . .'

The mistake and Rafinha's joke leave everyone feeling more relaxed but Pep's keen to get back to business as soon as the laughter subsides. He repeats his line-up, this time including Lahm instead of Rafa. He wants Benatia and Kimmich as central defenders, Xabi and Vidal will form a partnership in the middle of the park without Thiago and, given Robben's injury, Ribéry, not Coman will be on the wing. Pep then takes some time to explain why he thinks that Juventus will be actively looking for an 'incident', a one-off chance to score. It could be any of the many unplanned things that happen during a match: a slip in ball control, a corner, a momentary lapse of concentration . . . If they find a way to score, Bayern will be left with a mountain to climb. The Italian side has one of the strongest defences in Europe. Pep reminds his men that he wants to see precise passing, aggression in 50/50 challenges and confident clearances. Today more than ever.

It's bitterly cold outside so the warm-up lasts a bit longer than usual. Lahm and Müller go through the ritual they established at the start of the season: the captain crosses the ball to the striker who then tries to score with headers. Lahm sends eight crosses into the area but Müller fails to hit the target even once . . .

At 20.45, Pep shouts and gestures from the side-line. He's trying to catch the attention of Xabi, Lahm and Kimmich, the brains of his team. 'Five,' says the coach. 'Five,' he repeats waving his hand at them. Juve will be defending with five men. This had been Pep's only real doubt at the pre-match talk: whether the Italians would use four or five in defence. Pep's had a look at the way the Italians have positioned themselves ahead of kick-off and it's obvious that they've gone for five at the back. Alex Sandro will be going for a two v one by doubling up the cover on Douglas Costa. The match kicks off and Pep ensures Xabi's got the message. 'There's five in defence!' he yells over again.

In the first minute a nice effort from Vidal almost puts Bayern ahead. But it's a case of 'so near and yet so far' and things quickly start to unravel for the Germans. Juve don't have to wait long for their chance. It's only five minutes in when David Alaba makes a monumental error and hands the first goal on a platter to Pogba in front of an open goal. Alaba, despite his many extraordinary talents, often finds himself momentarily disorientated when he has to turn and run towards his own goal. And this is exactly what happens now: Khedira thumps the ball to Lichsteiner, forcing Alaba to turn. He loses sight of the ball for a second and also fails to notice that Neuer's sprinting out of his goal. The ball lands at Pogba's feet and he sends it straight into the empty goal. The Italian's chance has come in the first five minutes. It's exactly what Pep wanted to avoid. Bayern have played right into Juve's hands. It's already looking bad for the home side and things are about to get much, much worse . . .

Juventus begin to short-circuit Bayern's game plan. First Morata and Cuadrado press ferociously with Khedira, Pogba and Alex Sandro making up the second wave to back them up. Bayern are struggling to bring the ball out from the back and build the game the way they're used to. It's the first time this season that the Germans have failed to implement the plan: control the ball, set up camp in the rival's area and dominate the rhythm of the game. Things go from bad to worse when David Alaba loses an easy ball on the edge of the Juventus area and Morata sets off on an astonishing eighty metre slalom run, sprinting straight past Bayern players and mowing down all comers. Juventus are on fire and no-one can stop the Spanish striker. Not Alaba in the first forty metres of his run, or Benatia, when he passes the centre circle, nor Alonso as he attempts to tackle. Not even Vidal's emergency intervention can stop the Juve player as he sets the ball up sweetly for Cuadrado to score Juve's second goal. The score's now 0-2 and as the Bayern fans are plunged into stunned silence, Pep feels like it's the final nail in their coffin. Any kind of comeback looks impossible.

As always when things get rocky Manuel Neuer comes to the rescue and saves two more dangerous shots, either of which would have sounded Bayern's death knell. Cuadrado and Morata have a good chance each but the keeper gets to them both. The referee mistakenly calls Morata offside and disallows a goal although it's not the striker who's punished but the move leading to it. But Bayern are in pieces. They're making too many mistakes and failing to cope with the aggressive, brilliant football the Italians are producing. Even worse, their own game is being totally neutralised by Juve's defensive wall. They can't find any way to break through and look far too dispirited to come back from their disastrous first forty-five minutes.

Medhi Benatia, even more than Alaba, is the symbol of Bayern's chaos. He looks slow, sloppy and woefully short of confidence. The magnitude of the occasion is obviously getting to him and he's a bundle of nerves.

Bayern Munich crowds are similar to what you'll find at the Camp Nou or Real Madrid's Santiago Bernabéu. Quick to criticise and condemn, these supporters demand that their team excite and entertain. It's not for them to lift their team's spirits and cheer them on to a glorious fightback – it should be vice versa. And so it is tonight as a deathly hush descends on the Allianz Arena, only pierced by two thousand indefatigable, ever-noisy Ultras, who are the only section of the Bayern end prepared to match the cheers and songs of the ecstatic *tifosi*. The Italian supporters are having the time of their lives and they can almost taste the victory that now looks inevitable.

As the two teams go off to the dressing rooms at half-time, Mario Madzukic crosses paths with one of Bayern's technical staff and flashes him a triumphant smile as if to say, 'You made a big mistake with me and now you've no-one but yourselves to blame . . .'

Guardiola has five minutes in which to react. Inside the dressing room it feels like a wake. Out on the grass, Juan Bernat is just finishing his warm-up. Pep gave him the nod thirty-five minutes in, intending to bring him on for Benatia. It's the obvious change to make and his staff are all agreed. 'Sure, we need a goal to get back into the game but before that I'd like to see a bit more confidence and calm. We need more security at the back.'

Estiarte's talking about pulling their life jackets on and getting every man to the tiller, without thinking about it too much. Pep has two objectives: he wants to give the team more security and he thinks David Alaba needs calming down. He's less likely to become disorientated in the central defence position. Pep's also considering the idea of substituting Ribéry, who's had a dreadful first half, for Coman, but decides to make no more changes for now. He believes the team can still recover and start to perform.

The second half starts badly. Bayern still play poorly and only avoid conceding more goals thanks to Neuer's capable hands. Juve are on sparkling form. They know exactly what they're doing and are riding high on the two-goal lead. They continue to thwart Bayern at every turn and the home side are prevented from constructing their game. Pep's players stick steadfastly to their positions but their rhythm is off and their game fails to flow. The noose is slowly tightening around Guardiola's neck when, at the sixty-minute mark, he brings Coman on for Xabi Alonso.

'I was trying to think what Cruyff would do in my shoes and that's what popped into my mind,' Pep will tell Jorge Valdano over lunch tomorrow.

The change makes all the difference. Coman coming on as a right winger moves Costa up to the inside forward position and Bayern's game in this area suddenly picks up, despite the fact that Juve still have a three v two advantage. It's now that Bayern's players start to show how technically gifted they are. Costa drives forward, hammering continually at the Juve defence, weaving in and out, either alone or supported by Coman and Lahm. At first sight the wall of Italian defenders looks unbreachable and Coman's initial dribbles get nowhere but very gradually cracks begin to open up as Ribéry constantly sprints up and down the pitch in support.

It's better but not yet enough. They're up against the grandmasters of defensive organisation. Juve are so confident that Allegri goes ahead with two changes: Sturaro comes on for Khedira, who's totally exhausted and has been arriving late in his pressing for the last few minutes and Mandzukic substitutes the astounding Morata. Within a minute Lewandowski converts a Costa cross and everything suddenly looks very different. A heroic comeback is starting to look possible but it's up to Bayern to make it happen. Costa, Coman and Ribéry continue to harry the Italians.

In the eighty-fifth minute, Juve launch a big press on Bayern who respond by bringing the ball out with their customary patience and organisation: more speed, less haste, that's how it must be. Pep's men refuse to be rushed. They don't lob long balls into the distance, nor do they go for full frontal attack or any other similarly desperate tactics. This team will live or die with their playing model. In the stands, the fans clearly don't know whether to cheer them on or give them up for lost. The heart's gone out of them, a bit like Thiago, who's been warming up on the side for more than thirty minutes, initially at full tilt, then a little less energetically and now, looking decidedly dejected.

Then, in the ninetieth minute Coman reaches the byline and sends in a cross . . .

Tomorrow Pep will confess quietly, 'I had a nightmare last night about Coman's centre. I dreamt he got the ball, dribbled it forward and then sent it straight into the stands . . .'

But in real life the opposite happens. The ball curves majestically through the air over Bonucci's head, evading Barzagli's desperate efforts to block it, straight to Müller, the man who missed all those easy headers during the warm-up. This time however, he's right on target. The Allianz Arena explodes. Bayern celebrate. Juventus crumble.

In the short break before extra time Guardiola keeps his message short and sweet: the game's over and Juve's morale's completely broken.

Extra time starts with Thiago on for Ribéry and the Spaniard promptly loses his first two balls. He's a bundle of nerves and Pep's screaming at him from the touchline. There's no doubt that the coach treats him differently from the rest of his players. Thiago's his (football) son and he expects perfection from him. He won't tolerate the kind of slip-up he might overlook in someone else. Alaba, for example, who's made two serious errors tonight. But Pep refuses to let Thiago off the hook and gives him a furious talking to at the break. Thankfully, Thiago takes it all in his stride and ups his game accordingly.

Juventus still haven't recovered from Bayern's goal in the ninetieth minute and are obviously just clinging on for the penalty shoot-out. But Bayern are on a roll. They want to win in open play. They mount wave after wave of attacks against the Italian defence until suddenly it all comes together. Vidal steals the ball and Thiago penetrates the area where he teams up with Müller who picks this moment to turn on the magic only he, the world's most talented 'klutz', is capable of. Anywhere else on the pitch he might have lost control but here, in the box, Müller's at his brilliant best, transformed. With his left foot, he sends a gentle, perfectly aimed ball back to Thiago who puts Bayern's third goal away.

The whole stadium erupts. Bayern's supporters can hardly believe their eyes and, as their euphoric celebrations begin, Pep's men re-group, sticking to their positions and outnumbering their opponents in all the key areas. Two minutes later Coman's got the ball and he's charging up the pitch in a lethal counter-attack, which culminates in another goal for Bayern – eliminating the team which loaned him to them at the beginning of the season. Guardiola's agony is over.

'The noose was around our necks and suddenly Robin Hood appeared to save the day,' he'll say later over dinner.

Jérôme Boateng grabs Maria Guardiola and throws her up in the air. Pep's eldest daughter's face is shining with joy although she's cried right up to the final whistle. It's been a brutal tie. One for the history books. Maria clambers down a few steps and hugs her mother, who's also crying. Cristina has watched the game with Coman and Kimmich's parents and was so nervous during extra time that she incorrectly thought Juve still needed another goal to go through, even when Bayern led 4-2.

The tie has been a rollercoaster for both teams and the results show this. Bayern dominating, utterly, for an hour in Turin and leading 2-0. Then the following seventy-five minutes across the two matches showing an unstoppable Juve who led that period of the tie 4-0 [two goals in Turin and 2-0 ahead in Bavaria], then the last fifty minutes when it's Pep's team who score four astounding goals. It's been a tense but sensational tie and Jorge Valdano says later over a drink in the press room, 'The best film maker in the world couldn't have come up with a better plot. These guys have given us so many extraordinary performances. It's the very best that football can offer.'

For the first time ever the whole technical team end up in the lift at the same time. Guardiola, Torrent, Planchart and Estiarte are delighted. They ask for a photo to be taken as a memento of this unforgettable evening.

But when he arrives at the players' restaurant it's all too much and Pep collapses. Tonight he has no interest in the cheese platter or the hams or even a glass of champagne and contents himself with kissing Cristina and the kids and then collapsing on to the sofa with them. He doesn't utter a word for fully half an hour. Totally spaced out, he only manages a couple of words with Màrius, whilst his youngest daughter, Valentina stretches out, exhausted, across two chairs. Maria's complaining of a bad headache and asks her mum if she can take a taxi home and get to bed.

'No. I'm sorry Maria, we all have to stay until dad says it's time to go,' says Cristina.

Too exhausted to celebrate properly, Pep eventually asks for some pasta from Germano Gobbetti, the Italian chef. 'Give me something to eat before I faint.'

This has been the tensest match of his life and he's had to draw on all his internal resources to cope. The evening's events have also reinforced his belief that, no matter what he, as coach, does, it's the players who ultimately win or lose the game. Today it's all come down to a nineteen-year-old's ability to cross a ball without sending it into the stands and the skill of a striker who missed eight headers during the warm-up . . .

Around midnight Pep says something we thought we'd never hear. 'Dome, you'll have to do training tomorrow. I won't be capable . . .' He's absolutely drained. Everyone is. There's no celebrating, just a quiet sense of satisfaction. They haven't yet shaken off the emotional fatigue.

As it turns out, Pep's at Säbener Strasse by 9.00 am the next morning and he takes the training session after all. It's a sunny, warm, Mediterranean day and the coach is able now to express all the joy that wasn't possible last night. They'd beaten Juve.

'We were definitely lucky. If Coman had sent that ball into the stands or Müller's header had hit the post . . . But you've got to make your own luck. We played fifty minutes with five strikers against last season's finalists. We created our own luck with those five strikers.'

I remind Pep that it was still a massive risk and his answer makes me wonder. Does he know something the rest of us don't?

'You have to take risks like that, like playing with five strikers, for Johan Cruyff and the others like him. You have to do it for him. He was the one who taught us that you have to make your own luck.'

Just seven days later Pep sits down to write to his friends. It's a short message, just three words, 'Johan has died.'

# 11

# A FEROCIOUS COMPETITOR

When I'm white I win because I'm white.
When I'm black I win because I'm Bogoljubov.
*Efim Bogoljubov*

LET'S DEFINE SOME of the words we use when we talk about competition:

- Participate: to take part in an activity
- Compete: two or more competitors striving to outdo each other for a 'prize'
- Competition: the rivalry offered by a competitor in the market
- Competitive: the capacity of a certain strategy to give one competitor an advantage over the other
- Win: to gain victory in a game

One of Guardiola's great virtues is his ferocious competitive drive and he also inspires his players to higher and higher levels of competitive effort. His list of achievements is impressively long and he's won 65% of all the titles he's contested (twenty-two trophies in eight seasons: one with Barcelona B, fourteen with Barça, and seven with Bayern). What's even more striking is the fact that, in the thirty-four competitions he's contested since 2007, he's failed to make it to the semi-final or the final on only one occasion (Copa del Rey, 2010). That's the figure that tells us everything about this man's will to win: thirty-three times out of thirty-four he's been a finalist or a semi-finalist (champion on twenty-two occasions, runner-up on five and semi-finalist six times).

There's no doubt that Manchester City's new coach is a ruthless competitor who approaches every single tournament with the same killer instinct. Pep understands that an elite football team can never afford to coast, in any competition, and must fight for every game, every title. Just ten years ago this kind of attitude was relatively rare in football. Since 2009 we've had four treble winners (Barça twice and Inter and Bayern once each), exactly the same number we had in the fifty-five years prior to that date (Celtic, Ajax, PSV and Manchester United). Pep is one of the people who's helped to change people's attitudes and another elite coach has played a significant role in this process too. José Mourinho's combative style and bitter rivalry with the Catalan has given us astonishing displays of football down the years and now, with Mourinho in charge at Manchester United, we can expect even more epic battles between the two men. As Pep himself said at his first press conference, 'Great coaches like Mourinho have made me better at my job.'

As we've seen, being competitive isn't the same thing as winning. Unlike other sports, in football there isn't always a direct relationship between the relative talent and skill of the respective teams and the end result. This is less of an issue in league competitions where the need to sustain a consistently strong performance over a long period usually means that there are fewer surprises and the stronger, more tactically able teams triumph in the end. This doesn't apply to knock-out competitions, like the Champions League, or short term tournaments such as the Euros and the World Cup, which often produce the most unexpected of events. In fact, since the Champions League was established in its current form in 1992, no team has ever won it two years in a row.

Being a merciless competitor doesn't guarantee you victory but it can get you very close. Pep has won 328 of the 450 games he's managed (72.9%), with his best results coming in the league (76.4%) and the Cup (75%). It's highly unlikely that at City he'll hit the heights of his Barcelona days (victory in 76.3% of all league games) or produce as consistently good results as he did in Munich, where he won 82.3% of league games and 83.3% of Cup clashes. But, if City fans can't reasonably expect those kinds of results, they can be confident that the team will fight for every ball in every single game, no matter the opponent. Their coach may use five defenders or five strikers, the team may play well or badly, they may win or lose, but one thing's for sure, they will bring remorseless determination and maximum effort to everything they do. With Pep in charge City will never settle for second place.

## KILIAN JORNET
### Munich, 26 January 2016

Very few sportsmen have impacted on Guardiola as much as Kilian Jornet, the Spanish ski mountaineer and long distance runner. They first met in Munich at an event organised by Gore-Tex, who sponsor both men, and Pep was immediately fascinated by what Jornet had to say. He knew that there would be something he could take from Jornet's experience and adapt it to football.

At the time Kilian was preparing to scale Everest without oxygen, carrying a 10 kilo rucksack and running all the way from base camp to the summit. He told Pep that his preparations for this hazardous event had included trying to establish how many training sessions he could get through surviving on water alone. And he'd found that he could manage double the number of sessions he'd usually do over a five-day period. On the first two days he was able to train as normal but by the third day, he slipped, managing 75% of his usual intensity. By the fourth day, he was back at peak form for the morning session but dropped to 70% by the afternoon and on the fifth day noticed a sharp decline in his performance, although he was still able to manage the double session. He had subjected his body to this intense stress specifically to determine his physical limits before undertaking the extreme challenge ahead. Guardiola was blown away by his story and began to pose his own

> questions, 'What are the limits of a football team? What methods should we use to establish those limits? This is definitely something we need to work on . . .'

## AFTER EVEREST

When you reach the summit, you can go no further.
And yet, it's difficult to stop because basically,
there's nothing to do there and it's usually bad weather.
*Mijail Tal*

Garry Kaspárov looks at Rona Petrosian, the wife of the 1963 and 1969 World Chess Champion, Tigran Petrosian, as she approaches. If he's expecting effusive congratulations then he's about to be disappointed. It's 9 November 1985 and Kaspárov's just won the twenty-fourth game of his competition against Anatoli Kárpov. They've fought a long, fierce battle and Kaspárov, who's still just twenty-two, has emerged triumphant, the symbol of Mikhail Gorbachev's new Russia. He's taken on the Soviet establishment and won. The new World Chess Champion stands proudly in the Tchaikovsky Concert Hall enjoying the attentions of ecstatic well-wishers when Petrosian whispers in his ear, 'I feel so sorry for you. You've just experienced the biggest day of your life.'

Kaspárov pops up in Pep's life a lot. The two men used to meet over dinner in New York and Guardiola often mentions Kaspárov's views on many people's tendency to consider things to be 'impossible', a topic he'd first raised in 2012. Two years later Guardiola found himself in Säbener Strasse arguing with assistant coach, Domènec Torrent, on this very subject. 'Forget it Pep. It's impossible. You'll never get another team to play like that.'

'You're wrong Dome. It's definitely possible. Okay, maybe we'll never produce exactly the same game elsewhere but we're more than capable of achieving the same level of dominance. I promise you, we'll do it again. It's more than possible.'

The two men were discussing Barça's playing model which had produced six titles in 2009 (a feat still unmatched today) and fourteen trophies in four years. Today they weren't thinking about trophies and stats however, they were discussing the rudiments of the game and the level of dominance Barça had achieved. Neither man believed that recreating another 'Barça' was a realistic proposition but Pep was sure that he could build another team capable of that same domination.

For Guardiola, you get the results you want by sticking to your playing model. 'Our success and our trophies will always be a direct result of the kind of game we play.' Get the process right and the results will follow. Sure, sometimes things don't go to plan, you have a brilliant game and are still defeated but, in general, the quality of the football you play dictates the level of your success. Any team that can sustain a consistent level of superlative football over an extended period has certainly earned the right to be compared to the Barça side which dominated world football so absolutely. Once you reach the top however, there's nowhere else to go.

Manel Estiarte agrees, 'The word "treble" is going to be a burden for Guardiola. People will always remember his glorious early success but that kind of thing adds a lot of pressure. Having said that, it's the kind of pressure everyone wants. We'd all love to have achieved what he has done.'

There's a Mongolian proverb that fits the bill perfectly. 'If you've never risen, you've never fallen' expresses precisely Guardiola's attitude to the trophies he's won as well as the playing model he favours. What did Edmund Hillary feel after conquering Everest? That there was no higher mountain to scale (Everest is the highest mountain in the world, as we know) but he continued to tackle other mountains and conquered ten more which were over eight thousand metres high. Pep has a similar attitude. 'It's complicated. On the one hand I'm unlikely ever to repeat what I did there [at Barcelona] and that feels frustrating. But on the other hand I have this desperate need to try again and am genuinely convinced that it's possible to produce exceptional football with another team.'

And in Munich he did just that. Although he won fewer titles than with Barcelona (50% compared to 73%), Pep turned Bayern into a winning machine which achieved dominance in its game as well as producing some unforgettable nights of world-class football: against Manchester City, Roma, Arsenal, Juventus, Atlético . . . Bayern didn't manage the consistency and regularity of that exceptional Barcelona side, but, over the piece, they regularly produced high-quality, inventive, winning football. And it's that experience in Germany that drives Guardiola on, allowing him to push past any nagging doubts and strive for more and greater achievements. He understands that there's nowhere left to go once you've reached the top and accepts that his glory days may well already be behind him. But he wants to try. And he firmly believes that it's possible, 'It's not about the trophies you win. It's the way you make people feel. When people talk about Barça, they don't count up the trophies, they remember the way we played. The important thing is how you make people feel. It's all about the emotion, the passion!'


## RUN LIKE BASTARDS

Winners never give up
and those who give up never win.
*Vince Lombardi*


From time to time I've asked myself what exactly is involved in Guardiola's work method. The answer is deceptively simple: he works hard, develops new ideas and then adapts them, listens to his players and works to convince them. He also needs to be convinced himself and is always ready to change or discard ideas as long as his core philosophy is preserved. If he's sure of something then he'll insist on following it through, but he's also quite happy to change direction if necessary. In other words, rather like the rest of us, he's a human being in constant evolution, driven by his own ambition and inspired by the world around him, a man who constantly questions himself.

Guardiola is very, very demanding. There's no space for 'downtime' in a Guardiola training session (other than the pre-planned breaks he allows). He wants maximum effort. Always. Pep uses the term 'run like bastards' a lot and this can be misleading because he doesn't actually want his players doing loads of running during games. His idea is that the ball comes to them not the other way round. His meaning is qualitative rather than quantitative and refers to the effort he expects from his men. For Pep the word 'run' means 'put your backs into it' and he only tolerates players who are willing to push themselves to their absolute limits.

## I'VE GOT A GOOD FEELING
### Manchester, 5 July 2016

He misses football during the summer break. He craves it. It's only been forty-five days since his last training session in Munich but he's been desperate to get back to work and today, his first day in charge at Manchester City, he's fizzing with energy. He's working at full tilt, sparking with electricity as if he's waited years to be here on the pitch with his players and the ball. This is the start of his new project and he's feeling just as excited as he did when he started out at Barcelona or Bayern.

He knows that not all his current players will be sticking around but it makes no difference. He's on fire. Just a few days ago we got together in Barcelona and were chatting through his plans for City when he suddenly announced in that peculiar way of his, 'I've got this great feeling about [X]. I think he's a much better player than people give him credit for. Txiki's given me a few videos and I've really been impressed by him. He seems a great guy too, a real team player. Yeah, I definitely like him. Everyone's saying that I'm bound to get rid of him but not only am I going to keep him, I have a feeling that he's going to become one of the stars of the team.' (Apologies to my readers. I can't share the name of the player he was talking about.)

More than anything Guardiola is determined to transmit his high energy and warrior spirit to a City side which has lacked ambition and competitive drive of late. We're all aware that Pep demands high levels of technical and tactical performance from his players but not everyone understands that he's just as exacting about physical and mental effort. He won't tolerate anything less than total commitment and 100% exertion. He'll say, 'run like bastards' but what he means is, 'graft like you're a talentless nobody'. With Pep, you put your back into it or you're out, no matter who you are. He doesn't mind the fact that players sometimes fail, as long as they've put the effort in, but woe betide any man who turns up for the first day of pre-season carrying extra weight . . . Total professionalism, at all times. It's non-negotiable.

## NEVER RELAX, LEDECKY

Heaven, were man.
But constant, he were perfect.
*William Shakespeare*

Any team reflects the personality and state of mind of its coach. 'Of course it does,' says Pep. 'If I'm having an off-day, training never goes well but when I'm on top form I can really motivate the players, help them correct their mistakes, even give them a good talking to if they need it. And then they perform brilliantly. That's my big challenge this year. Never allow my own form to dip. No matter what happens. No matter how I'm feeling. That's my goal. You know I don't think it was good for me winning the league so early in the season over the last few years. I found it much harder to maintain my intensity and I think the team picked up on it. They sensed that I'd taken my foot off the pedal slightly because we'd won the title. It wasn't a huge slide but at this elite level if you even drop to 99% effort it can damage you. You lose a point here and there, you start to miss the small details and you end up paying for it. It's pretty basic. Never, ever relax. Maximum effort. Always.'

It's 15 August 2015 and Guardiola has just started his last season at Bayern. The team played its first league game of the season yesterday, beating Hamburg 5-0 ('Finally! A good performance to start the season!'). It's unbearably hot in Munich and the shades erected by the club only slightly lessen the feeling of being slowly baked alive.

'Rafa, what on earth have you got there?'

Rafinha's come out of the dressing room with a tub of ice-cream in his hand. Initially he thinks Pep's joking but the coach isn't laughing. 'Rafa, you know that every last detail counts. Ice-cream matters too. Sure, you can have a little bit but I don't want you putting on weight. Not even a gram. We can't afford to get this wrong.'

Rafinha immediately goes back into the dressing room and throws the ice-cream in the bin. There's going to be no let-up for anyone this year.

'You see? If I relax the team relaxes,' explains Guardiola.

He understands that sustaining your position at the top means never allowing the competitive tension to drop. There can be no respite and this too creates its own problems.

'It's very tough working with the same team for three years. Very, very hard. Unless you have a complete shake-up every year. We tend to exhaust each other, the players and the coach. It's inevitable because we're all giving it 100%. All of us have put our backs into this project, given it everything we've got and I'm pretty sure we're all going to end up absolutely done in.'

So that's it. That's Pep's 'magic formula'. Give 100% and never relax.

We're chatting in the room next to Bayern's dressing room and the conversation turns to the demands of elite competition and how important it is for all athletes to push themselves beyond their comfort zone. Manel Estiarte regales us with lurid tales about Dragan Matutinovic's harsh regime (the Croatian water polo coach led Estiarte and his teammates to silver medal position in the Olympics, World Cup and European Cup between 1991 and 1992), and Guardiola mentions Katie Ledecky, the sensational multi-medal-winning US swimming champion.

'I was reading an interview with her the other day, about how she finds the motivation and energy for her training routine: she swims at 4.45 every morning. Just imagine! 4.45 am! She said, "When I dive into the pool I tell myself that I'm the only person in the world capable of swimming like a mad thing every morning at that hour and that's the thought that keeps me going, keeps me motivated."'

All sportsmen must be extremely self-driven but coaches need highly developed motivational skills too, says athletics champion Loles Vives, who's also part of the conversation. But how does one maintain that level of energy and input?

Pep isn't clear, 'That's the million dollar question. It's the key to success. And I don't really know the answer. So many writers who don't know the first thing about me have written about my "magic formula" and it simply doesn't exist. I don't turn up at training every morning, click my fingers and make all the solutions appear. That's total rubbish. I don't have all the answers. All I know is that none of us can afford to relax. We're human beings and, like everyone else, we have our own internal impulses, the things that motivate each of us. What works for Katie Ledecky is the fact that she's the only person in the world willing to get up at that hour in the morning to slog away in the swimming pool. But maybe one day that'll change. She'll fall in love with some boy and then 4.45 sessions in the pool won't be so appealing and she'll switch to 6.00 am, which is also an impressively early start. But those seventy-five minutes will make all the difference and she might add fractions of a second to her time . . . There's just no magic formula that can keep you on top form. But you've got to try. For example, I get really hacked off with the way people criticise me but, at the same time, I understand that it's a good thing because it keeps me on my toes. So, on balance, I'm grateful for all the journalists and football pundits who slag me off. Michael Jordan used to say that if you don't already have a few enemies, you should make some. And he was right. In sport you need to be a bit wound up and tense. Feeling satisfied and full of yourself can be very damaging. It's constant movement and a bit of agitation that helps us maintain the right balance, not relaxation and downtime. That's why you have to avoid getting too comfortable. And that's why coaches have to give their players a kick up the backside every now and then. To stop them relaxing too much . . .'

Last night, as well as playing their first league game of the season, Bayern heard the results of the draw for the second round of the Cup at the end of October. The news couldn't have been worse and they've drawn last year's Cup winners VfL Wolfsburg (who were also runners-up in the Bundesliga last season).

We're standing in the team's private lift in the Allianz Arena. It's not particularly impressive: a rectangular metal box without a mirror or any other decorative touch. It's basically a service lift. The atmosphere inside is usually serious and thoughtful and Pep's got into the habit of sharing his thoughts about each game with me whilst we travel up and down together. He's also opened up a great deal about future plans, none of which I'm able to share.

Unlike most of his colleagues, Pep's happy with the results of the draw despite the fact that Bayern will be facing the champions in their own ground in just eleven weeks' time. 'Fucking brilliant. They'll really be feeling it by then. We'll have played ten league games by that time and we'll be well into the Champions League, playing three days a week. The pressure of those three games will be getting to them by then. They'll really be feeling it . . . In any case I'd rather have a tough opponent because it'll keep us sharp. We all know that we can't afford to take the pressure off and that's great. I can see how tense the players are. They're all coming to training determined to earn their place in the team. There are no guaranteed starters these days, except for Manu [Neuer]. Everyone else knows they have to work for their place. Every day. And that suits me just fine because it means I can push them to the limit.' (Pep mimes squeezing the juice out of an orange.)

A few weeks later Pep is called upon to oversee the oddest game of his career so far. The board has organised a friendly against Jahn Regensburg (in Ratisbona) bang in the middle of international leave and Pep has only five players from the first team available (keepers Ulreich and Starke plus Lahm, Alonso and Rode). The fixture is so badly timed that he can't even call on his B team players, who had a game yesterday and has had to take players from Bayern's youth categories. Rather than cancel the tie, Pep decides to approach the game with as much dignity as possible and tries to get the best he can out of the youngsters. This is Domènec Torrent's perspective on the whole affair. 'Good manners have always been important to Pep. He tries to do the right thing and is always prepared to put himself out. Look at what happened today with these kids representing Bayern. Any other coach would have refused flat out but Pep went through with it even though he knew we couldn't possibly win. He took it really seriously, gave the lads their instructions and put as much effort as ever into winning, for the badge and for the prestige of the club. He could have said no and taken ten days' leave but that's not his way. At the minute we've only got three outfield players here and it would have been perfectly reasonable for him to take the chance for a break. Anyone else would have done that in his shoes. But Pep preferred to fight on for the sake of the club. He opted to coach a bunch of seventeen-year-olds instead of going home and putting his feet up.'

And over the next few months Pep refuses to allow any easing off of the pressure. He rules with a rod of iron for the rest of the season. But then, that's the way it's always been.

In September 2015, in the middle of a game the coach spots

Lewandowski and Thiago arguing about who should take a free kick. He immediately tells them to shut up and follow protocol, yelling, 'Free kicks? You know damn well who takes them!' [Alonso and Alaba.]

When Vidal takes a knock to his knee during a training session in mid-October, the coach comments, 'Fine. He can have a rest and let it heal. But I won't put up with anyone not giving their best. They have to be full-on every second of every day. You get nothing for free in this life, and we can't give the players an inch . . . We play far too many games to allow the slightest relaxation.'

Even in November, when the goals are flying in and the team's producing win after win, he still insists, 'We can't afford to overlook anything, can't let ourselves become distracted. We must maintain the tension. No relaxation.'

Then in February 2016, Noel Sanvicente, former national coach of Venezuela, asks Pep how he'll manage to focus on Bayern until the end of the season. Surely he'll be thinking about Manchester City now?

'Don't you believe it! These four last months are going to be tougher than ever and I'm going to be even more focused. We need to be full-on, working harder than ever . . . I think the players know that I'm going to be demanding more and more of them. There can be no excuses. I've taught them everything they need to know to play my game and if, after three years of brutal training, they're still not up to it, then it's because they just don't want to make the effort. But I've no worries on that score. Every single one of them is totally committed and all of them are going to be giving their maximum over the next few months.'

And then in April 2016, as they approach the final sprint, he rallied them again. 'We have to be firing on all cylinders. At all times. At training, during every game, every minute of every day.'

'Never relax,' possibly Guardiola's favourite and most frequently used expression in Munich. No doubt City's players are also going to be hearing it a lot . . .

# DRESS FOR CEREMONY, PREPARE FOR BATTLE

Beauty is a form of performance.
*Juan Villoro*

For training he wears a tracksuit provided by his assistants and if it's cold, he'll throw on any old hat that's available. Pep's not particularly bothered about how he looks at work but everything changes for 'the big event'. For him, match day has a kind of magic and he treats it like a ceremonial occasion and therefore dresses accordingly. It might be because he's a bit vain and wants to look elegant in front of the fans but what's definitely true is the value he places on each game.

## FEAR
### Munich, 1 May 2016

Guardiola and David Trueba are talking about the kind of nerves you feel before going out to face an opponent. It's the sort of fear that galvanises you into performing at your best, not the kind that induces paralysis.

'Fear is the best stimulant there is,' says Guardiola. 'It's impossible to face a game properly if you don't fear your opponents. You have to believe that they're dangerous, that they've got something about them. It's the kind of fear that spurs you on rather than slows you down.'

'I agree,' says Trueba. 'And the same thing applies when you're working on something creative. When I'm making a film I always feel a bit of panic at the start. Will I be able to bring the script to life? Will I get the best from my actors and get the narrative flow right? It's the same for a composer of classical or rock music or for a football coach. Nobody can escape this kind of fear. I remember an anecdote about Billy Wilder and Ernst Lubitsch, two greats of the film world. Wilder had written forty scripts for Lubitsch and then he decided he wanted to make his own film. He was so worried that he phoned Lubitsch in a panic the night before filming started and told him he was having a heart attack. Lubitsch calmly told him, "I've made sixty films and I still panic every time I start a new one. But it's good that you're feeling like that. That's what keeps you alive . . .'"

In the hotel Pep wears a tracksuit like everyone else. The ceremony hasn't yet started and he sees this time as an extension of his planning and preparation for the main event. They don't spend much time there: Pep does the pre-match talk which usually lasts between ten and fifteen minutes and goes over the line-up and the game plan (or plans). He's already covered their opponent's strengths and weaknesses in earlier talks so now he focuses on how he wants his team to play. Fifteen minutes dedicated to the game plan without much, if anything, in the way of a motivational pep talk. From there they go to the bus and then on to the stadium. There will be no more contact between Guardiola and his players before kick-off.

An hour before the game starts Pep puts on his suit. He spends the time in the office he shares with Estiarte, whilst Domènec Torrent is available for the team in case of last minute emergencies. Torrent, who's eight years older than Pep, tends to have a cooler head at this stage of match day and the coach trusts him completely.

Torrent shares Pep's determination to learn as much as possible about future rivals. 'Times have changed and many old ideas are no longer relevant: nowadays you have to focus on your opponent, how they play, their strengths and weaknesses. You have to adapt to them. Sun Tzu says that even if your own army is better than your enemy's, you still have to know how to adapt to them. That's why it's so important for us to know how to beat any kind of tactics.'

Fifteen minutes before kick-off Estiarte leaves Pep alone with his thoughts. 'I like to concentrate on the match and I need a few minutes alone to get completely focused.'

For Guardiola, every match is the culmination of days of work and planning. He's in the process of creating his masterpiece and this is another small stage of it. That's why he approaches it with such a sense of ceremony. It's why he chooses to dress as if he were attending an important function. It's also a way of showing his players the value and significance he places on the game, no matter its importance in strictly competitive terms. It's the moment he presents his work to the world and it's vital that he looks the part.

With just three minutes to go before kick-off, he grabs two bottles of water and runs out to the bench. Let the show begin . . .

# BACKSTAGE 11

## A DILEMMA
Stuttgart, 9 April 2016

Once again Franck Ribéry's on sensational form just as his teammates, Lewandowski and Müller, continue to struggle. Both men look tired and their goal-scoring average has dipped dramatically. It's something that often happens to strikers but it's particularly bad news that they're going through this at the same time.

There's another reason for this decline and it relates to both the team's organisation and, paradoxically, to Ribéry's run of outstanding from. His formidable presence has somehow destroyed the delicate balance of the strikers' 'ecosystem' established by Pep a few months ago.

Let's remind ourselves how it worked. Two wingers playing on their natural side (Coman on the right and Costa on the left) plus two centre forwards (Lewandowski and Müller). The structure of the attack is pretty straightforward: the ball goes to Müller who'll drop as far as the centre circle to receive it, opening up space in the opponent's defence. He then sends the ball to one of the wingers and starts to move into the area in a different direction from Lewandowski. Meanwhile, one of the wingers is trying to get past his marker so that he can then pass the ball into the area to the feet of a striker.

The form of the two strikers is directly linked to the attacking 'ecosystem' but most specifically to the wingers.

Let's look at their goal averages (I've taken out stats relating to penalties):

• In September and October, without Robben and Ribéry (both injured) and with Coman and Costa playing on their natural sides Lewandowski averages 1.44 goals per game, and Müller, 0.33. So, between them they manage an average of 1.77 goals per game.
• In November, with Robben on the right wing and Costa on the left, his preferred position, their goal average is: Lewandowski 0.5 and Müller 1 goal per game making a combined total of 1.5 goals per match.
• In December, with both Robben and Costa out to injury and with Ribéry on for just sixty minutes, the ecosystem falls to pieces and their performance dips dramatically: Lewandowski 0.5; Müller 0.33. A combined total of 0.88 goals per match.
• In February, with Robben on the right and Costa back in position on the left, their scoring average increases: Lewandowski 1 and Müller 0.62, a combined total of 1.62 goals per match.
• In March and April, Ribéry returns to the left wing, Robben's injured and Costa's now having to play on the right and cut in. Their goal tally tumbles again: Lewandowski gets 0.33 and Müller 0.44. A combined total of 0.77 goals per match and their worst performance all season.

It's clear that Lewandowski and Müller are going through the kind of dry spell that can happen to any striker but the stats also suggest that their performance improves whenever their teammates on the wing are able to play off their better foot (and are thus more likely to send accurate balls to the area for them to convert). It therefore follows that the forwards produce fewer goals when the wingers are forced to play on their least favourite side.

So, paradoxically, Ribéry's return to the team, for all his energy, fabulous dribbling, speed and lethal passing, has a negative impact on the ecosystem that works so well for the strikers. With Ribéry playing on the left wing, Douglas Costa is forced on to the right and his diminished effectiveness impacts on the men up front.

It's exactly the kind of paradox that often occurs in a team throughout its life cycle and is one of the unexpected consequences of having to adapt to changing situations. A great player on his best form can, at times, have an unforeseen and negative impact on the group dynamic. But that's the unpredictability of football and it's also the coach's job to spot it when it happens, judge how serious the situation is and then make the best choices for the whole team. In this case it's clear that Guardiola would rather keep Ribéry in the team, even if this affects the output of the Lewandowski–Müller duo, whilst he sets about coming up with a new ecosystem which will work for everyone. It's not going to be easy because there are just seven weeks of competition left, leaving him very little time to create and develop another system.

Pep has a tricky dilemma on his hands and knows that you can never have everything in football. On the one hand, he wants the intimidating power of Robben and Ribéry on the wing. (Heynckes used both as wingers in his last season as did Pep in his first.) Robben's a sensational player who dribbles beautifully and scores lots of goals (twenty-one in Pep's first year). He's the kind of individually talented, ruthless footballer who's always determined to score. Ribéry too is prodigiously talented (sixteen goals in Pep's first year) and with his unstoppable dribbles and electric passing, he's the man who provides brilliant assists. Guardiola wants to organise Bayern's game around these two men. He wants the 'Bayern of wingers' (on other occasions it's also been the 'Bayern of full backs who play like inside forwards'). But from 2014 on both players suffer so many injury problems that they're rarely fit at the same time. So, many of Bayern's problems can be explained by the absence of these two men and a Barcelona defender confirms this, telling Bayern's technical team, 'The minute we saw that Robben and Ribéry were injured we knew we'd knock you out [of the Champions League semi-final]. When you see Müller or Götze coming towards you, you've a chance of stopping them but if it's Robben and Ribéry you just know they'll dribble round you and beat you. Those injuries gave us wings . . .'

The club and the coach therefore have to come up with some viable alternatives: Costa and Coman are the obvious answer and they perform even better than expected. Both of them bring speed, excellent dribbling, confident shooting plus a whole lot of creativity to their game. When they're on their natural side they improve Lewandowski and Müller's performances to such an extent that by autumn we're witnessing the best 'Bayern of wingers' we've ever seen. But their game is completely different from the one that Robben and Ribéry produce: Costa and Coman dedicate themselves exclusively to dribbling the ball and passing to the centre forwards.

Pep's no longer torn between the two choices: returning to the ecosystem that favours Lewandowski and Müller or going for Ribéry on the left combined with changes in the team's structure to facilitate the strikers' goal-scoring. It's a no-brainer and, given the choice between creating fluid organisation and maximising Bayern's levels of intimidation and threat, Pep prefers the latter. He really wants it all, but that's not going to happen. As one of the smartest minds in world football Professor Julio Garganta says, 'Sometimes you have to take the long view and accept that it's just not possible to reach all the keys on the piano at the same time.' Pep even considers putting Douglas Costa on as a false No.9 for the Lisbon match.

Guardiola now has only seven weeks to come up with a formula that combines the intimidation of his veteran wingers with the two youngsters' energy and the fluid attacking and sublime goal-scoring power of his striking duo. It won't be easy and he can't afford to keep using five strikers. They're facing far too many big games. If Pep's learned anything over the years it's the importance of understanding the level of risk inherent in each of his decisions and acting accordingly.

# 12

# BINGEING ON VICTORY

*The biggest cause of failure is our rush to succeed.*
*Success comes in its own good time, not before*
*José Luis Martínez*

Guardiola has three closely linked objectives:

• To win
• To play well
• To move and inspire people

He only feels completely satisfied if he manages to achieve all three and does so to the highest of standards. That's what success means for him (although inevitably the perfectionist in him will still find things he needs to address or improve).

But how do other people define success as it relates to the modern game? We've already heard Estiarte talk about the 'treble'. Before 2009 this was a term really only used to talk about historic achievements but nowadays people behave as if failing to win each of the three competitions is equivalent to failure. This attitude caused much of the criticism of Guardiola in Munich and of Luis Enrique in his second season at Barcelona. Bayern only won two European Cups in the period between 1976 and 2013 but nowadays the club's supporters appear to believe that they should take the trophy home every season. And it's the same story at Barça, a club which had never won the Champions League before 1992 and has now managed it five times but whose fans consider it a disaster of catastrophic proportions if they fail to win it year after year.

I like to call this phenomenon 'bingeing on victory' and although I can't say whether it's serious enough to be considered a medical condition, it's certainly something we should take very seriously. It's a 'syndrome' that prevents people enjoying their team's victories because they're immediately demanding the next trophy. The sufferer lives in a permanent state of anxiety about his/her team's results and the more they win the more obsessed they become until eventually everything else (how victory is achieved, who's playing and what they do to win) loses all significance. The level of obsession increases to the point that life becomes a permanent state of dissatisfaction with each goal providing fleeting moments of respite from the craving for more and greater triumphs.

In my opinion this obsession has been caused by the confluence of two very different but equally powerful forces: the global branding of football and the media's increasing need for sensationalism.

Some of our greatest football clubs are involved in the relentless process of repositioning themselves as 'producers of goods and services' and aim to become serious players in the world of commerce. Directors prioritise commercial interests over the fundamentals: the supporters, the club's history and the playing model of its team. Claiming to be simply responding to the opportunities offered by the massive industry sport has become, these clubs foster the compulsion to win. Set against the profits to be made, the team's playing model loses all importance and directors are unperturbed if their stadiums welcome more tourists than genuine fans and their own season ticket holders. The playing model isn't so important as long as we have famous players who will attract the tourists and sell lots of shirts. The only relevant number is the number of tickets sold and the more famous our players, the more numerous our victories, the better. This is an entirely new dynamic in which a football club's core business is no longer expressed in terms of the ball. It's now all about advertising space. It's about increasing revenue by building brand awareness. The players are commodities and their victories, just another part of the brand identity. The brand demands constant victory although how we win is less important and there's certainly never time to savour success.

The newspaper industry has also played a significant role in the spread of this reductionist attitude. Journalism, which not so long ago was an honourable, highly respected profession, has in the last ten years changed beyond all recognition. Old fashioned standards such as quality writing and detailed research are disappearing to be replaced by a demand for superficial, high speed, headline grabbing rubbish. There are still many excellent media outlets who produce good, high quality journalism but sadly these are no longer the norm. The modern media prefers attention grabbing banality and has driven football in precisely the same direction as the marketing men. Media outlets now work round the clock in a constant frenzied search for stories. Nobody pauses to reflect or check their sources and over the last five years there's been a vast increase in the number of damaging untruths published. In fact the number of inaccuracies published is on a par with the number of journalists who lose their jobs every year, as the quality and length of articles decreases proportionately.

If a tweet looks too long, slap a misleading headline on it so that people will click. The media's new core business is sensationalism. They've found that winding people up and provoking tensions is the single best way to boost sales.

All of this means that it's enormously difficult for any coach to have anything like an intelligent exchange with the media. And it looks like this particular battle is now lost forever. Just over a year ago I was at the pre-match press conference for the Bayern–Oporto game where Guardiola spent four minutes explaining how he expected the Portuguese team to play and detailing the particular qualities of each of its players. I then overheard two German journalists saying, 'Why would it matter to us how Oporto play?' Of course, in purely commercial terms, they were quite right. An in-depth knowledge of the opponents' tactics doesn't sell newspapers. Not in Germany, or England, or Spain or anywhere else . . . What does grab the headlines is a coach ripping his trousers mid-match or making a weird face or drinking champagne instead of wine. Those are the things people want to read about. But what about the game? What about football? The game has become just another part of 'big business'. As usual Marcelo Bielsa was right when he said, 'If one thing has damaged football's willingness to communicate with its public, it's the newspaper industry.' And please be clear, the problem does not lie with individual journalists, it's the whole industry which is at fault.

Your average football supporter is caught between these two great forces: the clubs and the media who bombard them with the same reductive message: it's only victory that counts. And they mean constant triumph, not the occasional, much celebrated and highly prized trophy we used to aspire to, but repeated, ongoing victory. Anything else is failure. These attitudes have pervaded all our lives to such an extent that the unreasonable demands made of football teams these days have come to be accepted as normal. Victorious fans have become blasé about their team's success whilst everyone else is permanently bitter and dissatisfied. Logically, there will always be more losers than winners and the disappointed masses seem condemned to look on in bitter frustration at their triumphant peers.

## WINNING IS THE EXCEPTION, NOT THE RULE
### Rome, 18 February 2010

Argentine coach Julio Velasco, a close friend of Guardiola's says, 'We can learn so much from sport, about losing as well as winning. It teaches us that in order to win, you have to perform well, you have to make sacrifices and you have to be efficient. Above all you have to pay attention to the little things as well as the big, no matter how difficult that is. You have to learn to lose as well and any competitor understands that you can't win every time. Winning constantly is the exception, not the rule and most of us will alternate between victory and defeat.'

The coach and his players who win constantly become the focus of attention in a world where phobias and compulsions are manipulated by forces desperate to whip up primitive emotions. The commercial interests of clubs and the media exert so much control over this process that concepts like ethics and balanced coverage are forgotten in the race for a quick buck as football teams are subjected to the kind of intense pressure that flies in the face of everything we know about development and learning.

Guardiola's very conscious of this. 'It's the same everywhere. You have to win or they slaughter you. Only winning matters and there's absolutely no respect for the work we coaches do.'

What then is the point of celebrating a victory today if I'm already obsessing about tomorrow's game and the prospect of another 'binge'? No victory will ever be enough to satisfy the voracious appetites of the media and the clubs' money men. This in turn creates a vicious circle in which the football fan is both the victim and a participant. Instead of celebrating victory and valuing the hard work and dedication put in to achieving it, we see it as rightfully ours. We celebrate for a second and then demand more. More trophies, more titles, more victory to gorge on.

This a modern malaise, an 'illness' born of the culture of instant gratification. I must have what I want now and I must feel in control at all times. Surely nothing could be further from the uncertain and constantly changing nature of football?

## ON THE SAME WAVELENGTH

Many say that utopias are nonsense
But at the very least they're vital nonsense.
Any teacher who fails to let his pupils think about utopias
And make mistakes
Is a very poor teacher indeed.
*Richard Sennett*

Manchester City isn't just another English football club. Its parent company is a global corporation with interests in several countries and, although its football may have some way to go, in business terms, the club is a major player on the world stage. We can say then that the club's core business is the production of 'products and services' with a view to extending market share and increasing profits. . The business model aims to build a global brand identity, which will encompass the brands currently being developed in other countries. But we've already seen the impact this level of commercialisation can have on the football they play.

We've yet to discover exactly what the club expects from Guardiola. If they expect continuous victory and a treble-winning first season, then they may well be disappointed because not even Pep Guardiola can wave a magic wand and guarantee instant success. Remember his chat with Braydon Bent in the back of that taxi? The young fan told him, 'With you in charge we'll win everything, all four trophies!' At the time it seemed nothing more than the charming enthusiasm of a young kid who loves his club but, more worryingly, it may also reflect the ambitions and expectations of the whole fan base.

Pep can promise them complete dedication, hard graft and total commitment to the job. He can give them a superb team that plays wonderful football and wins titles. What he can't do is guarantee constant and permanent victory.

## BIELSA'S FIVE REASONS
### Munich, 11 December 2014

The Peruvian coach Manuel Barreto has come to Munich and is watching training today. He's one of the many coaches who've made the journey to Säbener Strasse from all over the world to watch Guardiola at work and, as usual, the Catalan is more than delighted to spend some of his precious time chatting to him. Barreto's just come from Marseille where he watched a couple of

Marcelo Bielsa's training sessions. He tells Pep about the massive amount of information Bielsa had gathered on Marseille's next opponents, Nantes, and recounts how the Argentinian had come to training clutching his 'Nantes file'. He also shares some of Bielsa's insights, 'There are only five reasons why a team wins a game. Because it's the better side, because its players are in better shape, or have superior technical and tactical skills, or simply because they care more. And the fifth reason is this,' said Bielsa, waving the file at Barreto.

Guardiola's interested in Bielsa's comments, 'You know, I completely agree with him but I'd add a sixth factor: pure luck.'

The success of Guardiola's project at City will depend largely on the club's directors but it will also be hugely influenced by the attitude (and intelligence) of club president, Khaldoon Al Mubarak. We don't yet know if the focus will be on producing short-term success and immediate results or whether they aspire to creating stability and a long-term vision. But if Pep's mission relates to creating a competitive team with its own distinctive character and playing model the club must make every effort to ensure that their fans are on the same wavelength. In his biography of Picasso John Berger wrote, 'If a painting is to be successful, it's essential that the artist and his public agree on its meaning.' In the same way, City's directors and Pep will have to communicate clearly to the fans exactly what he has been employed to do. And this won't be easy. It's a bit like passing the ball in the middle of a game. If the pass is to be effective both players need to get it right: the man who passes and the player who receives it.

The club has already embarked on this task. Pep was presented to the supporters on Sunday 3 July, the culmination of a two-day fan event outside the Etihad Stadium. CEO Ferran Soriano organised the 'Cityzens Weekend' with one key objective: to create a sense of closeness between the fans and their new coach. The club wanted the fans to connect immediately with Pep who, dressed casually in sports gear, spent time chatting to supporters and answering their questions. It was a party atmosphere, with the beer flowing, and everyone was keen to know what they could expect from the new man in charge.

The event couldn't have been more different from his statesman-like arrival and presentation at Munich where Guardiola was hailed as the new 'messiah', a superhero come to save the day. Pep had drawn his own conclusions about that day and, having shared his thoughts with Soriano, was delighted that the event at Manchester City struck a completely different tone. The Cityzens Weekend was a festival, a chance for the fans to meet their new coach in a relaxed atmosphere. We then witnessed a similar attempt to give the fans an insight into Pep's character when he surprised Braydon Bent in the back of Chappy's taxi and met and chatted to City fan Noel Gallagher. The club and the coach are determined to establish direct communication between Pep and its fans from the start. It's all part of the strategic plan.

Pep was low-key in his first press conference, refusing to make outlandish promises or huge claims. He insisted that he'd not come to England to teach but to learn and shared his excitement at the prospect of getting to know the legendary clubs and stadia and people of the Premier League. His focus that day was on the team: building spirit, improving their game, thrilling their fans, making everyone proud to support Manchester City. He talked about victory but only in terms of being the end result of the process. It was a balanced, intelligent address and showed us just how savvy Pep has become.

# THOSE WHO WISH TO UNDERSTAND HIM
## WILL UNDERSTAND HIM

*. . . reject appearances,*
*look for the essence buried in the depths*
*'Faust', Goethe*

Guardiola has a tremendous gift for changing the entire positioning of his players on the pitch during a match but this brings problems of its own. His attitudes and approach clash with established beliefs and the traditions and customs that dominate football, a sport where anything unconventional or innovative is initially viewed with suspicion and hostility. People don't understand what they see on the pitch and, instead of being curious and trying to understand it, they dismiss and disparage it. Guardiola will therefore always be subjected to the scrutiny of conventional, pedestrian minds and those who don't understand his ideas will resort to dismissing or even ridiculing them.

Instead of admiring his ability to introduce changes mid-match and make constant tweaks to his team's organisation and development, people often criticise and condemn Pep's openness to change.

There's no doubt that much of what he does is challenging and you have to be pretty on-the-ball to keep up with Pep's thought processes. I'd go further and say that to understand him you don't even have to know too much about football. It's much more about curiosity, a willingness to accept a non-conventional mind and a readiness to challenge stereotypes. Rather than demanding to know why Guardiola has picked a particular line-up, or has used a certain formation, rather than whinging about the fact he keeps changing his starting XI and refuses to use the same players after a strong performance, we should be watching what he does and trying to work out the reasons behind his decisions. Come to his games with a telescope and a microscope, by all means, but above all, come with an open mind. Leave your prejudices at home.

We have to expect the unexpected from Pep. For him a full back doesn't necessarily play the way we're used to, his midfielders aren't tall and well-built and his keeper has to be as good with his feet as he is with his hands. Nothing is set in stone and anything can happen at any time in a match. 'Normality' for Guardiola is the unconventional. His ideology is all about evolution.

## THERE'S STILL A LOT WE NEED TO IMPROVE
### Barcelona, 27 June 2016

'Football has a lot of work to do to catch up with other sports, doesn't it?' I say.

'You're absolutely right,' replies Pep fervently. 'There's so much we can take from other sports that are way ahead of football and there's a lot to improve before we'll be on a par with many other disciplines. Obviously not in terms of everything we do, but in some areas, it's definitely true. It's not right to say that everything's been done already or at least we've not exploited all old ideas to the full. We've a long way to go in terms of innovation and improving what we do.'

It may be a result of the almost childlike curiosity with which he approaches life or his need to compete with his rivals and their constant attempts to outfox him but Pep sees football as a living thing in a permanent state of flux. Ask him about his current thinking, his preferred formation or his favourite starting line-up, and he'll tell you the same thing: 'it depends'. It depends on the moment, on his opponent and their weaknesses, on his current analysis of his own team's capabilities, the unity within his team, the strategies developed by others to thwart his own tactics, or just how he's feeling at the time . . .

For Pep, football isn't a fixed image, it's an ongoing story that changes every day. But Pep himself has attitudes and mannerisms that never change. That's the message for young Braydon Bent: if Pep scratches his head it's because he's worried about something but if he rubs his face or creases his forehead, it means he's looking for the right word to express an idea. During a match he doesn't get too bothered if a player makes a mistake but if he fails to execute something they've worked on in training, it's a different story. Pep will turn round towards the bench or throw himself down beside Torrent, furious at his player's failure to do something they've gone over a hundred times at training . . . Just like Antonio Conte, Pep 'plays' the match from the touchline. He still feels like a player and takes part in every move. That's why he moves constantly, waving his arms about and shouting, just like he did when he was a player.

He likes to produce multi-layered game plans and then reveal them one by one and will often choose to start in a certain way just to see how his opponent reacts. We tend to see football in terms of the more dominant side but it's a confrontation, a game of opposition. It's only if there's a huge difference between the relative abilities of each team that any one side can impose themselves fully and a football match is more usually a 'negotiation' between two rivals. The game is at its richest and best when it's the product of this process of negotiation. That's why Pep doesn't reveal all his plans before the game just as boxers test each other at the start of a match.

## BUTTERBEANS
### Barcelona, 11 November 2010

Guardiola uses an unusual metaphor to explain his team's 'sparring' at the start of a game. It's what he calls 'the butterbeans paradox' which he learned when he was a boy at the Barcelona Masia.

'Sometimes in a game you see immediately that things aren't going well and at those times I always think about something Charly Rexach used to say. He used to talk about throwing some hard, uncooked butterbeans on a plate and of course initially they're in a mess, all piled on top of each other but if you shake the plate really gently you'll find them one by one falling into place. It's exactly the same in football. It's brilliant. You're watching the game and you see that there's one guy not looking comfortable but you just say to yourself, "Don't worry, give him a bit of time and it'll all fall into place . . ." And usually that's exactly what happens.'

Should you use a player in a certain position because of what happens during a game? 'You place them according to how well they interact with each other. According to how much their interactions have improved and developed in response to what the opponent is doing,' explains Seirul.lo.

To fully understand how Guardiola plans a game you must approach it with an open mind. He's not a conventional thinker. He focuses hugely on the characteristics of his opponents which will heavily influence how he chooses his players and why his line-ups change constantly. It's the game plans that matter and he plans these with a flexible and varied approach. They will always be more important than how he distributes his men on the pitch. He will often apply old ideas to modern situations and his starting XI and game plan are often only the starting point, his way of testing his opponent and trying to get to the point where his team can play their own game and win.

Braydon Bent's parents will have to explain all of this very carefully to their son so that the lad understands how his team are now going to play under their new coach.

# BACKSTAGE 12

## THE CORNER IN LISBON
### Lisbon, 13 April 2016

Before every big game, the coaching team selects a set-piece move they want to use in the match and before playing Benfica in the Stadium of Light in the Champions League quarter-finals, Pep and his assistants decide on 'Javi's corner'. They then put the team through their paces and the players practise the move more than forty times. It needs to be executed perfectly and all the players involved also watch a special training video no less than twelve times.

The inspiration for the move arose out of an analysis of the Zénit–Benfica game in the last sixteen. Carles Planchart and Domènec Torrent had spotted some weaknesses in the Portuguese side's zonal defending at one of the seven corners taken by Zénit during the game. Benfica had all eleven men in the area defending: two in the six yard box towards the front post; four more forming the first line of defence on the edge of the small box plus three distributed around the penalty spot but all of them preparing for front post challenges.

There was just one Portuguese defender at the far post. For their part Zénit had their five strikers waiting out at the edge of the box. The corner had passed without incident in St Petersburg but the Bayern coaching staff had taken note and designed a strategy involving three key characteristics: distraction, precision and anticipation.

They have the players practise the sequence of moves twenty times on Monday and another twenty on Tuesday.

Sometimes with Costa taking it off his left foot, others via Alonso using his right foot. Only one Bayern striker takes up a position in amongst the clutch of Benfica defenders, the rest are on the edges of the box. The two best headers of the ball will be on the outer edge of the box towards the back post and the other three will be at the front edge of the area. To be effective, the corner needs to be taken powerfully and sent long – beyond the second post. The idea is that the back post header will be headed back along the front of the goal, almost along the goal line, and the Bayern player who arrives to finish the move off by scoring will be going in the opposite direction to all the Benfica players who'll have reacted by chasing the ball towards the back post. In training, without any real opposition, the strategy works around 60% of the time.

In the fifty-second minute of the game in Lisbon, Bayern get a second corner in their favour. This is the moment they've been waiting for. The strikers move into two groups.

To take advantage not only of the zonal marking but the fact that Benfica crowd their six yard box only Ribéry is situated in the penalty area and he's at the back post. This means that the eleven Benfica players who are crowded in and around the goalmouth leave the Bayern players who are on the semi-circle outside the box more or less unmarked. Javi Martínez and Vidal are towards the far post edge of the semi-circle while Müller, Thiago and Kimmich are in the same semi-circle but towards the front post – looking as if they'll be the first point of attack for the cross. But because the defence is zonal there's still space around them. Alonso takes the corner, it's long, high and curving from outside to in. It goes completely over the keeper and nine defenders in the direction of where Eliseu is marking the zone where Ribéry is. But his placement there is a dummy; the cross is for Javi Martínez who's made his run from the edge of the semi-circle to beyond the second post. If he heads directly at goal Ederson will probably save it. He's made a run to his second post. But so have all the other defenders who've had to turn 180 degrees from facing Alonso's set play to where Javi's receiving the corner. The Navarran 'passes' the ball with his exquisite header right into the path of the three Bayern men who've waited to run to the first post until the defence is running towards the back post and their teammate, alone and under no pressure, is serving the ball up back the way it came. Müller tucks it away but Kimmich and Thiago have made the right run too and either could have scored.

Bayern are ecstatic with the execution of the goal and the man responsible, Domènec Torrent, is the centre of attention. The minute the ball hits the back of the net Guardiola runs to give Torrent a hug, thanking him for coming up with such a brilliant idea. Ribéry does the same and within seconds, the rest of the team are crowded round the bench. They know that they've pretty much guaranteed themselves a place in the Champions League semi-final but they're also celebrating the fact that all the hard work of the last two days has paid off. They'd practised and practised the move and a few of them (Alonso, Javi Martínez, Ribéry, Müller and Thiago) had also watched the video several times more in Lisbon with Torrent and Planchart. 'Javi's corner' has won the day in Lisbon.

# 13

# THE BIGGEST CHALLENGE YET

*The more difficult the history,*
*the sweeter the victory.*
*Christian Thielemann*

DURING HIS TIME in Germany Pep began to perceive his role differently and was determined that at Manchester City his remit should be clearly established from the start. His own view is that 'the coach should really be the director general of the dressing room.' It's not that he aspires to being the club's 'general manager' who's responsible for hiring and firing players but he believes that, to be effective, he must have responsibility for many aspects of club life directly related to the success of his team: the medical unit, physiotherapy, rehab, nutrition, analysis, big data, the youth system . . .

This idea of the coach as 'manager' was pioneered in English football back in the 1920s when legendary coach Herbert Chapman, still remembered for his many tactical innovations (the 3-2-2-3, the WM), began to modernise other areas of the game, introducing many of the elements we take for granted today: numbering players' shirts, floodlighting stadia plus numerous changes relating to fitness, analysis and medical care. The figure of the football manager became well established in England although it took much longer to spread to Europe and even today there are still significant differences in the roles of club coaches.

In continental Europe many still insist that the coach's remit should not extend beyond the training and preparation of the current squad. It makes no sense, they argue, to entrust the direction of the club's sports policy to someone who may only be there for a brief time. For me, this seems a perfectly sensible argument. Others disagree and insist that, to be truly effective, the 'coach' (or 'manager') must have a degree of control beyond the strict boundaries of day-to-day coaching. My intention here is not to argue for one side or another and history has given us good and bad examples of both these approaches.

Manel Estiarte says, 'In sport, at the elite level, a tiny change can make a huge difference. It's maybe 1% of all that you do that makes the difference between winning a trophy or not.' And he's right. Think of the Champions League semi-final when Atlético's Godín managed to get back to full fitness in time whilst Bayern had to play without a vital asset like Robben. Elite sport is a bit like high-risk surgery: everything must be carried out to perfection and the slightest slip-up can mean the difference between survival or not. In elite sport there's a fine line between defeat and victory and even the smallest of changes can bring significant competitive advantage.

Although undoubtedly an historic moment for the club, City's Champions League semi-final in Madrid left many singularly unimpressed. Vicente Del Bosque has said that, 'apathy spreads like poison in a dressing room' and City's directors were particularly alarmed that night by their team's uninspired, lacklustre performance. It wasn't so much their playing model or the ideas behind it, it was the lack of effort, both physical and mental, made by the players. Their total lack of any sense of team spirit was plain for all to see.

It was that match that convinced City's board that a complete change of direction was required. And Guardiola was in full agreement: it wasn't about a few changes here and there, what the team needed was a complete overhaul. In a meeting in Dubai at the start of June he came to an agreement with club management that around ten new players would be needed. The squad which made it to the Champions League semi-final and achieved fourth place in the league worried him for several reasons:

- More than half the players (twelve out of twenty-three) were over thirty
- Seventeen of them were twenty-eight or older
- Only four men were twenty-five or younger

At the same meeting in Dubai, the coach also took the time to agree the playing model he would use and told the sports director and the president the kind of players he'd need, dividing his list into three separate categories:

- The defensive spine of the team
- New strikers
- The full backs

As ever, his priority was to create the nucleus of his defensive organisation, which would be composed of four men: the keeper, two central defenders and an organising midfielder. Pep had some players in mind and the club reacted at once. Some deals were immediately successful (Gündogan), whilst others turned out to be complete non-starters (Laporte) and the rest required many weeks of intense negotiation.

As well as putting together the defensive alterations Pep had requested, sports director, Txiki Begiristain, began work on securing the kind of forwards the new coach had identified, focusing principally on wingers (so vital to Pep's playing model). Although the media made exaggerated claims about the number of players the coach had demanded, in reality, Pep presented the chairman, Khaldoon Al Mubarak, and Txiki with a fairly modest list of names.

Once negotiations were complete and Guardiola was reassured that the nucleus of his squad was in place he was then able to assess which of the players currently at the club would most complement his playing model. Even before meeting them, he had already studied the players in detail and knew that there were several outstanding footballers already in place: Silva, De Bruyne, Agüero, Fernandinho and others.

During his presentation to the fans, Pep was asked what qualities he valued most in a player and replied, 'The first thing I look at is how good a teammate he is.' Just a year before he'd been chatting to his good friend Pato Ormazábal and said, 'In order to be successful any great team needs good substitutes. I'm always really interested in a player's track record as a substitute. I like to know how he behaves when things get tough and if he's been professional about being put on the subs' bench then that always impresses me. On the other hand if he's got a history of kicking up over that kind of thing, I'm usually not interested and won't have him in my team.'

## THE ALABA VIDEO
### Munich, 24 November 2015

David Alaba has published a Twitter video showing him celebrating his team's four goals against Olympiacos. The player was injured during the Schalke game three days ago and has had to watch the Champions League fixture from the stands.

Pep's impressed. 'Dome, we have to keep that video and use it one day in a team talk. It really shows what a team player David is. He's such a good example of the kind of humility I want to see in my players. And I want to use those images of Xabi Alonso running up to mark a guy a teammate should have been taking care of. It's important to show players making sacrifices by taking on things that aren't their responsibility.'

Back in Munich after training one morning Juanma Lillo and Pep were discussing their criteria for signing players. Lillo told him, 'Whenever we go to see a player I always look for what I see as a vital characteristic: that he's not intimidated by his opponents. I like to see how calm he is when the other team's pressurising him. There's a big difference between being pressurised and feeling pressurised. You get players who not only cope well with the proximity of their markers but who're also unfazed by any kind of intimidation. Guys like Andrés Iniesta, whose facial expression is always completely calm, as if he were enjoying a quiet cuppa rather than facing some big, threatening opponent . . . You get players who give the ball away far too easily under pressure and that's no use. You want someone who won't be affected by intimidation and pressure. That's the guy you need to sign!'

Guardiola explained his own approach, 'My first question is always, "Can this guy dribble?" I only want players who have that skill so that's always what I look at. I want full backs and central defenders and midfielders and inside forwards and wingers who can dribble. Because you can learn control and good passing . . . So, yeah, dribbling, that's the key.'

The new signings took up a significant part of Guardiola's summer, as did his work on the renovation of support services at the club. He had learned his lesson in Munich and insisted on taking immediate responsibility for the modernisation of the medical services at City, focusing on prevention and rehab, nutrition and analysis as well as a review of current personnel. Pep places enormous importance on his players' nutrition and believes that this has a huge impact on any sportsman's performance. Employing a hand-picked, expert nutritionist was therefore one of the first things he did at City.

Guardiola also insists on good habits. He expects his players to have breakfast and lunch at the club before and after training to guarantee peak fitness levels, physiologically as well as in terms of muscle development and effective recuperation.

For the same reason he insists that, after home games, the whole squad dine at the stadium restaurant where the menus have been devised by the club nutritionist. He insisted on this in Barcelona and continued the policy in Munich and no-one is exempt from this rule unless there are very special circumstances. On arriving in Manchester he realised it was even more vital than ever given that a couple of his players turned up at pre-season five or six kilos overweight. This is exactly the kind of unprofessional behaviour that Guardiola hopes to avoid.

Pep understands that full physiological recuperation means complete rehydration, recovery from muscle damage and the replenishment of muscle glycogen after exercise. He also knows how vital it is to take advantage of the 'metabolic window' (the period after exercise when the body is particularly receptive to the nutrients which can aid the process of recuperation). The coach wants his players to be lean and muscular without a gram of extra weight or fat. He also wants them to avoid muscular hypertrophy and therefore needs each of his players to have a personalised diet plan.

Club chairman, Khaldoon Al Mubarak told Citytv what he expects. 'There's no doubt in my mind that Pep will transform our team and take them to a whole new level. We expect great things precisely because of his passion and commitment. Our objectives for the next few years include fighting for the league title and, of course, doing our best to win the Champions League too.' Karl-Heinz Rummenigge said something similar in June 2013. 'For us, the Bundesliga is the primary objective because we have to play thirty-four league games every year. The biggest prize is obviously the Champions League although we recognise that it is, by its very nature, a very unpredictable competition where you can take nothing for granted.'

Interestingly, like Pep, Ferran Soriano (City's CEO) restricted himself to talking in terms of remaining competitive rather than promising the fans trophies. 'We want to be sure that we're still producing strong, competitive football in those crucial months of the season when titles are won and lost.'

It's clear then that the club expects great things from their new coach: a highly competitive team plus the league title as well as, if possible, the Champions League trophy. Not bad for a club which has won just four league titles in its entire history (two of them in the last six years) and only made it past the last sixteen in the Champions League for the first time last season. That said, these aims are entirely understandable. You don't hire Pep Guardiola if you lack ambition.

As he's always done, Pep will dedicate his life to City over the next three years. And his huge salary reflects the personal sacrifices he'll make. He expects this to be an enriching experience, not just financially but in terms of the opportunities to learn, experience and practise a different kind of football. In return he brings his own inimitable playing model: high possession, passing, positional organisation, constant attacking combined with superb defensive organisation and an unrelenting competitive drive. The City project also promises to be his greatest challenge ever.

Barcelona represented a huge challenge for a young inexperienced coach who was taking on a great team that had lost its way. And he handled it beautifully, signing players who would complement his playing model and work well with the core group of home-grown talent. He also used players like Xavi and Iniesta to showcase Messi's formidable talent. This happy confluence of a group of super-talented players and a brilliant coach resulted in an unprecedented level of success.

In Munich Pep had to adapt to circumstances and expectations that were radically different to what he had been used to at Barcelona (interestingly, he was initially hired by Bayern when the German side were in the doldrums but when he actually took up his appointment they had just won the treble). He brought new, challenging ideas which he implemented with the assistance and dedication of his players. With them onside he managed to transform the team's playing model and lead them to repeated success – although he failed to conquer the supreme title.

This latest appointment is the one that presents the most risk. As he starts his new project, City lack the power and dominance of Bayern or Barca. The team also has a significantly busier calendar than his former clubs and many of his main players were absent from his initial preparation and have therefore had less exposure to the new playing model.

There are no absolutes in football. Everything's relative and the game is in constant flux. No-one can predict how Guardiola will do at City and there's no way to tell how many trophies and titles he'll bring to Manchester. It's highly likely however that it will take him at least eighteen months to fully develop his playing model and, without claiming clairvoyant powers, I'd say that it will be from March 2018 onwards that we'll start to see the fruits of his labour. Win or lose however, the coach is definitely facing his biggest challenge ever.

## HOW WILL GUARDIOLA'S CITY PLAY?

It's not enough just to have the ball;
you need to know what to do with it
*Johan Cruyff*

On his first day at training in Manchester, Pep tells me that he hasn't yet got a clear vision of what his team's going to be like. 'I just can't visualise it. I can't imagine what the team will be like or how we'll play. Right now I don't know which players I'll keep and which ones I'll let go.'

I've talked a lot with Pep about his new job over recent weeks and it's clear he feels this is the most high risk job he's ever taken on, largely because he doesn't yet know which players he'll have in his squad. But his intentions there are obvious given that he wants a new goalkeeper, two central defenders, an organising midfielder and two wingers.

Let's look at how he's likely to use each of these positions:

The goalkeeper. Pep likes his keeper to initiate his team's play. It's not all about using his feet well. That's definitely part of it but it's not the most important consideration. Guardiola likes a goalkeeper with super-fast reactions and, obviously, he must also be pretty good at saving goals. All these characteristics are increasingly the norm in the world of elite football and any keeper lacking any of these skills is likely to struggle at this level. When he appoints a keeper, however, Pep is looking for something more than this. He needs his man to be able to read the game, show high levels of concentration combined with an audacious spirit and a willingness to contribute to the organisation of the team. Guardiola's game starts with the goalkeeper's decisions regarding the direction of the play and it's therefore not about a keeper who 'plays well with his feet' but a footballer who plays brilliant football. It's not about possessing one or two skills, it's about his all-round capabilities. For Guardiola his keeper's still a specialist but he's also the complete player. He's his No.1 'team' player.

Central defenders. Again, Guardiola asks for that something extra from his central defenders. Of course their job is to defend their area but they must also be capable of bringing the ball out efficiently and cleanly. Without these players Pep's positional play would founder and his teams would not be able to install themselves, and impose themselves, in the opponents' half as well as they do.

The defenders are the players who initiate the team's push forward into their rival's area and, once the attack is underway, and their teammates are established well up the pitch, they position themselves near the centre circle, fifty metres from their goalkeeper so that they can continue pressing. This is obviously a high-risk strategy and Guardiola needs men who are fast, daring and not afraid to cope with danger.

Midfielders. This was Guardiola's position and his own experiences have influenced his current thinking. Gündogan, who was the first player signed by City after Pep's arrival, is the kind of footballer who facilitates the 'construction of the game' in the middle of the pitch, ensuring that his teammates 'move forward together' towards the rival penalty box. He's also highly effective at using his skill at running with the ball to draw opponents away and creating sequences of passes to disorganise them. He isn't a defensive midfielder, nor is he like Busquets, Alonso or Weigl, all of whom tend to maintain a very fixed position. Pep will be able to play Gündogan as an organising midfielder or an inside forward and is clearly planning to deploy his midfielders in a variety of ways to achieve the objective of dominating inside the opponents' half.

Wingers. After seeing his work with Bayern, it's impossible to imagine Guardiola's game without his wingers wide and open on the wing. These guys need to be prepared to wait for the ball patiently on the wing and be capable of producing the fast, effective dribbling that will get them past their marker.

So, we can already predict the kind of game City will play: the keeper directs the initial build-up, the central defenders play the ball out until the team is set up in the rival's half, the midfielder/inside forwards impose themselves close to the opposition's box and the wingers wait for the ball so that they can give the assist pass for the goal.

Pep ensured that his 'core' players were in place at City by the end of the summer so that he could build the team from there, either by using current players or by identifying new signings he required. Having this core group in place meant that he could start to establish his playing philosophy and from the first day began to train his players in the tactical skills they'll have to master: the rondos, bringing the ball out from the back, pressing to win the ball back.

Pep also made it absolutely clear to the team that first day that he expects maximum effort at all times. Gael Clichy explained what Pep expects from his defenders, 'Pep wants us to play a very offensive game and that means that we defenders have to work constantly to help in the recuperation of the ball. This is really new for us because in the past we've tended to be really open and would concede a lot of goals on the counter-attack. He wants us to be an attacking team but very well organised defensively.'

No surprises there then.

The coach also spent much of his summer learning about the 'hidden side' of the players. With information provided by the club, he analysed the behaviour of the squad 'behind closed doors', looking at each player's weight, their daily progress and timekeeping . . . He was also keen to see how players recovered from injury, examining the number of rehab sessions each had required and checking to see how many training sessions had been missed. Having examined the information in depth Pep arrived at City's training ground with a pretty clear impression of his players' behaviour during the previous season. None of his technical team were therefore surprised when he told a fan that the quality he values most in a player is being 'a good teammate' and immediately set about establishing the standards he expects in three areas of dressing room life:

- Work ethic
- Team spirit
- A demanding programme (diet and injury prevention)

Pep expects every single one of his players to work hard to develop their talent and give of their very best in everything they do. He sees team spirit as the essential foundation for the culture of mutual co-operation that will guarantee long-term success and believes that he has to impose a tough, demanding regime in order to avoid the inertia and apathy of last season and establish new, healthy habits and more positive dynamics.

Pep is extremely tough on himself and he's therefore likely to be just as relentless when it comes to his players, regardless of who they are or how much they've achieved. Everyone will have to earn his place in the team and the coach will have no hesitation in using talented youngsters from City's academy (one of the best in England).

Under Pep, the rules are clear: nobody is guaranteed his place and anyone has the chance to make it to the starting XI. Back in June he told me, 'I still can't visualise "my" City because I don't know which players I'll have but I'll tell you one thing, anyone who's not prepared to work his arse off will be out and I'll put one of the youngsters in. We've got some talented kids in the youth team.'


PLAYING WITH PATIENCE . . . AND WINGERS

There's nothing truly new. It's all just old things we've forgotten
*Dante Panzeri*

Pep dedicates himself totally to his players and he expects the same level of commitment from them. He also asks for lots of sacrifices, particularly from his centre forwards (whether they're false No.9s or traditional centre forwards). Take Robert Lewandowski's role at Bayern for example. In a typical game Pep would ask the Pole to use his acceleration to confuse and unravel the opposition, allowing the teammates around him to continue their passing game. The player would be in constant movement, sprinting forward and suddenly changing direction but that also meant that he had very few touches of the ball: twenty-five on average per match, ten fewer than Neuer and a quarter of Alonso and Lahm's time on the ball. Moreover, around twenty of his touches would be used to return the ball to a teammate in a better position and he usually managed just five shots on goal in any one game, with, on average, one going in. The striker, an intelligent and articulate man, understood why the coach expected him to run himself into the ground every game for very little personal return (he ran on average 11 km per match including eighty-five high velocity sprints) and accepted that sacrifices had to be made, commenting, 'The game we play demands a lot of patience.'

City fans should expect their team to be called upon to show this same level of patience under Guardiola. And no-one will need more patience than his wingers. For Pep, wingers and goalkeepers are a class apart. He sees them as the team's 'specialists' and expects them to fulfil a very specific remit. Pep explained how he uses wingers over dinner with Noel Sanvicente, former national coach of Venezuela. 'In my playing model the wingers have to spend a lot of time alone out on the wing almost immovable, without intervening in the game, without touching the ball. They have to wait. Just like the keeper. Manu [Neuer] can spend forty minutes without touching a single ball and then he'll leap into action and make a miraculous save. In my teams wingers have to have those same very special qualities.'

Pep likes his wingers high up the pitch, on the touchline, right at the edge of the pitch, watching and waiting to strike. They trot about, occasionally getting the ball and passing inside or back to another team mate or doing the odd feint and very little else. They are the team's 'silent' players. They bide their time until the team has confused and disorganised their opponents so much that they've lost all sense of order.

And that's when they strike. The ball comes to them and they react instantly with clinical precision. At Bayern, Costa and Coman fulfilled this role to perfection, waiting on the wing until the time was right. Robben struggled more and his frustration was often very evident but he had enough professionalism to follow orders and wait for the perfect pass. Ribéry, on the other hand, tended to show decidedly less patience and often broke the rules to go looking for the ball rather than staying put and waiting for it to come to him.

## ZONAL ATTACKING
Munich, 31 January 2016

Hoffenheim have only managed a couple of shots at Neuer's goal but their tactical approach to the game is providential. 'Juventus are going to play like Hoffenheim have today. Banked defence. They'll use Morata and Dybala to try and squeeze Xabi and Lahm out of the game so our "free" men will be Kimmich and Alaba. And if we get things right like today then we can ensure they have difficulty getting out of their area.'

Pep's using his analysis of today's game to plan how he'll deal with Juve, something which is habitual for him – juggling two scenarios at the same time: the immediate plus the important.

'Juve close themselves up in a five defenders plus three midfielders formation – up front there's barely any space for you to get through. They're a compact mass that's impossible to penetrate. The Hoffenheim game's been the perfect trial run and what we'll need to do against Juve is drag one of the central defenders away from his position and then penetrate through the space he leaves.'

Sometimes Pep has two objectives when he plans a match. On one level he prepares the tactics that he hopes will win the current game but sometimes he wants to use the game for strategic purposes, to test the weapons that he'll use in another, more decisive game.

Most people think that 'zonal play' only applies in defence but that's not true. There's also zonal attack. When you've got your strikers at a distance from the ball, waiting for possession to come to them after a determined series of moves and actions rather than going looking for the ball, that's zonal attack. Some call it positional play but really it's a zonal game. Waiting in a predetermined area for the ball to arrive rather than seeking it.

Guardiola told Sanvicente, 'You have to be very careful about how you handle your wingers. It's not enough to tell them how I want them to play and expect it all to work immediately. An eighteen-year-old kid has an ego and you have to convince him that if he shows enough humility as well as developing super-fast reactions, he'll be a great success. You tell him, "Wait right out there as far as you can go until the moment comes. Then you have to react. How many opponents will you have to get past? Just one. We've made sure of that by the way we've built the game up to this point. So you'll just have to get past one guy or sometimes there might even be nobody there. But if you don't follow instructions and get involved too early, how many men will you have to beat? Four!"

'Don't get me wrong. It's great to have a winger who comes inside successfully but there are very few who have that knack and tactical know-how. You have men coming at you from all over the place if you're cutting inside, from in front, behind you and both sides. There are very few wingers who can handle the space-time balance just right. Most wingers prefer not having too much to think about. The touchline, a couple of opponents and when they go into the box they'll be attacked on all sides . . . There are very few who are capable of receiving the ball correctly, coming inside and participating well in an attack.'

'Robben's one of them,' says Sanvicente. 'He knows how to start outside, make a diagonal inside run then cut back outside once again.'

'You're right,' replies Pep. 'And I told Arjen, "You're only going to get on the ball once from every ten moves the team makes but I need you to turn that one opportunity into a goal. Because if you attack from outside to in and your two strikers move correctly then it's undefendable. There's no more perfect attacking movement than that."'

'So Robben's role is completely different from say Douglas Costa's?' asks Sanvicente. 'Robben's an all-out winger but Costa's more of an inside forward who dribbles?'

'Look at Messi when he's in this situation,' says Pep. 'It looks like he's walking. And it seems like he's alone, detached. Or when he sees the defenders are watching him he'll wander off into a space of his own. Messi spends the match making a mental X-ray of every space, every moment. It looks like he's just ambling around and maybe he's the guy who runs least in the Spanish league but, boy, when that ball reaches him he knows the complete time-space X-ray of who's where. Then . . . pow!'

'Yes, Pep, I've noticed you trust young wingers. You had Tello and Cuenca at Barça . . .'

'I like wingers in general – not just classical wingers but those who master making diagonal runs. The classic Barça winger has always had the inside-to-out run totally mastered. But I also want my wingers to generate the outside-to-in runs: it's why we signed David Villa.'

'Sure. And Neymar's brilliant at both things,' agrees Sanvicente. 'But Brazilian players are like that. They're multi-talented and play with pausa [control] and great speed at the same time.'

'You're right. Look at Romario, Ronaldinho, Douglas Costa, Neymar . . . They all seem to have the same skinny ankles with strong muscular calves. They're wiry yet strong and muscular at the same time. It's the cultural melting pot of generation after generation of different races and that's why Brazil's produced so many great players down the decades.'

Using wingers like this dates right back almost to the origins of football but it's something that fell out of fashion as the sport evolved until eventually they were nearly extinct. Their gradual disappearance was largely due to the conservative attitudes that dominated tactical thinking in football and which led to the systematic reduction of the number of attackers used. In 1963 Argentine writer Dante Panzeri argued, 'Winger's don't get factory produced. They're the consequence of how many forwards a team wants to play with. So if the front line which used to be four suddenly becomes three and then changes to two can we really hope that, given the number of defensive players in front of them, there'll be a player on either touchline – wingers? No. Football's objective is the goalmouth. It's stuck bang in the middle of a sixty-metre-wide pitch. Thus the instinctive, sensible and obvious thing to do is to tighten up into the middle. To bring the players more closely together. In which case the wingers get abandoned. Everyone crams into the middle and there's no chance of maintaining those two wide players when they're so far apart and the only means of communicating between them would be by phone. Wingers were staples of the old game and now modern coaches and directors of football want rid of them. Those who actually know how to play want a different version of football to that. Those guys want the pitch as wide as possible, to open up space because intelligent footballers and smart coaches know how best to take advantage of it.' It's certainly true that when the number of attackers drop, the wingers can become a threatened species.

But Guardiola's doctrine is: 'For a winger to perform well there needs to be certain conditions. Teammates need to be near him. The centre forward who's tying up a central defender with his movement or physique, the playmaker or false 9 who draws another central defender out of position, your own centre half who's made a run up the pitch to show for a cross . . . All these vital movements are only possible if your team is located high up the pitch and the lines of players are close together. If you've pushed up high between the wingers who are hugging the touchline then you push the two full backs inside next to the organising midfielder and you've blocked off all the channels into which the opponent can counter. All of them. Your wingers bring equilibrium to positional play.'

'Yeah, fine,' says Sanvicente. 'But if just one of the players makes a wrong positional move then . . . Ciao!'

'Obviously, of course. You have to know which zone you're attacking and what space there is between you and your nearest teammate. But behind you there's fifty metres of space and if you lose the ball you MUST win it back high up the pitch because it's vital to avoid the rival bombing through into that huge empty space behind you. You mustn't allow them to counter-attack.'


## WHAT AWAITS HIM IN THE PREMIER LEAGUE

Constant surprises never surprise
*Alejandro Dolina*

Guardiola knows that the Premier League is different from the Bundesliga in numerous ways and he's been very honest about this, talking openly before his debut match against Sunderland about how challenging it's going to be to impose his ideology in a new, unfamiliar setting.

His greatest challenge, however, lies in the quality of the competition in England and he'll be facing many top-class teams led by outstanding coaches. You only have to hear some of the names (José Mourinho, Jürgen Klopp, Slaven Bilic, Claudio Ranieri, Ronald Koeman and Mauricio Pochettino) to know to expect superb football this year. And the talent isn't limited to these 'big name' coaches. In fact Pep may find his greatest challenger is Chelsea's Antonio Conte.

I remember asking him back in 2015 to name two coaches with the greatest potential and, without a second's hesitation, he said, 'Tuchel and Conte.'

He sees a lot of himself in Conte: his passion, his aggression, work ethic and determination to have the ball as much as possible, the intensity of his game and his competitive drive. 'Conte plays positional football too. It's very different from my own but it's a game of position and he does it very, very well.'

In private, Pep's gone as far as identifying Chelsea as one of the favourites to win the league this year. The team has a superb coach, excellent players, and a preferential calendar without any European competition and therefore lots and lots of time to concentrate on training and preparation for each game. He may well be proven wrong but before the league kicked off Pep certainly saw Conte as one of his biggest threats. And, to my mind, there's another good reason to take the Italian very seriously: his playing model, like Mourinho's, requires far less time to implement than Guardiola's and we can therefore expect Chelsea to reach cruising speed long before Manchester City.

Pep will be facing a complex variety of playing styles in the Premier League but Juanma Lillo has identified certain common patterns that differ greatly from German football. 'German football, for the longest time, has been a high speed game, lots of running on the ball and direct attacking. When a player on the ball sees space in front of him he'll run . . . and keep running. Normally that player will be shrewd enough to choose which inside channel to attack to keep the counter-attack alive. It's just like in basketball. If he chooses well then the teammate accompanying him on the counter-attack can overlap inside or outside in order to keep the move flowing. This is why Pep quickly realised that the best way to stop these counters was to play the full backs 'inside', tucked into the pivot midfielder. Position them well, teach them well and then every time an opponent begins a counter they'll always be there waiting to block it off.

'In the Premier League he'll find substantial differences,' continues Lillo. 'In England, football isn't so much about dominating possession and the counter-attacks tend not to come because one team sees an opportunity to do that. Instead it's the case that almost all of the teams counter-attack each other all the time – mutually and endlessly. It's a counter-attack culture because there tends not to be long passing sequences to get in the way. These are different counter-attacks to those found in Germany. Generally it'll consist of the ball played long up the pitch to find someone. Then it's laid off to a teammate who'll pass to the 'third man' whose run is in a wide channel and there'll usually be one guy making an inside run to receive the ball. This will oblige Pep to stick to his traditional values like immediate, coordinated pressing of the ball when it's lost high up the pitch and it'll probably be useful that he uses his full backs "tucked in".

'But they'll have to watch much more, and very closely, the rivals who are left up the pitch. They might even need to get in front of them and mark from that position. The counter-attack team will then find it tough to put the ball long over the defenders' heads to make them turn but a one-two pass to a forward high up the pitch who lays it off wide and then turns to run – that they can do. That means City will have to break the counter-attack either by pressing and winning the ball back high up or blocking the path of the counter-attacking rival who wants to feed a breakaway pass to one of the opponents who's been left up the pitch and has dropped deep to link the counter-attack to an overlapping winger or wing back. This can't be allowed to happen.'

# BACKSTAGE 13

## THE LAST TRAINING SESSION
### Munich, 19 May 2016

Pep picks up the balls one by one and puts them in the bag. The youth team players who'd come along today to help the first team practise for Saturday's match against Borussia Dortmund have said their goodbyes to the coach and headed off to the showers. Outside there's only Pep and a couple of janitors, who've come to take down the tarpaulin that screens the pitch from the public. All alone, Pep continues to gather up the balls. Just as it was on his first day in Munich almost three years ago, it's pouring with rain.

'Was it raining that first day too? I don't remember. But I suppose it makes sense, I started in a downpour, might as well finish in a downpour . . . And it's worked out so that my first and last opponents have been Dortmund! But this time I've got Neuer and Ribéry.'

This has been Pep's last-ever training session with Bayern and not even the pressure of playing the Cup Final in forty-eight hours can prevent him feeling a bit nostalgic.

'I've had such a brilliant time here over the last three years. I've loved it and have learned so much.'

Ever the pessimist, Pep isn't completely reassured by the team's fine performance at training today where their free kicks and corners have been absolutely spot on. 'Let's just hope that they score like that on Saturday.'

He's got all the balls together now so he closes the bag and deposits it at the door of the dressing room, where it's usually left by one of the players. Today he insisted on doing it himself. Maybe it was just a whim or perhaps he wanted to mark his last day in charge. Someone approaches and asks him to write a dedication in a book for a certain Garry Kaspárov. He's delighted and, sheltering from the rain under a small awning, takes the pen and writes, 'For Garry, my idol'.

Having enjoyed the celebrations for their fourth consecutive league title, the team's trained hard today. Guardiola's run the technical-tactical side of things and Lorenzo Buenaventura has prepared a structured four-day plan focusing on fitness:

- Tuesday. Core and torso work plus upper arms
- Wednesday. Legs and explosive power
- Thursday. Resistance training (thirty minute game)
- Friday. A few explosive power exercises

Ironically, fate provides another parallel with Guardiola's first season. In his first Cup Final then (May 2014), David Alaba was injured during the last training session before the game and sure enough, now in May 2016 the player hobbles off the training pitch having gone over on his ankle. The good news is that this time the medics are immediately on the spot and they'll work on the injury over the next twenty-four hours to ensure that he's able to play with his ankle heavily bandaged. A very different outcome from 2014 . . .

Pep's always uptight and worried before a big game. In private he'll share his concerns about the opponents' abilities and express doubt about his own game plan. He can't stop thinking about the other team and how he's going to thwart them and it's hard to get him on to any other subject. This is one of the reasons that he wants to leave early for Berlin, where the final will be played.

'I want to leave in a couple of hours. I always like to get there early when we're playing a final. It's good to walk about the city a bit and soak up the atmosphere before the game. It's a habit I've got into.'

The dinner on Thursday in Berlin is very emotional. The players have prepared a presentation for the technical team plus Mona Nemmer, the nutritionist and Andy Kornmayer, the fitness coach who's about to take up a job at Liverpool. It feels like the high point of their three years together and Lahm makes a beautiful speech, followed by a few kind words from Neuer and Müller's comedy routine. The players then produce a load of presents for the coaches.

It's a great night but Saturday's going to be even better. When they win the Cup.

# 14

# IT TAKES TIME

*Art never progresses, it evolves.*
*Raúl Soldi*

BETWEEN JULY AND September 2013 I became sceptical about what Guardiola was doing at Bayern. I watched training sessions and couldn't see a lot of improvement in the team. The rondos, positional play, the mini training games, match day performances, the players' body language and Pep's constant head scratching all gave the impression that the process of learning and assimilation was failing. Pep's pessimism didn't help either. I don't mean that he's an out and out pessimist, it's more that his job requires him to be aware of the very real dangers presented by his opponents as well as his own team's weaknesses. He's constantly mentally reviewing all potential risks and this not only makes him very careful about the decisions he makes, it also gives him an air of pessimism.

His first weeks at Manchester City have been as challenging as those early days at Bayern. The process of adaptation was similarly slow and we've seen a great deal of Pep's more pessimistic side. Guardiola needs to implant a vast quantity of software in his new squad: a new playing model, a different rhythm, greater cohesion, competitive drive, a new team culture and greater consistency of performance . . . And he'll be working on all of this whilst coping with the demands of the Premier League. Pep's had to hit the ground running and it's perhaps understandable that, at the moment, he's not constantly full of the joys of spring.

You should know however that, regardless of City's immediate results, the really exciting work will be going on behind closed doors as the team take their first slow, disjointed steps towards their ultimate destination. Think of this as a work of art. The artist has just begun and as yet all we can make out are a few strange and confusing brush strokes. We'll see the games (and their results) but what we won't be aware of is the complex learning process going on behind the scenes. Arguably, in these early weeks and months, Pep will rely to a large extent on the players' innate abilities (and perhaps a bit of luck) to win games. But in the long term it will be the coaching team's strategic and tactical vision which will allow City to take a qualitative leap forward.

The players and coach must come to an agreement about the conditions in which they'll carry out their shared 'project'. This is the only way to get the most from the teaching-learning process and maximise their collective talent and energy. Greatness comes not from the application of each man's talents but from the synergy this creates.

A crowded calendar mitigates against this process. Seirul.lo says, 'Teams must prepare themselves tactically for the battles they fight every three days and this becomes a barrier to the absorption of new strategic information. It makes it especially hard to assimilate the playing model, which isn't learned as part of a distinct learning process but is assimilated gradually by following the instructions for each game.' Lorenzo Buenaventura also has experience of this, 'The key is to optimise everything you do. Nowadays we think less in terms of training the team and more in terms of training each player.'

Julen Castellano and David Casamichana sum up the importance of training: 'In order to maximise the collective performance of a football team you must optimise all the elements which make up the system and the subsystem and then manage the way they interact. You have twenty-five different men (each with his own distinct and fixed past, a personal and unique present and an unknown and relatively unpredictable future) all working on the same project with the same objective: to compete at the highest level possible. That's why you have to train.'

The coach must solve this problem by combining training exercises which prepare his men for the coming game with work that fits the strategic plan. Almost inevitably, much of what he does will be misunderstood by the outside world, particularly if the team isn't immediately successful. New systems, formations or positioning of players are just some of the things that will challenge established norms and the idea of approaching each game differently whilst maintaining a certain style of play will prove challenging for many in the early days. As Lillo says, 'We're naturally contemptuous of anything new that we don't fully understand, particularly if we perceive the information to be aggressively intellectual. It's easy to reject and deride anything unfamiliar and difficult especially if it appears intellectually beyond us. We "get" the guy whose every second word is "bollocks". He may be a bit rough around the edges but we understand him and it's therefore easier to accept what he says. If the things you say seem a bit over my head however, forget it, it must be nonsense. Someone talking about his scrotum is absolutely fine but please, on no account ask us to open our minds and attempt to understand anything new and challenging . . . So if a team's positional play doesn't get the right results immediately, they're condemned and mocked because people simply don't understand what they're doing.'

## FOOTBALL IN CONSTANT FLUX

Football, like life, is in continuous movement.
*Miljan Miljanic*

Football is in a constant state of flux where the absence of progress means inevitable decline and clinging to outdated ideas will sooner or later lead to defeat. This process of gradual, silent transformation takes place in private, away from prying eyes, and is all too easily muffled by the strident sound of victory. Stefan Zweig, the Austrian novelist, playwright, and journalist wrote, 'In silence, I can absorb all that is great; with premeditation, I lend all my endeavours intelligence and guile.'

Not so long ago, I was lucky enough to witness one of Guardiola and Seirul.lo's exchanges on this very subject.

Guardiola: 'It's difficult to see from the outside but things are constantly changing in football. Today's game is not the same as it was four years ago. Change happens constantly and it's important to regularly take stock of where you are. That's not easy when you have a game every three days.'

Seirul.lo: 'There are so many games at the end of the season that teams almost have no time to train or improve. It's all about recuperation and there's very little time to make real progress. What happens is that there are a lot of outstanding players around whose talent conceals the fact that many teams are worse today than the teams of twenty years ago.'

Guardiola: 'We have to completely overhaul the way we manage training. When you're playing every three days you can only really cover recuperation exercises and run over a few tactical concepts in between matches. That's why we need to learn the tactics right at the start, in pre-season. And the day after a match, you can work on tactics with the subs and other guys who haven't played much whilst your starting XI recuperates.'

Seirul.lo: 'Players have helped football evolve but sadly some coaches have contributed to its regression. In some countries there are still coaches who restrict what the players do on the pitch in the interests of "defensive security". That's how they win. Things can only move forward if coaches have the guts to say, "Okay, I'm about to do something that's going to confuse people and they may take a long time to understand the ideas behind it." It's those guys who've helped the game evolve down the years and I'm not referring to specific nations like Germany or Sweden or Hungary who've excelled in some way on the world stage, I'm talking about the coaches who put progress before trophies and could therefore make the changes needed to bring the game along. It's always been about defending your own goal and attacking your opponent's. It's like leading an army into battle. You have lines of players who have specific roles. There are the "destroyers" who prevent your opponents from breaking through (the defenders); then there are those who construct your game whilst exploiting the rival's disorganisation (the midfielders) and the last group keeps your opponents' goal under constant siege in order to achieve the ultimate objective: a goal. Football has evolved in these four areas: defend, construct, rebuild, besiege.'

Guardiola: 'Take our full backs for example. They can be absolutely decisive players depending on the role you give them. Now, I don't want full backs to play like wing backs. What I want are full backs who play as inside midfielders. And I want midfielders who play where the full backs once were. That kind of player was vital to my game at Bayern: Lahm was super smart and Alaba, multi-talented. Rafinha had the versatility I needed and Bernat was like a whirlwind of energy. Those players were like a gift to me. That's why we could play with five strikers, put away so many goals and win so many games. It was vital that my full backs defended in a line of three close to the central midfielder because that way my inside midfielders were pushed higher up the pitch and became much more dangerous. Playing with the full backs tucked in tight let me use midfielders who might have less technical finesse but who were better at timing a dangerous run into the box and who were better finishers. They'd be playing with more defensive cover behind them.'

Seirul.lo: 'In other sports there's been far greater development and documentation of the different playing models possible. People in football are so involved in the day to day work, in bringing their players along that they don't stop to ask "why?", only "how?" "How can I neutralise my rival's threat?" And they usually conclude that the answer lies in attacking and defending. They don't ask, "Why do they play the way they do? What are the key elements of their game?"'

Guardiola: 'It's important to speak out about this. Football is always changing and we have to adapt to that. Constant evolution. Look at Conte's Italy. They used positional play. Imagine that! Italy playing positionally! A very different kind of game from how I employed it but positional none the less. And I really admire Conte for it. And his players – Buffon, Bonucci, Chiellini and the rest. Everyone still wants to apply the old labels to what we do (tiquitaca, catenaccio), but those terms are nothing more than clichés. And I'll say it again, in my teams my defenders are a key part of the game. We can no longer think of them as the guys who defend on the touchline and run up from time to time to attack through a specific channel. Now they have to play more like midfielders who switch between giving support to the pivot in the middle of the pitch and moving back to the touchline to defend when it's called for.'

Seirul.lo: 'People tend to talk about the phases of play and that's influenced the way football's evolved. There's obviously been no great cataclysm which has swept everything away and forced us to start again from scratch. But for us, concepts like "attack" and "defence" actually have very little meaning. I know that's a big statement to make but I think it's important to explain to people that what happens on the pitch isn't "attack" and "defence".

'In the 150 year history of football, the game has evolved because some players are capable not just of scoring but also providing assists; and others have shown a talent for defending and for building the game. And as these kinds of players emerged, so too did the coaches who could use these talents to create a different playing model.'

Guardiola: 'I like my teams to play good positional football but also to have the ability to defend tightly in their own half if the situation demands it. And to be able to switch from attacking through positional play to crossing to their forwards so that they can score with headers. That's the kind of flexibility I want to see and it's something I need to keep working on, although I did get Bayern very far down that road. My ideal is that my team is able to switch between all these different approaches and be confident and comfortable in each.'

Seirul.lo: 'It's definitely true that evolution only happens when you have coaches with unconventional ideas. But these men also need to evaluate the impact of their ideas in action. And you do that by using players who haven't been disciplined to think only in terms of attack and defence. It's those kinds of players who've shown that it's possible to do things differently and that in turn has allowed coaches to develop the game using a range of diverse ideas and playing models.'

MP: 'So it's "undisciplined" players who are the basis of all this evolution?'

Seirul.lo: 'To my mind, yes. These are the guys who've excited the coach's curiosity, whose attitudes have inspired him to observe, reflect and analyse and then make specific changes. Obviously a more conventional coach isn't going to come up with these ideas and he's also unlikely to see the potential in an undisciplined player (I mean undisciplined in the sense of the idea of not being hidebound in the idea of attack-defence). In reality of course this type of player is the catalyst for change because a smart, imaginative coach will watch him and suddenly have a light bulb moment. He'll say, "Aha, so it's possible to do this differently!" And that's when he begins to develop new ideas and constructs which lead to the introduction of innovative tactics and strategies. And that means the whole game advances.'

Guardiola: 'I don't expect to play the same way as I did in 2009 or 2011 because, although I know I'm a better coach today than I was then, so are Conte and Klopp and all the rest of them. And the players all know so much more than they did four years ago too. They have much more expertise these days.'

So how do we define the ongoing development of football? Well, I'd say it's the process of synthesising all the disparate playing models – although this never happens in a linear or continuous way. If you look back there have been seasons where attacking teams and teams who play positional football have dominated but at other times it's all been about the defensive sides or those who play a very direct game or even those who just know how to play given the particular circumstances of a game and exploit every chance they get (like Portugal in the 2016 Euros).

This is how it's always been and will continue to be but we mustn't confuse a 'trend' with what's really happening in terms of the game's long-term development.

We'll see different trends come and go and a particular style of game may flourish in any one season for a thousand different reasons. This may happen year after year and go on for a long time but it won't change the 'direction' of football which has been the same for the last eighty years. Football will continue to try to integrate every single playing model until we have achieved the ultimate aim: integrated or 'total football', the kind of 'liquid football' I've referred to before.

Let's look at some specific examples of what I'm talking about.

In the 1940s, Carlos Peucelle, the brilliant player who was the inspiration for River Plate's 'Maquina', aspired to playing this kind of 'total football'. 'Everyone [all players] should be markers when they lose the ball and be attackers when they have it . . . Discipline in football isn't a rigid thing, it's elastic. Elastic discipline! The tactic of the line-up should be 1-10: a keeper and ten outfield players – ten outfield players who can fit anywhere, play any role. Not a rigid formation which only works if you use it against another rigid formation. It's the only method that's really effective. As soon as you know that you have the right kind of footballers, you organise your team so that everyone goes up the pitch and everyone goes back, you can change any player for any other player: it's football for all times and all places.'

Peucelle clearly advocated the 1-10 formation: the seed of total football.

About fifteen years after Peucelle was speaking, Hungary trounced England 6-3 in a match at Wembley, thereby provoking an ideological crisis in a nation which considered itself the birthplace of football. At the time Hungarian coach Gusztáv Sebes explained, 'I planned to go out and attack, using the four strikers plus [Nándor] Hidegkuti [an attacking midfielder]. I kept a certain fluidity in terms of my players' positions and the English defenders were totally nonplussed . . . I wanted my wingers, Budai and Czibor, to go back down to help the defence whenever necessary whilst Puskas, Kocsis and Hidegkuti moved all over the field, drawing the English defenders with them. That then left lots of gaps and I instructed Bozsik to take advantage of those spaces. That was my plan.' That Hungary side played a new, challenging kind of game which came pretty close to 'total football'.

Two years after the Wembley defeat Willy Meisl wrote *Soccer Revolution* in which he explained how he saw the football of the future. Meisl was a highly respected journalist and an expert in football. He was also the younger brother of Hugo Meisl, one of the most significant figures in football in the first part of the twentieth century who managed the astounding Austrian national team of the 1930s, the *Wunderteam*, and who coached with Englishman Jimmy Hogan, who himself was the inspiration behind the Marvellous Magyars.

In his book Meisl says, 'It's necessary to substitute individualism with the wider fundamentals of team play. The model of the future will be the whirl. I don't think of the "whirl" as being a system. It's more like a tactical approach that will do away with all the individual systems of football. Players have to see the team as an orchestra . . . Primitive football will be transformed into a fast, breathless game which is very specialised. Continuous action and constant changes will be the norm. The game, which until recently was mostly about individual talent, will become a collective game which can be summed up in one phrase: integrated talent. Tactics in the future will be about the flow of the game, and football will move very fluidly in every direction. There are so many examples of this already starting to happen. To execute "the whirl", which will demand constant motion, every player will be required to match the work rate of his teammates without any time limit.'

Almost nobody in England at the time took any heed of Meisl's words and, in the main, no useful lessons were learned from the Hungarians' dazzling performance at Wembley. Interestingly, Manchester City was the only English club to react and between 1954 and 1956, they implemented the 'Revie plan', initially at youth level and later in the first team which at the time was coached by Les McDowall. The plan basically consisted of converting Don Revie into the false No.9 of the team.

This search for total football lost its momentum for a while but eventually the idea returned, driven forward by Alfredo Di Stéfano's Real Madrid, Helmut Schön in Germany, the Soviet school of trio Maslov-Beskov-Lobanovsky and, to a certain extent, by Pelé's Santos.

Arrigo Sacchi and Johan Cruyff then emerged to lead what became a football revolution, creating a game of positional play which inspired Louis Van Gaal's 1995 Ajax side. But no team represents this style more than the Clockwork Orange, the Dutch national team coached by Rinus Michels and starring Cruyff which was defeated in Munich in the 1974 World Cup Final.

Michels explains, 'In the 70s I was famous for using two strategies relating to the construction of the game and attack. These definitely left their mark on the evolution of football in a couple of ways: 1) the so called "total football" (Ajax of 1970); 2) attacking, pressing football in which we "hunted" the ball (1974 World Cup). Total football came about as a consequence of my efforts to find a way to break down strong defences. I believed that this required a lot of movement during the build-up phase and the attack which would take our opponents by surprise. That's why I chose to change positions so much, inside and between the three lines. We wanted all our players to take part in the construction of the game and our attack as well as seeing to their defensive responsibilities.'

The direction of football really hasn't changed since the start of the 1940s when River Plate began their search for an integrated style of game which would combine all the diverse playing models in one. The search continues today and Guardiola is one of those in the modern game who is determined to see it through.


*TEMPUS FUGIT*

Pat Garrett: Times change . . .
Billy the Kid: No, times don't change. We change.
*Sam Peckinpah*

There's a general belief in football that's now become a mantra: there's no time. There's never time. It's become an almost universal belief and, therefore, a self-fulfilling prophecy, which is unfortunate because it's not necessarily true. Even Guardiola told the press when he first arrived at Manchester City, 'I know that there's never enough time in football . . .'

But, why is there no time? Why is there no time at City? What's causing this pressure? The club? The fans? I don't think so. From 2012 onwards the Manchester City board made repeated attempts to sign Guardiola and eventually had to wait four years for him to accept. Can anyone really argue then that a club that's been prepared to wait so long to sign him will expect Guardiola to turn everything around in three months? The idea's nonsensical and, if there's one thing that the power-brokers at City (Al Mubarak, Soriano, Begiristain et al) have, it's plenty of common sense.

So it must be the fans who are putting on the pressure. In a club which has won just four league titles in its entire history? Absurd. City's supporters are well aware that there will be ups and downs, days when they think they've got the best team in the country and days when quite the reverse seems to be true. They also know that their team and coach will work themselves into the ground for them as well as bringing passion and commitment to everything they do. Perhaps it's young Braydon Bent who's exerting all this pressure?

The truth is that not only do City possess vast quantities of money and ambition, they also have plenty of time to realise those ambitions. Guardiola can be confident that he'll have all the time he needs to develop his project. The club and the supporters have gifted him this breathing space.

In reality it's the newspaper industry that applies the greatest pressure on teams and coaches. I've already talked about the forces that drive the media: people's insatiable need to win plus their own desire for sensationalist headlines. To keep the hamster wheel turning everything must be fast, superficial and rushed. In order to achieve their own objectives the press must keep every coach (and club and player) under constant pressure, as if there's never enough time. And that's not to mention the football agents who, in the interests of lining their own pockets, push their players to change clubs every year.

Time and patience, the coach's great allies, don't suit this purpose which is why the media constantly seeks to interfere. (I'll say again that I'm referring to the newspaper industry as a whole and not to individual journalists. There are still many examples of fine journalism but these are the exception, not the rule.)

This doesn't just happen to Guardiola. Mourinho, Conte, Klopp and the rest encounter exactly the same problems in England and many other countries. It shouldn't surprise us then that so many football and basketball coaches (Popovich, Obradovic, Guardiola, Luis Enrique . . .) have adopted the same position: every single one of them has actively rejected any attempt by the media to influence the work they do.

There's no coach who goes into the dressing room, says the magic words and transforms his men into superstars. There are no short cuts, no trade secrets they're keeping from us. And anyone who says otherwise is, frankly, lying. A team will only play like superstars (or at least in the way the coach wants) after they've suffered (and I do mean suffered) a long process of learning, correction, adaptation and modification until every piece, movement and interaction fits together perfectly. Only then, and not a minute before. This process is a fundamental part of any sport. Why then does the media work so hard to wreck it? It's not because they don't understand it. Ask any journalist and he'll tell you that he accepts that all of this (the ongoing work of the team) is as vital to sport as the aging process of a good wine. Basically, they try to disrupt the process because the media's entire purpose is to appeal to our baser emotions and prevent the consolidation of healthy and successful enterprises. The press needs to create 'monsters' and must therefore ensure that ongoing processes are interrupted so that new ones have to be created. It's the only way to feed the 'monster'. One of the best ways to achieve all this of course is to create a non-existent threat, in this case, an imaginary, desperate lack of time.

Of course we're all familiar with clubs and supporters who refuse to allow their coach the time he needs to achieve his objectives but there are also numerous examples of great clubs who do value gradual, steady progress: in Munich and Dortmund; Barcelona and Villarreal; Turin and Lisbon, Seville and Eindhoven.

Manchester City are ready to give Pep all the time he needs and if you read or hear someone say that the opposite is true then, please, reject it out of hand. It's merely the empty claim of someone who doesn't want Pep to succeed. And it's completely untrue. The kind of changes that Guardiola proposes can't be rushed and his players must be allowed as much time as they need to assimilate them. His playing model is proactive and constructive. It's not about exploiting the gaps left by his opponents or destroying the other team, it's an attacking model that's based on the slow, careful construction of the game backed up by a well-organised defence. Would you demand that a new high rise be thrown up as quickly as possible or would you expect security concerns to be the priority? The effective execution of this style of game isn't learned quickly under pressure and the City players must be allowed to learn at the right pace. The club and its fans must have the patience to allow them to fully grasp the demands of the game of position and to master it completely. Even if it takes twenty months to get there.

## OUR WORK IS A PROCESS
### Munich, 18 March 2016

Although winning is absolutely vital, Pep still sees it as part of the evolutionary process, in football and in another sport he's passionate about, basketball. 'Gregg Popovich, the brilliant coach of San Antonio Spurs, said that success needs time. Our work is a process.'

It's another question entirely whether it's possible to fully realise Guardiola's and the club's objectives in three years. It certainly seems to me that this won't be long enough for Pep to finish the complex and ambitious project he's started. He may well need more time and it will be for him to make that decision in the years to come. I'm not speculating here about a contract extension, this is definitely not the moment for that, but merely expressing the opinion that three years will not be sufficient to achieve everything he's set out to do. Let's remind ourselves of his objectives:

- Develop a detailed strategic plan
- Implant a defined and detailed playing model
- Develop team spirit in a unified and competitive group
- Establish a clear football identity at City
- Establish a unique 'language' in the City academy
- Win trophies

These are ambitious plans that he must realise in a high-pressure demanding league and it's therefore not impossible that Guardiola will change his mind and stay on longer. He'll also have to be careful about the amount of pressure he exerts on his players. Domènec Torrent often uses the image of Pep stretching an elastic band when he talks about the coach's relationship with his players. Pep stretches each of his players to their limits in his determination to get the very best out of them but this always runs the risks of wearing them out (as well as wearing himself out in the process). That's why it's important to ease off from time to time and this is something he still needs to master.

Pep will require a high level of creativity at City because he's set out to achieve something that he's never done before: develop his players and win titles but also rebuild the team and everything this implies – competitive drive, character, philosophy and rituals.

I agree with Santiago Coca that 'the footballer owns the game' but I disagree with the general belief that football belongs to the players. In fact it doesn't belong to players or coaches, or to the fans or even the directors. It belongs to the teams.

A football team is a living thing: the combined result of a number of different forces including players, coaches, fans, directors plus the context they play in (rivals, journalists, luck and time). A team has to be brought into being. A 'we' has to be created from numerous 'me's. It must be created and given clear direction. Football is a pact and it belongs to the teams.

Good coaches live two lives: their own and the life of their team. That's why so many of them age prematurely.

It was Kaspárov who told Pep, during one of their dinners in New York, what his biggest threat would be, 'Time, Pep, your biggest enemy is time.' And now, at Manchester City, Guardiola must give himself all the time he needs to be the coach he wants to be.